# The Hidden Cost of Being

# African American

# The Hidden Cost of Being
# African American

## How Wealth Perpetuates Inequality

## Thomas M. Shapiro

OXFORD
UNIVERSITY PRESS

# OXFORD
UNIVERSITY PRESS

Oxford   New York
Auckland   Bangkok   Buenos Aires   Cape Town   Chennai
Dar es Salaam   Delhi   Hong Kong   Istanbul   Karachi   Kolkata
Kuala Lumpur   Madrid   Melbourne   Mexico City   Mumbai   Nairobi
São Paulo   Shanghai   Taipei   Tokyo   Toronto

Copyright © 2004 by Thomas M. Shapiro
First published by Oxford University Press, Inc., 2004
198 Madison Avenue, New York, New York 10016
www.oup.com

First issued as an Oxford University Press paperback, 2005
ISBN-13: 978-0-19-518138-8

The Library of Congress has cataloged the cloth edition as follows:
Shapiro, Thomas M.
The hidden cost of being African American : how wealth
perpetuates inequality / Thomas M. Shapiro.
p.  cm.
Includes bibliographical references and index.
ISBN-13: 978-0-19-515147-3

1. African Americans—Economic conditions.
2. African Americans—Social conditions—1975-.
3. Wealth—United States. 4. Equality—United States.
5. United States—Economic conditions—1981-2001.
6. United States—Economic conditions—2001-.
7. United States—Race relations—Economic aspects.
8. Racism—Economic aspects—United States.
9. Interviews—United States. I. Title.
E185.8.S53   2004
330.973'0089'96073—dc21   2003046742


7 9 8
Printed in the United States of America

To
Ruth and Izak,
the real wealth in my life

# Contents

# Preface

I MET RICHARD AND KERI BROOKINS in a bookstore in St. Louis. Black and middle class, until recently they had high-paying jobs in the telecommunications industry, working their way up the corporate ladder. Both had worked and taken out loans to get through college, Richard at Webster College and Keri at the University of Maryland and then George Washington University. They began their family and professional lives together in St. Louis. Everything was going according to plan. But when the company they worked for was bought out and departments merged, they both lost their jobs. They had purchased a home a year earlier, cashing out Richard's retirement plan for the down payment. With two young, school-age children, modest savings, and $33,000 in school loans, this college-educated, middle-class family that had built a good life was forced to start over again. Richard decided it was the right time to pursue his dream of starting his own consulting company, but business was so slow during the holiday months that they started living off savings. Keri decided to freelance and found temporary employment. When they drew their savings account down to $2,000, Richard hedged on his dream and started looking for full-time work.

Describing themselves as optimists, Richard and Keri hope that they will not be forced to sell their home or borrow against it to pay living expenses and keep their children in Montessori school. Our conversation ends with Richard telling me that cashing out his 401(k) retirement account to buy their house was a gamble but that it should pay off. The difference between the Brookins family and many white middle-class families came not in their ambitions, education, achievements, personal decisions, or even incomes but in the family assistance and financial safety net they had behind them.

The experience of the Brookins family and others like them provides powerful insights into the question that drives this book: Why is racial inequality increasing after an era in which civil rights and opportunities expanded?

The ideas for this project began percolating as my previous book, *Black Wealth/White Wealth*, coauthored with Melvin Oliver, started to receive public attention. *Black Wealth/White Wealth* shows the huge wealth gap between otherwise equally achieving blacks and whites: The average African American family holds 10 cents of wealth for every dollar that whites possess. Black and white professionals in the same occupation earning the same salary typically move through life with significantly unequal housing, residential, and educational prospects, which means that their children are not really on the same playing field. This represents a challenge to our belief in growing racial equality and to our core notions of equality and social justice. We have grappled for decades with the long history of racial inequality. *Black Wealth/White Wealth* demonstrated that the racial wealth gap is not just a product of differences in education, jobs, and income but rather a kind of inequality passed from one generation to the next. The book succeeded not so much because we produced something new but because we gave voice to what many people already instinctively "knew" was happening and backed it up with convincing evidence.

My coauthor and I traveled across the country in 1995 and 1996 talking and lecturing about our work, and this gave us the opportunity to talk to people ranging from unemployed single mothers to bankers to congressional representatives. These conversations challenged me to think more deeply about advancing the analysis to include a more sophisticated account of the role of private family money in passing inequality along. The enduring question involves passing racial inequality from generation to generation—and that question is at the heart of this book.

While *Black Wealth/White Wealth* provided the numbers behind racial inequality, I could not help feeling that the stories of people were the best way to learn how families use their assets to secure further advantages and better opportunities—just as the lack of financial resources severely limits opportunities and makes improving family well-being more difficult. And so for this book I sought long and deep conversations with black and white, middle-class and struggling, urban and suburban families to see how the phenomenon described in *Black Wealth/White Wealth* played out. Their stories speak more powerfully than cold statistics about how American families think about schools, communities, and bettering themselves and how they act upon those thoughts.

The American Dream promises that Americans who work hard will achieve success and just rewards. But, of course, this depends in part on your starting point. Parents want to give their children a good start in life. As I spoke to families in different cities, I became increasingly aware of the profound difference between those who have a tremendous head start in life because of their family wealth and those who struggle just to obtain opportunities for themselves and their children. I believe that if we are to discuss inequality and personal responsibility we must put forward an intellectual, political, and moral distinction between families who better themselves by means of their own achievements and merits and families who move up because unearned, often inherited, advantages have been passed along.

Racial inequality persists in the United States, even if it does not have an urgent place on our national agenda and it is not fashionable to discuss it, and I hope that this book will compel people to reevaluate our commitment to social and economic justice. I am convinced that a perspective focused on assets brings new insights and understanding to the race dilemma that has plagued the American experience throughout our history and has left our great experiment with democracy unfinished. I also believe that asset-based public policy can provide fresh approaches and new impetus to attacking poverty, racial inequality, and social injustice.

Writing *Black Wealth/White Wealth* allowed me access to an emerging intellectual movement concerning wealth studies and a swelling grassroots movement building around asset policy. This has given me the opportunity to convene conferences, commission papers, conduct extensive and expensive research, sit on research evaluation boards that oversee national demonstration projects, discuss policy proposals with a "brain trust" of asset policy experts, present papers and lecture widely, and, most of all, listen to the thinking of wise people with broad visions. These experiences, along with my interviews with more than

180 families, have provided a wellspring of stimulation, encouragement, and understanding.

At the outset, I should disclose a pronoun problem. This project has been the center of my intellectual, personal, and political universe for years. Writing may well be solitary work, but this work stands on the shoulders of others involved in all phases of the lengthy research project. So I periodically shift from the use of "I" to "we" or "our" in the text: It is one small way to recognize the contributions of a fabulous research team that made this book possible. Deborah Murgia, Patricia Stoddard, Claudia Mora, and Ingrid Castro are talented interviewers, and in writing up these interviews I often inserted myself as if I actually conducted all the interviews single-handedly. I hope that these fine young scholars take my usurpation of their splendid talents as a compliment.

Interviews with people like Moszela Tessler, a 53-year-old struggling black woman, provide the meat of this book. She poured out her heart describing her hopes for the future of her 12-year-old grandson, Derek, whom she is raising. She works part-time helping take care of a disabled man; she fears crime and drugs on her block and how they are influencing Derek. She dreams about a home in a safe neighborhood and a good school for him. This book is primarily about her and 182 other families who graciously took us into their homes and lives and so generously shared their stories, dreams, struggles, triumphs, and tears. To protect the anonymity of individuals and families, I have taken some creative license with identities and demographics, even constructing a composite or two, and I have tried mightily to keep their individual identities hidden while allowing them to speak for many others just like them. If the reader sees part of himself or herself in the interviews, then I have succeeded.

# Acknowledgments

My NAME APPEARS ON THE COVER OF THIS BOOK, but that is misleading. The only part of this project I did alone was write words on paper. From the first ideas to planning the study to carrying it out to figuring out what we had learned to revising my drafts, exceptional people have been my partners, and they deserve a lot of credit. This final product owes so much to so many. It is my awesome responsibility to live up to their stellar contributions and faith in my abilities. I hope they are proud when they read this book; if they are not, it is my failing entirely. I will name them, knowing that I can never really give them their due credit for all they have given me.

I start with the research team that put the interview together, recruited the families, conducted the interviews, and helped analyze them. Claudia Mora, Ingrid Castro, Tamara Ochoa, and Debbie McCarthy helped me in Boston. In Los Angeles, I benefited from the superb interviewing skills and advice of Deborah Murguia, a graduate student at UCLA. In St. Louis, Patricia Stoddard, a graduate student in the George Warren Brown School of Social Work at Washington University, took charge of the St. Louis interviews and produced an exceptional dataset.

The interviews often took me to Los Angeles and St. Louis, where I was most fortunate to benefit from the friendship and keen abilities of two colleagues. Abel Valenzuela helped to monitor and supervise in Los Angeles, and during my visits we conducted many qualitative methods seminars over breakfast. Michael Sherraden made me feel as if I never left St. Louis, providing a base away from home for this project. Michael was a great listener and a better adviser.

I wish that I had found Jessica Kenty earlier. Her quantitative methodological skills, statistical expertise, ability to organize and manage large databases, and plain good sense were exactly what I needed to examine two national surveys. As a doctoral student in sociology at Northeastern University, she became a collaborator. She helped to keep me focused on the importance of the conditions of education.

Heather Beth Johnson guided my understanding of the interviews. She took charge of organizing the family interviews into a qualitative database, listened to all of them, coded the interviews, read the transcripts, and wrote summaries for each interview. As an exceptionally talented graduate assistant, she took charge of this part of the project, becoming a colleague and coauthor, and I am certain that her account of the interviews will push my own understanding. She was always most interested in the ideological material—how families justify advantage and teach their children about inequality. It is in these areas that my debts to Heather are most profound.

My Social Stratification seminar at Northeastern University read an early version and provided helpful comments. Wini Breines, Alan Klein, and Debbie Kaufman have been very supportive of my work, helping to give me the space and encouragement I needed.

I had the pleasure of working with Tim Bartlett at Oxford University Press. Tim was an early supporter of the research and a strong advocate for the book, and he provided important insights and criticisms of several drafts. I owe Tim heartfelt thanks for making this book easier to read. India Cooper, a superb copyeditor, provided clarity for my writing. My agent, Geri Toma, provided support and encouragement, not least in the way she helped move the project to Oxford University Press.

The Ford Foundation supported this research with several grants. Without their assistance, this costly and time-consuming research would not have been possible, and I thank them for their support and generosity. It has been a great partnership. The Asset Building and Community Development division, under the leadership of Melvin Oliver, is at the forefront of the asset-building policy movement. It has been a pleasure to be part of that effort. As a part of my funding from Ford, under Janice Petrovich's initiative, I had the extraordinary opportunity to meet some of the best minds in the country concerned with equity-based educational reform. Meeting with this group was like a super-seminar on educational reform and gave me the chance to listen to the ideas of very wise people and discuss my work with Amy Stuart Wells, Roslyn Mickelson, Jeannie Oakes, and others. George McCarthy provided valuable insights into the housing and home mortgage materials.

I began this project in collaboration with Melvin Oliver. We started the journey on wealth and race together, wrote a book and several articles jointly, and became even closer friends. Unfortunately, time and commitments did not allow us to collaborate on this book. In many ways, it is still a product of our association; we have had countless discussions about the research, his support has been indispensable, and the book bears his strong imprint, although the final responsibility rests with me. Melvin continues to be a good friend and admired colleague, and maybe someday we will get the chance to collaborate again.

I owe a large debt to a group of special readers: Ruth Birnberg, Heather Beth Johnson, George Lipsitz, Melvin Oliver, Mark Rank, and Michael Sherraden read the manuscript and made challenging, critical, insightful, and clarifying suggestions. The book is much improved because of their gracious contributions.

To my mother and father I owe special thanks, again, for all their support and the superb accommodations in Los Angeles. Finally, again, the twin loves of my life, Ruth and Izak, more than endured my grumpy moods to provide the home support to sustain me throughout a project that often kept me away from home.

# The Hidden Cost of Being African American

# Introduction

## At the Assets Crossroads

I MET FRANK AND SUZANNE CONWAY during the late-afternoon rush hour at a restaurant in Los Angeles. Recently laid off from a communications marketing firm and now taking courses to become certified to teach elementary school, Frank arrived after picking up their daughter, Logan, from day care. Suzanne arrived from her job as an operations supervisor for a money management company. The Conways loved their home in the diverse urban neighborhood of Jefferson Park, near the University of Southern California, but were gravely concerned about sending Logan to weak public schools. They talked to me at length over coffee about this community-school dilemma, their high educational hopes, and their future plans. The Conways' story and their solution to their dilemma turned out to be more common than anticipated. Because they receive generous help from their families, they are considering moving to a suburban community with highly regarded schools. Home prices there start at four times those where they live now, and Logan would grow up and go to school in a far more homogenous community—family wealth makes these decisions logical and desirable for some families.

Of course, as with the nearly one in three American families without financial assets, many of the family interviews did not brim over with optimistic choices and options but rather turned on how lack of family wealth severely restricts community, housing, and schooling opportunities. Like the Conways, Alice and Bob Bryant work at professional jobs and earn a middle-class income, but they do not have access to family wealth—they are asset-poor. Living in the working-class Dorchester section of Boston, they are frustrated about their inability to afford to move to a neighborhood with better schools. Doing the best they can, they are highly aware that their son, Mathew, attends only "halfway decent schools" and is not getting the "best education." The Bryants' hopes for Mathew are no different from the Conways' for Logan. What is different is their capacity to follow through on their hopes and deliver opportunities. The Conways are white and the Bryants are black. Because their incomes, professional status, and educations are nearly identical, conventional wisdom suggests that race should be at most a minor factor in opportunities available to these two families, but we will see tangible connections between family assets and race. Differing family asset capacity, which has more to do with race than with merits or accomplishments, most likely will translate into different worlds for Mathew and Logan.

Demonstrating the unique and diverse social circumstances that blacks and whites face is the best way to understand racial differences in wealth holding. The ideas I develop in this book also push the sociology of wealth in another important direction, namely, an exploration of how the uses of wealth perpetuate inequality. Together, wealth accumulation and utilization highlight the ways in which the opportunity structure contributes to massive racial wealth inequality that worsens racial inequality.

My argument is grounded in three big ideas. First, I argue that family inheritance and continuing racial discrimination in crucial areas like homeownership are reversing gains earned in schools and on jobs and making racial inequality worse. Family inheritance is more encompassing than money passed at death, because for young adults it often includes paying for college, substantial down-payment assistance in buying a first home, and other continuing parental financial assistance. Consequently, it is virtually impossible for people of color to earn their way to equal wealth through wages. No matter how much blacks earn, they cannot preserve their occupational status for their children; they cannot outearn the wealth gap. Many believe that African Americans do not do as well as whites, other minorities, or immigrants because they spend too much money rather than save and invest in the future. They are unable to defer gratification, do not sacrifice for the future, and consume excessively. We will see how the facts speak otherwise. Second, these inheritances frequently amount to what I call transformative assets. This involves the capacity of unearned, inherited wealth to lift a family economically and socially beyond where their own achievements, jobs, and earnings would place them. These head-start assets set up different starting lines, establish different rules for success, fix different rewards for accomplishments, and ultimately perpetuate inequality. Third, the way families use head-start assets to transform their own lives—within current structures that reward them for doing so—has racial and class consequences for the homes they buy, the communities they live in, and the quality of schools their children attend. The same set of processes typically advantages whites while disadvantaging African Americans. My family interviews point to critical mechanisms of denial that insulate whites from privilege.

Homeownership is one of the bedrocks of the American Dream, and I explore homeownership as a prime way of delving into these big ideas. We are a nation of homeowners. In 2002 the homeownership rate was 68 percent, a historic high. Homeownership is by far the single most important way families accumulate wealth. Homeownership also is the way families gain access to the nicest communities, the best public services, and, most important for my argument, quality education. Homeownership is the most critical pathway for transformative assets; hence examining homeownership also keeps our eyes on contemporary discrimination in mortgage markets, the cost of home loans, residential segregation, and the way families accumulate wealth through home appreciation, all of which systematically disadvantage blacks. Homeownership appears critical to success in other areas of life as well, from how well a child does in school to better marital stability to positive civic participation to decreased domestic violence.[1] How young families acquire homes is one of the most tangible ways that the historical legacy of race plays out in the present generation and projects well into future. Understanding how young families can afford to buy homes and how this contributes greatly to the racial wealth gap brings us back full circle to the importance of family legacies.

These big ideas help us understand one of the most important issues facing America as we start the twenty-first century. African Americans were frozen out of the mainstream of American life over the first half of the last century, but since 1954 the civil rights movement has won many battles against racial injustice, and America has reached a broad national consensus in favor of a more tolerant, more inclusive society. Yet we live with a great paradox: Why is racial inequality increasing in this new era?

## The Context of Rising Inequality

To fully appreciate the decisions American families like the Conways and Bryants face, we need to understand the extent, causes, and consequences of the vast increase in inequality that has taken place since the early 1970s. Inequality has increased during both Democratic and Republican administrations. Those at the top of the income distribution have increased their share the most. In fact, the slice of the income pie received by the top 1 percent of families is nearly twice as large as it was 30 years ago, and their share now is about as large as the share of the bottom 40 percent. This is not news. In *Nickel and Dimed,* liberal critic Barbara Ehrenreich tells her story of working at low-skill jobs in America's booming service sector, jobs like waitressing, cleaning houses, and retail sales. These are the fastest-growing jobs in America, and they highlight our current work-to-welfare reform strategy. Ehrenreich's experiences illustrate how hard it is to get by in America on poverty wages. More than anything else, perhaps, Ehrenreich's personal experiences demonstrate that in today's America more than hard work is necessary for economic success. I talked to many families who live these lives for real, and we will see how rising inequality makes assets even more critical for success.

In *Wealth and Democracy,* conservative strategist Kevin Phillips argues that current laissez-faire policies are pretenses to further enrich wealthy and powerful families. Rather than philosophical principles, conservative policies of tax cuts for the wealthy, gutting the inheritance tax, and less business regulation favor wealth and property at the expense of middle-class success. The Bush administration's gradual phase-out of the estate tax privileges unearned, inherited wealth over opportunity, hard work, and accomplishment. President Bush's 2003 tax stimulus package carved 39 percent of the benefits for the wealthiest 1 percent. I will broaden the discussion of rising inequality by bringing family wealth back into the picture. Phillips concludes his book with a dire warning: "Either democracy must be renewed, with politics brought back to life, or wealth is likely to cement a new and less democratic regime—plutocracy by some other name."

An ideology that equated personal gain with benefits to society accompanied the great economic boom of the last part of the twentieth century. Even though inequality increased in the past 20 years, despite loud words and little action, policies such as affordable housing and equitable school funding that challenged that mindset simply had no chance of getting off the ground. Ironically, historically low unemployment rates went hand-in-hand with rising inequality in an America where hard work no longer means economic success. Success includes harder work, less family time, and probably more stress. The average middle-income, two-parent family now works the equivalent of 16 more weeks than it did in 1979 due to longer hours, second jobs, and working spouses.[2] The years of economic stagnation subsequent to the boom produced a dramatic increase in the number of working poor, and working homeless families are a growing concern.[3] Since late 2001, in a period marked by a declining stock market and rising unemployment, an abundance of data has provided strong evidence that lower-income households are under severe economic stress: Personal bankruptcies, automobile repossessions, mortgage foreclosures, and other indicators of bad debt all reached records in 2002.[4]

What is the role of wealth and inheritance in rising inequality? The baby boom generation, which grew up during a long period of economic prosperity right after World War II, is in the midst of benefiting from the greatest inheritance of wealth in history. One reliable source estimates that parents will bequeath $9 trillion to their adult children between 1990 and 2030.[5] Given this fact, it is no wonder that an already ineffective estate tax (due to tax planning, family trusts, and loopholes), which takes 50 percent of estates worth more than $1 million, came under such ferocious political attack during the second Clinton administration and has been effectively repealed by the Bush administration.

This wealth inheritance will exacerbate already rising inequality. Economists Robert Avery and Michael Rendall presented a benchmark statistical study in 1993 showing that most inherited wealth will be pocketed by only a few.[6] According to the study, one-third of the money will go to 1 percent of the baby boomers, who will receive about $1.6 million apiece. Another third, representing an average bequest of $336,000, will go to the next 9 percent. The final slice, divided by the remaining 90 percent of the generation, will run about $40,000 apiece. We will see how this baby boomer inheritance not only fuels inequality but also intensifies racial inequality. Few people now talk about the profound effects—economic, social, and political—of that widening gap. We can argue for the privilege of passing along more unearned inequality, or we can take a stand for fairness and equality.

## The Context of Racial Inequality

Writing at the beginning of the twentieth century, historian W.E.B. Du Bois emphatically declared that the problem of the century was the problem of the color line. Writing again at midcentury, Du Bois reviewed what African Americans had accomplished in education, civil rights, voting rights, occupation, income, housing, literature and arts, and science. African Americans had made progress, he noted, although it was unequal, incomplete, and accompanied by wide gaps and temporary retreats. At about the same time that Du Bois was penning his assessment in a black newspaper, the *Pittsburgh Courier*, the Nobel economist Gunnar Myrdal published the widely read *An American Dilemma*. This influential and lengthy study documented the living conditions for African Americans during the first half of the century, revealing to many for the first time the impact of systematic discrimination in the United States. These two giants helped to define racial inequality in terms of equal opportunity and discrimination and to place these issues at the heart of a nation's concern. The twisted, politically narrow, and bureaucratically unfortunate notion of "affirmative action" substituted for equal opportunity by century's end, and affirmative action continues to frame our hopes and distrust regarding race. Even though the struggle for equal opportunity is far from completed, the single-minded and narrow focus on affirmative action forces compromises with our past, obscures our present understanding of racial inequality, and restricts policy in the future.

Du Bois and Myrdal correctly identified a color line of opportunity and discrimination at the core of the twentieth-century racial equality agenda in the United States. The agenda in the twenty-first century must go further to include the challenge of closing the wealth gap, which currently is 10 cents on the dollar, if we are to make real progress toward racial equality and democracy. Understanding the racial wealth gap is the key to understanding how racial inequality is passed along from generation to generation.

The enigma of racial inequality is still a festering public and private conversation in American society. After the country's dismantling of the most oppressive racist policies and practices of its past, many have come to believe that the United States has moved beyond race and that our most pressing racial concerns should center now on race-neutrality and color-blindness. Proclaiming the success of the civil rights agenda and the dawning of a postracial age in America, books by Shelby Steele, Abigail and Stephan Thernstrom, and others influenced not only the academic debates but elite and popular opinion as well.[7] Indeed, a review of the record shows impressive gains, most particularly in the areas of law, education, jobs, and earnings. Even though progress is real, this new political sensibility about racial progress and equality incorporates illusions that mask an enduring and robust racial hierarchy and continue to hinder efforts to achieve our ideals of democracy and justice.

In fact, we can consider seriously the declining economic significance of race because the measures we have traditionally used to gauge racial inequality focus almost exclusively on salaries. The black-white earnings gap narrowed considerably throughout the 1960s and 1970s. The earnings gap has remained relatively stable since then, with inequality rising again in the 1980s and closing once more during tight labor markets in the 1990s.[8] The average black family earned 55 cents for every dollar earned by the average white family in 1989; by 2000 it reached an all-time high of 64 cents on the dollar.[9] For black men working full-time, the gains are more impressive, as their wages reached 67 percent of those of fully employed white men, up from 62 percent in 1980 and only 50 percent in 1960.[10] How much the racial wage gap has closed, why it has closed, and what it means are the subjects of academic and political debate. One study, for example, argues that the racial wage gap is really 23 percent higher than the official figures because incarceration rates hide low wages and joblessness among blacks.[11] At comparable incomes, more African American family members work to earn the same money as white families. Working longer hours and more weeks per year means that middle-income black families worked the equivalent of 12 more weeks than white families to earn the same money in 2000.[12]

The tremendous growth of the black middle class often is cited as a triumphant sign of progress toward racial equality. Indeed, the raw numbers appear to justify celebration: In 1960 a little more than three-quarters of a million black men and women were employed in middle-class occupations; by 1980 the number increased to nearly three and a third million; and nearly seven million African Americans worked in middle-class jobs in 1995.[13] This impressive growth in achieving upward mobility, however, does not tell the whole story, as some argue that stagnating economic conditions and blacks' lower-middle-class occupational profile have stalled the march into the middle class since the mid-1970s.[14]

The real story of the meaning of race in modern America, however, must include a serious consideration of how one generation passes advantage and disadvantage to the next—how individuals' starting points are determined. While ending the old ways of outright exclusion, subjugation, segregation, custom, discrimination, racist ideology, and violence, our nation continues to reproduce racial inequality, racial hierarchy, and social injustice that is very real and formidable for those who experience it. This book will explore the bedrock of racial inequality.

In law, in public policy, in custom, in education, in jobs, in health, indeed, in achievements, one could argue that America is more equal today than at any time in our past. Analysts and advocates scour the annual release of official government statistics on income to detect the latest trends in racial inequality. Traditional measures of economic well-being and inequality, such as income, education, and jobs, show authentic and impressive progress toward racial equality from the mid-1960s through the early 1980s and stagnation since.[15] This is not to suggest by any stretch of the imagination that we have seen the dawning of the age of racial parity in the United States, because, indeed, wide racial gaps and discrimination persist in all of these domains. Employment discrimination, educational discrimination, environmental discrimination, and discriminatory immigration, taxation, health, welfare, and transportation policies continue.[16] Despite the passage of major civil rights reforms, most whites and blacks continue to live in highly segregated communities. To achieve perfectly integrated communities, two-thirds of either all black or all white residents would have to move across racial boundaries.[17] The same indicators show too that progress toward racial equality has halted since the early 1980s. Vast wealth differences and hence enormous disparities in opportunities remain between equally achieving and meritorious white and black families.[18] Progress made since the early 1960s has stalled short of equality. Familiar for Du Bois and Myrdal is the dilemma that, despite narrowed gaps in so many important areas, new generations of whites and blacks still start with vastly different sets of options and opportunities. An asset perspective examines a modern element of the American dilemma: Similar achievements by people of similar abilities do not yield comparable results.

## The World of Assets

### *Inheritance and Transformative Assets*

Sometimes an over-the-top public incident crystallizes our understanding of the causes and consequences of inequality. Yet, if the story seems outlandish and exaggerated, it also serves what sociologists call a boundary-setting function; that is, it pushes society's moral boundary line between what we consider right and wrong further toward an extreme edge. The Jack Grubman tale is a perfect example. Grubman, a securities analyst for Citigroup Corporation, lowered Citigroup's stock rating for AT&T. Citigroup's CEO wanted further business dealings with AT&T, and since he knew that AT&T was very sensitive about its stock rating, he suggested that Mr. Grubman take a fresh look. Upon the urging of his boss, Mr. Grubman's new evaluation restored AT&T to its previous rosy status, and the two Fortune 500 corporations did more business with each other.

In return, Citigroup pledged $1 million to the 92nd Street Y, which also runs an exclusive nursery school in Manhattan, to secure admission for Grubman's twin daughters to a program that had previously turned them down. Newspapers and magazines had a lot of fun writing about upper-class corruption, upper-middle-class ultra-anxiety about schools, and the connections necessary for getting 2-year-olds into the right preschools. Indeed, there seemed to be a lot of sympathy for a family doing everything they could to put their children on the road to success; after all, the right preschools lead to the right private schools, which lead to Ivy League colleges. The problem was the million dollars, the connections, and the fix. My perspective is different because an outlandish amount of money is not the only issue and diverts attention away from critical practices. An asset perspective examines how families routinely use financial resources for purposes very similar to Mr. Grubman's to gain significant advantages.

This book will highlight the crucial role that private family wealth plays in our communities and in our schools to perpetuate inequality from one generation to the next. I will argue that because of these dynamics—which have virtually nothing to do with achievement or merit—racial inequality is increasing and will continue to increase as long as present practices remain unchanged. While the U-turn in racial progress has many sources, I will present evidence that inherited money, particularly the way families use it to achieve and maintain class and community status and provide educational advantage, plays a primary role in reversing hard-earned, merit-based racial progress in jobs and income. Continuing institutional bias and public policy, along with family legacies, subvert advancements in the classrooms and on the job. Before World War II, only the children of upper-class American families received substantial inheritances, and we continue to view such legacies primarily as the sole province of the upper class. In fact, as a result of the tremendous postwar economic prosperity and public policies promoting middle-class homeownership, today inheritances are commonplace for middle-class families. Our traditional idea of inheritance involved wills, large estates, and trusts, distributing assets after death, among a fortunate few wealthy families. We will not only examine how much more commonplace inheritance is among the middle class, but we will also expand the common notion of inheritance to include down payments and closing costs for first-time homebuyers, college tuition payments, large cash gifts, and loans, as well as old-fashioned bequests at death.

To get a better analytic handle on this phenomenon, I will use the concept of *transformative assets:* inherited wealth lifting a family beyond their own achievements. This concept of transformative assets is not meant to belittle achievements or successes of families who inherit significant amounts, but it does suggest that in many cases there is something else involved. Many of the families I spoke to relied on transformative assets to acquire their class standing, social status, homeownership, the kind of community they live in, and their children's schooling.

When we look at assets rather than just earnings, we recognize that financial resources beyond a weekly paycheck are an essential building block of a family's capacity to better itself, create and take advantage of opportunities, feel secure economically and take risks, and identify itself. Most Americans survive on their incomes while assets feed dreams of a better life, offer hope for the future, and are the key resources for launching upward mobility, as well as providing important real and psychological safety nets. Focusing on assets also allows us to consider how the historical legacy of the past acts upon the present and, possibly, the future. It provides insight into the persistence of racial inequality into the modern post-civil-rights era by exploring how families use their assets to build and maintain adequate standards of living and how they attempt to secure advantageous opportunities for them and their children.

## Class and Racial Identity

A family's assets, consisting of financial resources like savings accounts, stocks, bonds, home equity, and other investments, are not merely means through which they measure success or make a life. These assets also define a family's community and class status and racial identity. Our conversations with families will illustrate how they use assets to establish class, community, and race boundaries. While it is no longer legal to deny access to housing based on race, there is no law against keeping out people who cannot afford a mortgage and thus hoarding community and educational opportunities. The home we own, how big that home is, and its location are key statements in our class identity. Immigrants, Asian Americans, Hispanics, and others form racial identities in large measure by the characteristics of the communities they live in. For example, Hispanics who live in predominantly upper-middle-class white communities and whose children attend white schools are far more likely to be treated as and identify as white than those living in poor nonwhite communities. In contrast, African Americans can use assets to achieve class status, but where they live has little consequence for their racial identities. Widespread residential segregation further restricts African American families from using assets to break out of racial boundaries.

Assets give families the capacity and flexibility to act and the capacity to engage more fruitfully and meaningfully with the world, enhancing their ability to improve their place in it. Families use assets to create opportunities that others do not have, such as moving to neighborhoods with better schools, providing cultural and social experiences for their children, making career changes, or taking advantage of business opportunities. By focusing on the central role of assets, I hope to bring new insight to the ways in which families' assets often determine their ability to choose communities and schools for their children. I will examine closely the relationship between how families use their assets and persistently high levels of residential and educational segregation. I will be looking at how families use assets to solidify their class standing and how differences in wealth set whites and blacks farther apart. This asset framework underscores how asset acquisition and asset building in the context of modern American life defines social class and race in a way that more often than not reproduces the inequalities of the past. I focus in this book on how wealth perpetuates racial inequality, yet I also will be mindful of how wealth perpetuates class inequalities among both whites and African Americans.

## Assets, Freedom, and Segregation

The sociologist Georg Simmel writes that money is central to every aspect of life and culture. He calls money "the frightful leveler" because it strips the core and value away from everything, leaving only a scorecard of accomplishment.[19] Money tends to neutralize the relevance of other roles, such as family, religion, and political party. It is a frightful leveler because value is established in terms of how much, not the position or characteristics of individuals. The acquisition and accumulation of money also allows people the freedom (within constraints) to choose how, when, where, and with whom to use their money to satisfy needs and fancies. People with money also are freer from the will of others and can elude more easily the limits of weak or undesirable public policy. This marketplace notion of success means that those with more assets have more freedom and liberty.[20] They can thus exercise the freedom to buy out of neighborhood problems like crime, weakly supported public services, or undesirable levels of integration. This rampant sense of individualistic freedom and liberty clashes with the collective social injustice of racial inequality. Freedom exercised by money also produces a privatized notion of citizenship in which communities, families, and individuals try to capture or purchase resources and services for their own benefit rather than invest in an infrastructure that would help everyone.

Many whites continue to reap advantages from the historical, institutional, structural, and personal dynamics of racial inequality, and they are either unaware of these advantages or deny they exist. Black Americans in particular pay a very steep tax for this uneven playing field and outcome, as well as for the denial of white advantage. In housing markets, for example, we will see that it is harder for equally creditworthy black families to qualify for home mortgages, that blacks receive far less family financial assistance with down payments and closing costs, that black homeowners pay higher mortgage rates, and that homes in African American communities appreciate less in value. Many whites either refuse to acknowledge these advantages or are unaware of them, and this inhibits our national dialogue and forestalls a national reconciliation.

Social justice, in my view, requires coming to grips with the ways in which inequality passes from generation to generation for people of all races. My interviews reinforce the wisdom of historian George Lipsitz's observation that modern racism often is seen in universal or neutral terms without any personal benefits or overt racist intent. In this way, individuals evade personal responsibility for any resulting inequality.[21] I spoke to many families, for example, who see no paradox in using inherited wealth to leverage advantages and opportunities unavailable to others. Their insistence upon how hard they work and how much they deserve their station in life seems to trump any recognition that unearned successes and benefits come at a price for others. This insistence upon wrapping advantage in the American Dream blurs the difference between thinking you are self-made and being self-made. Coming from families living in homes and communities they can afford only because of inherited wealth, the constant admonitions to the poor to take responsibility betray and distort the dream.

*Making Inequality*

In the United States, progressives have traditionally seen racial hostility as a strategy fostered by ruling elites to divide people with common economic interests from joining together to contest their power. My interviews complicate this understanding because they show how a certain quest for middle-class success contributes to racial inequality. Most white middle-class families with whom I spoke emphasized their desire to move up and better themselves; most middle-class black families with whom I spoke seek to better themselves too, but residential segregation, conflicting community-race-class tugs, and lack of family assets make their quest more complicated. The white families I spoke to often sought to improve their children's education by moving to communities with better schools, rather than by improving schools for all children. In the race to secure quality education and competitive advantage, families and communities often treat this valuable resource as a scarce commodity and hoard it. The children of families with resources necessary for such moves receive better educational opportunities along with all of the benefits they bring, but the inferior schools they leave behind continue to teach those unable to move. Part of the paradox is that it is difficult for families with these choices to act differently because to do so would be to act irrationally and outside the strictures of the American Dream.

I talked to many families who face tough choices between what is best for their children and their belief in the American Dream. Through this research, I have come to a sharper understanding about how rational, individual actions like moving to more successful communities to attend higher-quality schools result in further class and racial inequality. Americans have traditionally bettered themselves by moving up. What is different now is the extent to which Americans define good schools and communities in racial terms and how baby boomers use family assets to transform their status. If these observations are accurate, then by presuming that race no longer matters we remain oblivious to disadvantage and sanction racist consequences. The conflict between inheritance and the American value of fair play intensifies in this moment.

Deeply embedded policies, such as those underlying the Federal Housing Administration and locally funded schools, and market incentives, such as property values, shape how we think about neighborhoods, what we mean by integration, and how we think about educational prospects in ways that reward discrimination. Real estate and mortgage markets and educational environments contribute significantly to the racial wealth gap by structuring racially different opportunities in home-ownership, wealth created by homeownership, and educational quality. The point I wish to emphasize here is that in the current structure there is a huge hidden cost of being African American, just as current policies and structures reward the individual actions of many white families.

## Talking to Families

My interviews allow me to tell the stories behind how families use assets to expand opportunities for themselves and their children. We designed the interviews to raise questions and elicit answers particu-larly about family assets, community and school decisions, and inheritance. I got to know Frank and Suzanne Conway, Alice and Bob Bryant, and many other families in the course of interviewing nearly 200 families in Boston, Los Angeles, and St. Louis. I had interviewed a handful of Boston families for my previous book, and I live in Boston, so this city was a logical choice. Likewise, we had a handful of Los Angeles interviews from my previous book, and Los Angeles represents another region and a different urban growth pattern, so it was another logical choice. I chose St. Louis as the third city primarily because of its comparable size and its location, to balance out an East Coast–West Coast bias. Since I do not claim that the families I interviewed repre-sent a random sample of all American families, pragmatics of place and my ability to monitor these sites were more important than all-inclusiveness.

My colleagues and I interviewed white, black, and Hispanic families over the course of a year and a half. We chose families with school-age children because we wanted to focus on families facing critical schooling, housing, and community choices. About half the families we interviewed live in the city, and the other half live in suburbs. Three-quarters of the families are middle class in terms of income, job, or educational criteria; the others are working-class and poor families. I designed the research in this way so I could compare equally situated white and black families to best highlight asset differences and the difference assets make. We interviewed a smaller, supplemental sample of Hispanic families in Los Angeles and Boston.[22]

We worried initially that people would not be open about their financial resources. In this age of relentless telemarketing and intrusive dinnertime sales pitches, who would even allow us the time to ask? We worried that it would be an overwhelming challenge to find and interview families willing to talk to us. We worried too that those who did agree to talk with us would give us "politically correct" answers when we asked searching questions about sensitive topics like race, schools, and community. Almost as soon as we heard the first interviews, however, we knew we had a treasure to mine. The frank nature of the responses, which often crossed politically acceptable boundaries and shocked my interviewers and research assistants, indicated that we had touched something really important in their lives. Most people were willing to talk to us so enthusiastically because they were sharing hopes about their family and children, and people love to talk about their kids. These interviews show in a way that no statistics or survey could how families attempt to use assets to make better lives for themselves, just as they show the disadvantage of not having ample assets.

On average, the interviews took almost two hours each and resulted in about 400 hours of audiotapes to listen to and 7,000 pages of transcribed data to read and analyze. I use family interviews from all three cities, but of the extended family cases I present, the reader will get to know more St. Louis families than those in Boston and Los Angeles. The St. Louis discussions about race, class, community, and schools were the sharpest and bluntest and thus best exemplify these concerns. I think this reflects St. Louis's sharper race, class, and city-suburban divisions. If I am correct, this means that working- and lower-middle-class St. Louisans have fewer community and school options than Boston or Los Angeles parents.

My colleagues and I designed questions to test ideas about how assets affect opportunities, to find patterns and trends, and to flesh out the whys of families' asset-behavior, the role assets play in their well-being, and their thinking about assets. Such interviews alone, however, do not establish baseline information about wealth inequality, nor do they allow for the kind of sophisticated statistical analysis that we need to see the big picture. The second source of material supporting this book thus draws on national data sources, especially two surveys of households across the nation that ask systematic questions about family assets and liabilities. I also needed to get a valid snapshot in time to establish baseline facts about age, education, family, jobs, and income so that I could assess wealth and racial inequality. In addition, the ability to examine families over a period of time is vital to answering some of the most important questions about wealth accumulation. Thus we can explore more fully what accounts for changes in wealth, how families use wealth, and the role it plays in a family's quest to better itself. The chief advantage of these quantitative data is that we can follow families and watch changes in wealth and examine the effects on family stability, school performance, and risk-taking behavior. This ability to follow a large number of families over an extended period allows a far more thoroughgoing and reliable foundation for my argument. When I bring together my in-depth family interviews with the survey data, I am able to explore the profound importance of assets in shaping modern racial inequality in America. We need both of these databases because, in my estimation, each is most appropriate for different critical tasks.[23]

Since the mid-1990s, the debate on race and inequality has been shifting to incorporate the challenge of the racial wealth gap. My hope is that this book not only strengthens the legitimacy of this change in our understanding of racial inequality and public policy by exploring how racial inequality is passed along but that it also poses new, serious challenges to the current understanding about equality and public policy. I am arguing nothing less than asset-based public policy. In conjunction with living wages and adequate social assistance, policies that motivate families to accumulate assets for education, homeownership, business development, retirement, and emergencies can best launch family mobility, well-being, and self-reliance. Asset-based public policy, I firmly believe, is one of those new and rare big ideas with the potential of reframing public debate. The distinction between income-based survival policies and asset-based mobility strategies clearly isolates the main shortcoming of contemporary welfare reform policies, which confuse welfare caseload reduction with lifting families out of poverty. Families may understand this better than politicians and academics. I talked to a single mother who called income "life support" and referred to assets as "moving-ahead money."

No doubt, many readers will be uneasy with the implication that individual white middle-class families benefit from racial inequality. I am. This was not a starting point for the study. However, I cannot evade the inescapable conclusion that families make important choices that maintain residential and school segregation because it provides benefits and advantages to them personally. Such choices, in turn, help to fortify class and race inequality while passing inequality along to future generations. Discussing my work with friends and colleagues invariably leads them to ask if the study is about them, or to tell the story of why they moved or placed their children in a better school. While the study is not about them we all need to pay attention to how our actions are shaped and the consequences of our actions, if we are to fix undesirable inequality. My concern is about our commitment to equality, social justice, and fairness. A rekindling of these core values requires a tough, bold, critical appraisal of public policies that promote these ideals, instead of actions that continue to move us further away.

# Part I
# ASSETS

# 1

## The Color of the Safety Net

### Vivian and Kathryn

*There's nothin' I can do about it. . . . Maybe I might meet a millionaire or somethin', you know, but I doubt that very seriously. I wish that I wasn't in a lot of debt, though, because I had got out of debt, and now I'm back in debt.*

VIVIAN ARRORA, 40 YEARS OLD, is the struggling single mother of a young teenage son, Lamar, and 4-year-old twin girls, Bria and Brittany. Vivian, who is African American, grew up in Watts, which is one of the poorest sections of Los Angeles and where about one in every three families falls below the government's poverty line. Several moves have inched her family away from this poverty-stricken black community toward more middle-class West L.A. She tells me she has been attacked and raped several times. With tenacity and determination, she has bootstrapped her family and, as she says, "branched further west, out of a gang-infested area, a drug area." She dreams of owning a house in "peaceful" and middle-class Culver City.

"After I gave birth to the twins, I was just ready to go to work because just receiving AFDC [welfare] just wasn't the thing to do," Vivian begins, "and all my life I've been receiving AFDC." She took vocational classes at a technical school because she "wanted to learn how to do the computer." She completed the program and earned her certificate, acquiring substantial student loans along the way.

The next step was to find a job. "I was out lookin' for a job, and it seemed like nobody wanted to hire me and I got kind of discouraged, and I just kept lookin', I just kept lookin'." A friend then suggested going to a temporary agency.

*We went to the temp agency on a Wednesday. It was raining, and we just kept on. We kept on going, and the rain didn't stop us. . . . I went in on a Wednesday, and they called me that Thursday and told me to start work that Monday. And I've been working ever since. And I'm like: Am I really, really ready to go to work? Mentally? But once I started, I just, I've been on a roll ever since.*

All this occurred two years before we talked. Vivian worked as a temp for a year and then was hired by the county to work full-time, with some medical benefits, processing adoption papers. She is proud of having worked herself off AFDC, declaring, "I'm worth more than 700 dollars a month. I'm worth more than that!" But this clerical work does not pay much—a tad under $20,000 per year, which is about $500 above the official poverty line for her family of four. She may be a poster girl for welfare reform because she successfully transitioned off welfare, but she has joined the swelling ranks of the working poor.

Vivian's job is very important because it provides skills, habits, stability, and self-worth that she said had not existed before, but she still is very concerned about crime and safety where they live and wants to move into a better place, even own her own home someday. Working hard and bootstrapping her family off welfare has neither lifted her out of poverty nor put the American Dream within her reach. I asked her how she found the neighborhood and apartment where she is living now; her answer reminds us of the fragile and precarious living situations of those without safety nets. She was forced out of her last place with 30 days' notice, and the family just

*landed right here. This is not where I really wanted to be, but I was tired when I was looking because I was working full-time, and by the time I got off it was too late to go look, you know, to be out at night, in there with the kids, nobody to baby-sit, so I have to come home and cook. It's just me. I don't really like the surroundings. I don't like the traffic over here either. Sometimes when I come home I see a lot of guys, they hang out down here at the corner.*

She would like to buy a home in a safer neighborhood for Lamar and the twin girls. It would be the next step up on her mobility ladder because it would solidify her present stability and provide improved services for her family and better schools for her children. She faces serious obstacles. She has lots of debt and ruined credit. She does not seem to have the resources or capabilities to work out of her debt trap, at least not on poverty-level wages. Nonetheless, she is thinking about buying a home through a funding program that requires education, training, and clearing her credit. She wonders how she can find the time to do all this while working full-time, because it would mean finding costly day care for Bria and Brittany.

A modest, even small, amount of assets, together with day care provision, would make a huge difference in securing a better future for this resolute full-time working woman and stabilizing this family's mobility up from poverty. For example, if she had assets put aside, Vivian could acquire job skills and training, and these enhanced skills in turn might well lead to a better-paying job. In the view of mortgage lenders, difficulty in getting out of debt reveals a high credit risk, so if she could get out of debt, she would be in a better position to consider seriously buying a home. Vivian's story gives us glimpses of the kind of life that so many others like her live. Her struggles anchor a starting point regarding some broader asset themes of this book. Poverty is not merely the lack of adequate income for daily needs and survival; for the Arrora family it means difficulties around community, housing, crime and safety, debt, environment, child care, and schools. While it is no doubt true that there are some people whom no amount of assets could help, because of handicaps or inclination, given how far she has taken the family already, I firmly believe that Vivian Arrora's family is poised for mobility and self-reliance. Lack of assets holds her back.

Kathryn MacDonald, like Vivian, is in her 40s and earning a salary close to the poverty line. She too is a single mother, but her life struggle tells a very different story. Kathryn works about 30 hours a week as a freelance contractor in publishing, earning approximately $16,000 a year. Her boyfriend left her just before her son, Evan, was born and she has raised him alone. She prefers to work part-time so she can spend part of her day with Evan, who she says has attention deficit disorder. According to her this was a major reason why she moved from New Jersey to St. Louis in 1995.

Kathryn and Evan MacDonald live in Florissant, a traditionally working-class and middle-income community in north St. Louis

County. Kathryn worked at a large publishing house in Manhattan before moving. She grew weary of the city's frantic work pace, expensive New Jersey housing, and spending so much time away from her son, so they moved. Now Kathryn does the same work in her St. Louis home that she used to do in a Manhattan skyscraper, matching Library of Congress book subject headings to subject titles for publishers. Freelancing half-time at home allows her to spend much more time with Evan and to watch over his educational and social development. She also enjoys the freedom and autonomy of working at home. Kathryn earns a lot less than when she worked full-time in New York, but she is far happier with her life now, even if her earnings only amount to poverty wages. She likes the community and schools, which are largely white.

Kathryn clearly is pleased that things have worked out so well.

*We're in a good neighborhood. My son can go out to play and I don't have to worry about what he's going to get into or who he is going to be encountering. I don't have to worry about him being abducted. . . . I don't have to worry too much about drive-by shootings. I don't have to worry that something terrible is going to happen to him just because he was out on the street.*

Kathryn is especially pleased with Evan's school situation. Evan is smart, just a notch below getting into gifted programs, and the system has special programs for bright kids like him. The school also has understanding and knowledgeable teachers working in small-group settings who can help him overcome his ADD.

Normally, $16,000 does not afford a great deal more than what Kathryn calls "life support," much less the kinds of services and opportunities available in middle-class communities. What makes Kathryn's life so different from Vivian Arrora's? How is she able to live on essentially poverty wages and yet plan for a future that looks to have better prospects? How is she able to live in a place that is safe for herself and Evan? How is Kathryn able to find a school where Evan can thrive? It is not as simple as that one is white and the other is black. The answer is transformative assets.

For one thing, Kathryn is free of debt. Her brother has been sending $100 a month for several years to help her out with Evan's educational and day care expenses. She lost a job several years ago, when Evan was 2, but was able to move in with her father for five years. She has no school loans because her family paid her college bills. Even today, unlike the average American, she does not owe any credit card debt.

But her financial stability goes far beyond just lack of debt, Kathryn explains. She has inherited money from her family.

> *I have the proceeds from my father's estate, and also my grandmother. I don't even pretend to understand this—my cousin the lawyer handles all this—but if her estate gets to a certain size, she is liable for more estate taxes, so every so often he has to disburse some of that money.*

Kathryn tells us that she has already inherited about $125,000, of which about $90,000 remains, and will inherit another $80,000 when her 94-year-old grandmother passes away. "That could be when I buy a house. That could be what pushes me over the top. With that plus with the mortgage I could get, I could get something decent." She hopes to buy a home with her new boyfriend, who will not be able to contribute much because he pays alimony to a first wife.

When her father died, "the first thing I did was take some money out, and we took a vacation." When another chunk of money came from her grandmother's estate, she and Evan took off to a family wedding in Alaska. She dips into the inheritance every few months as bills mount up, especially when her quarterly estimated income tax is due. She is looking into magnet schools and even private schooling for Evan, in case the local public schools cannot continue to meet his special needs and provide an environment in which he can thrive.

If Kathryn MacDonald did not have assets, one might think of her in an entirely different light, and many questions might arise. For instance: What is she doing to better herself? Why is she not working full-time? Why are her ambitions so low? If she were black, the questions might have a harsher tone, and we can imagine the social condemnation and scorn this single mom might face. Although one might question some of Kathryn's choices, her story is an example of how financial inheritance can provide advantages and a head start in life. Maybe even more important for Kathryn MacDonald, assets supply an anchor for her family's middle-class status and identity that her work and income cannot.

Vivian Arrora's and Kathryn MacDonald's stories provide a concrete starting point for considering how racial inequality is passed from one generation to the next. In many ways they are so alike; yet in many other ways their lives are so different. Vivian's legacy is growing up black in a welfare family in Watts and becoming a single mother herself. She is the first in her family to go to college. The big issues for her are work, debt and bad credit, finding time for the kids, the fear of violence, drugs, and gangs, and figuring out a way to buy a home in a stable and safer community. Hers is a remarkable success story, but her mobility from welfare to working poor may have reached its own limit. Her children go to weak urban schools where getting ahead is a difficult task accomplished only by a few. Lamar, Bria, and Brittany will inherit America's lack of commitment to equal education for all.

Kathryn's situation, if not her accomplishments, is very different. She does not worry about drugs, violence, and gangs, the adequacy of the public schools, or finding time to spend with her child. Her upper-middle-class inheritance includes a debt-free present, a substantial amount of assets, and palpable prospects of inheriting considerably more in the near future. Her inheritance, one could argue, includes class standing that sustains her comfortable and respectable middle-class situation. In looking at these legacies and inheritances, we begin to see that family assets are more than mere money; they also provide a pathway for handing down racial legacies from generation to generation.

Finally, Vivian's greatest dream is to own a home in a safe place with decent schools for her kids. As far as I can tell, this is not likely to happen, unless she actually meets and marries her millionaire—or unless a bold and imaginative policy helps to make her hard work pay off. Kathryn's dream home most likely will become a reality after her grandmother passes away. The lives and opportunities of their children already are being acted out upon different stages, and the gulf between Evan and Lamar is likely to widen further. What the two boys make of their lives from these different starting points will be their own doing, but let us not delude ourselves that Kathryn and Evan and Vivian, Lamar, and the twins share even remotely similar opportunities.

## The Ackerman Family

*This is a step up from our starter home. We looked at the city, and the bottom line was we weren't happy with the schools. We wanted to be in a public school in the county. The benefits. The tax benefit; the ownership and not having a neighbor right on your next wall; privacy. We didn't end up here, we chose to be here. We were definitely trying to buy our life house.*

Chris and Peter Ackerman and their three children are middle-class residents of south suburban St. Louis. Chris is a plant accounting manager, and Peter is a technical service manager; together their incomes top $80,000. Through "working and saving, working and saving" they have built their net worth to more than $100,000. As is true for most American families, their largest pool of wealth is their home equity, accounting for about $67,000 of their assets. They also own about $60,000 in various retirement programs, which, as they note, carry heavy tax and withdrawal penalties if used before retirement.

In our conversation, Chris and Peter express a keen sense of economic security and the firm belief that their children have a bright future: Because they both work for a large organization that promises to pay college tuition for long-standing employees, they will not have to dip into their assets or take out loans for college. Like most Americans, they believe their assets put them right in the middle of the wealth distribution, but when I tell them they own more than most Americans, Chris remarks, "Good."

Because these college graduates come from middle class families, are not burdened with student loans, and are good credit risks, they were able to get a mortgage for a classic starter home. Peter's parents helped with the down payment, which allowed them to buy in the community of their choosing. As with many families, the increased property value in their starter home provided a sizable portion of the down payment when they moved up to their present suburban home.

It was a pivotal moment for them, as it is for many American families. With three children reaching school age, the Ackermans' space, community, and schooling needs were changing and growing. The flexibility families with assets have at these times sorts them and their children onto different life trajectories from those without assets. Chris begins explaining how they approached these important issues.

*I had cousins growing up in the city, and—this is my own blood, but basically they turned out really trashy. Their friends were trashy. [I] did not even want sometimes to bring my own children around my cousins, because their lifestyles were different, their values were different. Things that were important to us were not important to them.*

Peter talks about those things that were important to them.

*It seemed like the areas we could afford in the city, the neighborhoods were different. One street would be really nice, clean-kept houses, and two streets over there would be boarded-up houses or just really trashy houses. And we just thought, the mix of the group and then all of these people going to the same school, it did not fit with what we wanted for our family.*

The Ackermans wanted to live in a community where more people were like them and had the same standards. Community for Chris also means a place where

*you are intertwined, with "Hi, Martha" in the store. You see her in the store. Okay, then you go to day care that morning and you see her and her kids, and you say, "Hi, little Timmy," or, "Hi, little Johnny," and then you are out on the street and they have got their little lemonade stand or whatever.*

Peter and Chris bought a home in a suburban part of St. Louis where nearly everybody owns a home built since the 1950s and families have similar incomes, in the $60,000 to $80,000 range. The community they chose is almost all white; less than one percent blacks and Hispanics live in their zip code. When I ask about the diversity of their community, Peter explains:

*It is unfortunate that it is bound by race too. As far as I am concerned, that has nothing to do with it [lack of diversity]. I think it's economic because it's the same issue we dealt with when we lived in the city. It didn't matter if our neighbors were white or black, as long as they had the same standards we had.*

The Ackermans' assets—help with the down payment, no college loans, and especially the equity built up from their starter home—along with stable jobs and high-quality benefits allow them to own a home in the suburban community of their choice, one up to their "standards," and to select the kind of schools they want for their kids. Most middle-class families with school-age children face similar school, community, and space issues. Of all the options available to Peter and Chris Ackerman, they chose a segregated suburb and segregated schools. And in later chapters we will see the kinds of strong incentives built into home-owning markets and public policies that reward their choices.

### "Worlds Away"

Elizabeth Wainwright Cummings works part-time as an accountant; her husband teaches in the same city schools that drove the Ackermans to the suburbs. Their incomes do not cover their expenses, which include a mortgage on a large, historic home, day care for 4-year-old Anna, and exclusive schooling and private tutoring for 9-year-old Alexander. Their incomes are supplemented by $30,000 a year in interest from an inheritance, and her parents are paying the private school bills. She explains that the family money goes way, way back—it is money her father inherited—and it will last a long time. She already has inherited about $350,000, with "more than a million dollars sitting there with my name on it." Their home is in a suburban school district that she feels is not strong. This didn't matter, she explains, because "we knew we weren't using the school district." Her comment is a good example of a privatized notion of citizenship: Since she can use ample family wealth for her own benefit, she does not have to worry about or invest in the public infrastructure that would help everyone.

Although, "once we are inside our house, we love it," she is wary of her largely middle-class neighborhood, because not all the homes look like hers and some of her neighbors are still at early points in their careers. Elizabeth is planning to move to an upper-class neighborhood that fits her class identity better and where she is more comfortable with the neighbors. As she puts it, she has her "eye on this area really close to our house but *worlds* away."

Perhaps because she comes from a family that has handed down money for generations, Elizabeth is conscious of how wealth confers privileges and advantages. At the end of our conversation, I say that I have just one last, big, complex question: How do you feel that wealth has impacted your life?

> *No question about it. I mean, if my parents hadn't had the money to send my kids to* [the private] *Hills School, we couldn't have considered it. We would have had to really do belt tightening, and financial aid, and many more loans, more mortgages. It would have been very difficult and a real strain on us, especially with two. And we probably would have felt like we just couldn't swing it as a family. So, I don't know, I would have had to have gone out and gotten a job that would pay enough to justify two kids in private school. With that, it would have meant not being able to mother them as much myself. Or my husband having to change work, and all the soul-searching that would have meant for him. It's unimaginable. I can't envision a path that we would have been able to so comfortably just sail on over to Hills School. And, yeah,* [we would have had to] *go through a lot of heart-wrenching decisions about Alexander* [school and tutors]. *But they never had to do with money. None of these decisions have had to do with money. I can't imagine it being any other way.*

The world that Elizabeth has trouble imagining includes difficulty paying a mortgage out of earnings, working full-time, working at a job you may not like, public school, family budgeting and making choices, and worrying about money issues. The world she cannot imagine is reality for most Americans. The Cummings family is a possibly excessive but nonetheless illustrative example of how a reservoir of wealth and expected inheritance opens the door to all opportunities and can make dreams come true more easily.

## Families and Safety Nets

Let us ask a question of the four families we have met thus far that penetrates further the ways in which assets matter. What if these families lost their jobs? Vivian Arrora has nothing to fall back on and might well find herself back on welfare or worse. The consequences for Kathryn and Evan MacDonald, on the other hand, would be less catastrophic. She could sustain her present lifestyle for several years while progressively drawing more money from her inherited assets. Soon, however, if they were not replenished from other expected inheritances, she would need to tap her assets for everyday living. Without a full-time or higher-paying job, she would have to postpone becoming a homeowner. The Ackermans' financial assets provide a resource cushion that can absorb economic shocks and personal misfortune. They could survive on their nest egg for some time, but it would mean scaling back the lifestyle they treasure—fewer vacations, giving up their boat—and even then they could not endure a prolonged absence of income. More important, their resources secure a desired status for them and educational opportunities for their children. The wealthy Cummings family probably would not notice the financial impact for a long time because the interest on Elizabeth's inheritance alone gives them more money than Vivian Arrora earns working a full-time job.

The stories of these four families introduce themes that I will weave throughout the text. I want to use the cases just presented to expand the idea of transformative assets. Wealth is critical to a family's class standing, social status, whether they own or rent housing, the kind of community they live in, and the quality of their children's schools. Based upon a thorough familiarity with the textured lives of the families we interviewed, I suggest that it is possible to distinguish whether a family's current position and life trajectory is based upon earnings and achievements, or wealth and family legacies, or some combination. The notion of transformative assets is most trenchant for our purposes when the financial resources that make current status possible are inherited in some fashion. In the families we have heard about already, Kathryn MacDonald provides the clearest example of the power of inherited assets to transform her current position far beyond what she earns. The Cummings family illustrates the old-fashioned and better-understood notion of very wealthy families handing down resources. The Ackerman case is not so clear-cut. They enjoyed a head start because their families paid the college bills, and they received family financial assistance on their first home. At the same time, the Ackermans' assets also represent the fruits of savings and investments based upon their earned achievements in the workplace. Vivian Arrora works as hard as anyone in these four families—and has the least to show for it. Lack of assets, much less family money, caps her family's mobility.

These four accounts highlight the role that assets—or lack of them—

play in a family's quest for well-being and promoting opportunities for their children. When asked to name the primary benefit of money, 87 percent of affluent baby boomers in one survey answered, "It enables you to give advantages to your children."

American families are in the process of passing along a $9 trillion legacy from one generation to the next. This is a lot of money, but it is distributed very unevenly. Most whites do not inherit considerable wealth; an even smaller percentage of African Americans benefit. Hand in hand with this money, I submit, what is really being handed down from generation to generation is the profound legacy of reproducing racial inequality. This legacy will be difficult to discern because the language of family heritage hides it from our political consciousness. Mainstream sociological theory sees differences in jobs, skills, and education as the primary causes of inequality, and substantial wealth transfers embarrass this theory. The classical sociologist Emil Durkheim, for example, predicted that family inheritances would decline over time in favor of giving to charitable and nonprofit organizations, but studies examining actual bequests invalidate this prediction.[1] Andrew Carnegie's belief that giving relatives money only makes them lazy (a belief he put into action) may correspond with this perspective, but the empirical evidence tells a different story. In 1989 charitable bequests constituted less than 10 percent of proceeds of estates valued over $600,000 in the United States.[2] Even Karl Marx was more concerned with production and the circulation of money than with property and family legacies.

## The Asset Perspective

A core part of my argument is that wealth, as distinct from income, offers the key to understanding racial stratification. Thus a wealth perspective provides a fresh way to examine the "playing field." Indeed, I believe that this perspective challenges a standard part of the American credo—that similar accomplishments result in roughly equal rewards—which needs serious reexamination. First, however, I need to outline this wealth perspective and why I believe it is so important.

By wealth I mean the total value of things families own minus their debts. Income, on the other hand, includes earnings from work, interest and dividends, pensions, and transfer payments. The distinction between wealth and income is significant because one signifies ownership and control of resources and the other represents salary or its replacement. However, the difference between the two is often muddled in the public mind, and only recently have the social sciences begun to treat wealth as an intrinsically important indicator of family well-being that is quite different from income. Another perspective on advantage and disadvantage emerges when wealth is used as an indicator of racial inequality. Wealth represents a more permanent capacity to secure advantages in both the short and long term, and it is transferred across generations. Income data is collected regularly, and vast stores of it exist. In contrast, wealth data has not been collected systematically, and issues such as how to value a home, how to view home equity, whether retirement plans should be counted, and how to value a business make it harder to measure.

Wealth has been a neglected dimension of the social sciences' concern with the economic and social status of Americans in general and racial minorities in particular. We have been much more comfortable describing and analyzing occupational, educational, and income inequality than examining the economic foundation of a capitalist society, "private property." When wealth surveys became available in the mid-1980s, journalists and social scientists began to pay more attention to the issue of wealth. The growing concentration of wealth at the top and the growing racial wealth gap have become important public policy issues that undergird many political debates but, unfortunately, not many policy discussions.[3]

Social scientists typically analyze racial inequality as imbalances in the distribution of power, economic resources, and opportunities. Most research on racial inequality has focused on the economic dimension. This economic component has emphasized jobs and wages. Until very recently, the social sciences and the policy arena neglected the effect of wealth disparity and inheritance on the differing opportunities and well-being of white and black families. We are suggesting that wealth motivates much of what Americans do, grounds their life chances, and provides enduring advantages and disadvantages across generations. Wealth ownership is the single dimension on which whites and blacks are most persistently unequal.[4]

Our understanding of racial inequality comes typically from data on income. Primarily this represents earnings from work, but it also includes social assistance and pensions. Income is a tidy and valuable gauge of present inequality. Indeed, a very strong case can be made that reducing racial discrimination in the workplace has resulted in narrowing the *hourly wage gap* between whites and racial minorities.[5] Reducing discrimination in jobs, promotion, and pay is an effective way to narrow racial inequality. The average American family uses income for food, shelter, clothing, and other necessities. Wealth is different, and I will argue that it is used differently than income. Wealth is what families own, a storehouse of resources. Wealth signifies a command over financial resources that when combined with income can produce the opportunity to secure the "good life" in whatever form is needed—education, business, training, justice, health, comfort, and so on. In this sense wealth is a special form of money not usually used to purchase milk and shoes or other life necessities. More often it is used to create opportunities, secure a desired stature and standard of living, or pass class status along to one's children. It is obvious that the positions of two families with the same income but widely different wealth assets are not identical, and it is time for us to take this into account in public policy.

The importance of wealth was borne out in the stories we heard from families about how they think about assets, how they strategize about acquiring wealth, how they plan to use assets, and how they actually use them. I want to emphasize that families consider income and wealth very differently so that wealth is seen as a special kind of money. We asked families directly if they treated wealth differently than income. The pattern of answers is resoundingly affirmative, especially among families with ample assets. Kathryn MacDonald summed it up succinctly by saying, "Income supplies life support, assets provide opportunities." A middle-class Bostonian put it this way: "My income is limited. My assets I want to hang on to for future needs." Jen Doucette of Los Angeles, whom we will meet in Chapter 2, captured the thinking of many we interviewed when she said that wealth "is definitely long term. We act as if it's not even there." Another person added, "We figure like the income is what we got to work with. Try and live within it." We asked one Boston family if they ever used assets for expenses, and the answer was a Benjamin Franklinesque scolding:

"Absolutely not. We are New Englanders. Never touch principal.... To me income is to pay bills; assets are to keep."

The way that families with few financial assets replied to questions about the role assets play in their plans to get ahead clearly indicates class differences. Some scoffed or simply laughed at the question because they have no assets to distinguish from income. Even among those with small amounts, though, assets are viewed as resources not to be touched so that they can face emergencies. In fact, we heard the words "emergencies," "unexpected," "rainy day," and "cushion" more often from families who have few or no assets than from families with more. These families view their limited assets as cushions or safety nets against unexpected events like paying for a child's orthodontic work that is not covered on the family health policy or family crises like helping a recently unemployed sister pay her rent, not as tools of opportunity. Working-class and poor families use wealth for life support, to cushion bad times, and to meet emergencies. Middle-class families, in contrast, use their assets to provide better opportunities that advantage them. In our conversations about the power of assets, working-class and asset-poor families dream that assets will give them freedom from a situation, ease a difficulty, relieve a fear, or overcome a hardship. Middle-class and asset-wealthy families see assets as power and freedom to leverage opportunities.

I have made much of the distinction between income and wealth, but this would only be an academic distinction if the two were highly correlated, that is, if a family's income were a reliable predictor of its wealth, and if savings were the primary source of wealth accumulation. If this were the case, we could continue to tell the income story as a sort of proxy for all resources, as we have in the past. If they are not powerfully correlated, however, fusing them prevents us from addressing an important basis of racial inequality, the increasing concentration of wealth, and public policies that mitigate the consequences of such inequalities. Sociologist Lisa Keister's *Wealth in America* reviews this issue and concludes that the correlation between income and wealth is weak. This suggests that, according to Keister, "studies that focus solely on income miss a large part of the story of advantage and disadvantage in America."[6]

Because wealth sometimes represents inequalities from the past, it not only is a measure of differences in contemporary resources but also suggests inequalities that will play out in the future. Looking at racial inequality through wealth changes our conception of its nature and magnitude and of whether it is declining or increasing. Most recent analyses have concluded that continuing racial inequality primarily results from disparities in educational achievement and jobs. Sociologist Christopher Jencks, for instance, argues that improving educational performance for African Americans would be the biggest step toward racial equality. William Julius Wilson has consistently maintained in several books that advances in the workplace are the linchpin of racial equality. The asset perspective does not neglect the importance of these powerful insights. I maintain, however, that exclusively focusing on contemporary class-based factors like jobs and education disregards the currency of the historical legacy of African Americans. A focus on wealth sheds light on both historical and contemporary impacts not only of class but also of race. Income is an indicator of the current status of racial inequality; I argue that an examination of wealth discloses the consequences of the racial patterning of opportunities.

The legacy of the American dilemma of democracy and race continues to haunt the American scene. The dynamics of race and class intertwine in a way that becomes more clearly explicable upon examining how families use private wealth to expand their chances and—just as important—how lack of assets dampens aspirations. Americans highly value two cherished but contradictory notions: equal opportunity and a family's ability to pass along advantages to their children. By focusing on assets rather than exclusively on income, we can unravel this legacy and examine how it affects racial inequality.

In summary, I argue that we have been seriously underestimating racial inequality by focusing primarily on workplace and income and that an examination of wealth is an indispensable part of understanding inequality. Tragically, polices based solely in the workplace that seek to narrow differences will fail to close the breach. Taken together, however, asset and labor market approaches open new windows of possibility, an approach I will elaborate in the closing chapter.

## An Asset Poverty Line

One of the disappointments of attempts to allay poverty is that policies only consider jobs and transfers that substitute for income. Changing the lens of analysis to wealth dramatically shifts our perspective on poverty and gives us new tools. The official poverty rate, based on annual income, dropped from 15.2 percent in 1983 to 12.8 percent in 1989 and to 11.7 percent in 2001 ($18,104 for a family of four). Using these numbers we could say that the rising tide of the long boom during the 1990s seemed to lift many, if not all, boats. The government releases these official numbers annually, and they give us a good idea of the scope and nature of poverty for that year.[7] But sociologist Mark Rank suggests that to understand the true nature of poverty, we must see it in a different light.[8] He argues that we should be looking at American families that will experience at least one year of poverty. Poverty touches a surprisingly high number of Americans, as 59 percent will spend at least one year below the official poverty line. While this number puts the economic fragility of America's families in a new light, the shocking statistic is that nine of every ten black Americans will encounter poverty during their working adult years.

If we think about poverty as a lifetime event and shift the perspective to examine family assets, our understanding of poverty and inequality and what needs to be done changes dramatically. And, as we will see shortly, the asset-poverty perspective captures the fragile economic status of American families, embracing nearly two in five families and over half of all African American families.

The Nobel economist Amartya Sen highlights the affect of asset-poverty on the ability to avoid elementary deprivations including premature mortality, significant undernourishment, persistent illness, widespread illiteracy.[9] His argument is that poverty is more than just lacking an adequate income; rather, poverty includes lacking the basic capacities for building and sustaining a better life.

The Asset Poverty Line (APL) helps us understand the asset condition of American families. (See Figure 1.1, page 39.) The fundamental idea is to determine an amount of assets a family needs to meet its basic needs over a specified period, under the extreme condition that no other sources of income are available. We decided to tie this figure to the official income-poverty standard. In 1999 the official U.S. government poverty line for a family of four stood at $1,392 a month. In order to live at that poverty line for three months, a family of four needs a private safety net of at least $4,175. Families with less than

$4,175 in net financial assets in 1999, then, are "asset-poor." And this is a conservative standard because it incorporates the official government poverty line, which many believe underestimates the actual scope of poverty, as the basis for our calculation. It also employs a three-month standard even though one could argue just as reasonably for a six-month standard. Although I believe my built-in assumptions underestimate asset poverty among America's families, I want to stay focused on the basic idea of asset poverty. It is my hope that as these ideas are accepted, bolder conceptions will follow.

The APL measure allows an examination of asset-poor families since 1984, so we can track trends in asset wealth. *Black Wealth/White Wealth* reported the rate of asset poverty in America for 1988, and the result was truly appalling. One could argue that it has gotten even worse since. In 1984, 41 percent of American families fell below the Asset Poverty Line; and the rate held fairly stable until it dipped several points to 36 percent in 1999. Nearly four households in every ten in the world's wealthiest nation do not own enough assets to live a poverty lifestyle for three months. The boom years of the 1990s, which produced enormous wealth and record-low unemployment, lifted only 7 percent out of asset-poverty. The Asset Poverty Line shows that the effects of the tremendous run-up in the stock market in the 1990s that created over $8 trillion in equity barely trickled down to typical families.

The Asset Poverty Line also contains information on the official income-poverty line, which illustrates that looking at poverty through the asset lens changes the scope, magnitude, and understanding of what poverty means, not just the definition. One can view income-poverty as a phenomenon affecting a relatively small percentage of Americans, who, perhaps, have educational and skill deficits, physical disabilities, or personal deficiencies. But if poverty is something that affects not just one in every eight, nine, or ten families but four in ten, then we need to think about poverty very differently because it is much more characteristic of American families.

Over half of black American families fell below the Asset Poverty Line in 1999. This represents a positive trend for black families, as it was 67 percent in 1984 and has declined steadily over 15 years. This downward trend is encouraging, although an asset poverty rate of 54 percent is shamefully high and more than twice the rate of white families. In 1984

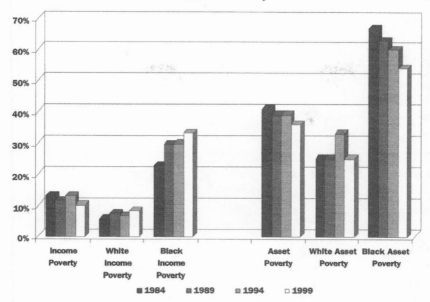

**Figure 1.1   Asset Poverty Line\***
**Percent Below Poverty Line**

\*Net financial assets below three-month poverty standard
Source: PSID, 1984–1999

one in four white families fell below the Asset Poverty Line; this rate remained steady in 1989, rose in 1994 to 33 percent, and then fell back to 25 percent in 1999.

Figure 1.2 below provides information on children in asset-poor families. Thirty-nine percent of America's children are being raised in families that fall below the Asset Poverty Line. Vivian Arrora's children—Lamar, Bria, and Brittany—are growing up in an asset-impoverished family, and instead of viewing their circumstances as tragic or extraordinary, the reality is that this family represents the genuine asset circumstances and incapacities for two of every five children in America. The Arrora family is a good illustration of how much more difficult it is to permanently leave asset poverty than it is to escape income poverty. Vivian Arrora's income barely extends past the official government poverty line, but on a personal and statistical level hers is a success story. It will take many, many years of working full-time, getting raises, and being promoted before her children will receive any benefits that go along with assets, unless she meets her millionaire.

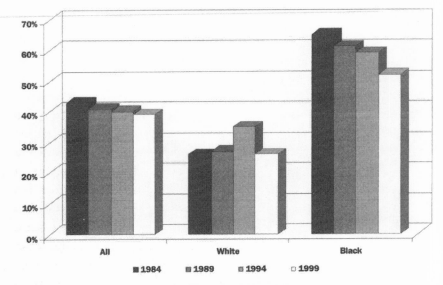

**Figure 1.2   Children Growing Up Asset-Poor**

Source: PSID, 1984, 1989, 1994, 1999

A further analysis of this already disturbing data discloses imposing and powerful racial and ethnic cleavages. In 1999, 26 percent of all white children grew up in asset-poor households, compared to 52 percent of black American children and 54 percent of Hispanic children. The rate for whites has held steady since 1984 at about one-quarter while the rate for Hispanic children has risen and the rate for blacks has fallen. An annual report card on the nation's asset health would be a good start because it would provide information on family asset poverty and a regular tally on the extent to which important segments of the population lack this private cushion.[10]

In this chapter we got to know the Arrora, MacDonald, Ackerman, and Cummings families. As my argument takes shape in the rest of this book I will draw upon some of the other 178 families we interviewed. The detailed private information these families shared with us is the basis for our understanding of how families use assets to promote their betterment. Just as significantly, as we already have begun to learn, lack of financial assets typically acts as a critical barrier to advancement or launching social mobility. I will use the household surveys to examine questions about financial wealth in the United States, demonstrating that private wealth is the hidden fault line in American society and that a racial wealth gap persists. The next key step in my argument explores the lives of middle-class Americans to consider in greater detail the impact of private wealth on successful white and black families. After that, I examine the main routes by which past wealth inequality becomes the foundation for modern racial inequality. To accomplish this I focus on one of the bedrocks of the American Dream—homeownership. How young families acquire homes is one of the most tangible ways that the historical legacy of race plays out in the present generation and projects well into future. To understand how young families can afford to buy homes and how this contributes greatly to the racial wealth gap, we need to unravel the legacies of inheritance. Sorting out a modern notion of inheritance brings the racial legacy into closer view. An important element of my argument details how families leverage resources to position themselves in communities they deem to be advantageous in both class and race terms. I develop this theme further by describing the extraordinary extent to which families make sacrifices and expend resources to place their children in educational environments that give them important competitive advantages. Finally, I connect what we have learned to public policy recommendations, most particularly in the areas of homeownership, equitable schooling, asset development, and minimizing the ability of wealth to perpetuate inequality.

# 2

# The Cost of Being Black
# and the Advantage of Being White

## Wealth and Inequality

WHAT PORTION OF THE RACIAL WEALTH GAP results from merit-based differences like education, jobs, and earnings, and what portion springs from nonmerit-based sources, like inheritance, institutional discrimination, and discriminatory public policy? This question is crucial not because we can hope to explain all causes of the racial wealth gap but rather because it allows us to identify some significant sources of the gap. A commonsense explanation of why some people have more wealth than others is that wealth is accumulated primarily through high salaries, wise and timely investments, and prudent spending. Many contend that the racial wealth gap principally results from income inequality.[1] That is, people with similar incomes will have similar wealth, regardless of race. Do differences in income explain nearly all the racial differences in wealth? If so, then policies need to continue focusing primarily on the workplace to further narrow job and earnings inequality. If not, however, then public policy must address dynamics outside the labor market as well as those within.

The remarkable growth of wealth resulting from the sustained economic prosperity after World War II changed forever its role in American society. Until the baby boomers started coming of age, family wealth was the prerogative of a tiny minority of upper-crust American families. In the baby boom years, between 1946 and 1964, a significant number of middle-class families accumulated substantial amounts of wealth for the first time. Middle-class families now are passing along about $9 trillion to their adult children. How they use this unprecedented wealth transfer is an important part of the increasing inequality and racial inequality stories.

When we discuss a family's *net worth,* we mean all assets minus all debts and specifically include home equity. Net worth, then, is like a family's total asset balance sheet and indicates all of its financial resources. The median (or typical; half of all families have more and half have less) and mean (average) net worth of families in 1999 was $40,000 and $179,800, respectively.[2] *Net financial assets,* on the other hand, are restricted to liquid assets (those immediately available), specifically excluding home equity and cars. Net financial assets indicate those resources immediately available to families, and net worth gives a better idea of those resources that might be available to the next generation. Median and mean net financial assets in 1999 stood at $15,000 and $134,700. Which is a better sense of what the "average" American family possesses: $15,000 or $134,700? In the case of the latter, adding a billionaire's wealth raises the statistical average substantially. It does not affect the median.

The significant difference between net worth and net financial assets is the inclusion or exclusion of home equity. Because net worth indicates wealth that may be bequeathed at death to the next generation and net financial assets indicate resources available today, I will present both throughout.

The remarkable post–World War II growth in wealth saw average net worth increase nearly $60,000 per household between 1962 and 1995. Of course, this figure is misleading, because the growth in wealth did not occur evenly for all families. Net worth increased from $31,000 to $39,000 for typical families during this period. The huge difference here between the mean and median figures demonstrates again the lopsided nature of wealth accumulation.[3] Meanwhile, net financial assets for typical families remained unchanged between 1962 and 1995, although the average figures, again, show a hefty increase from $92,000 to $135,000. Keeping the important top-heavy caveat in mind, it does mean that larger shares of wealth created by the tremendous postwar prosperity in America spread out into more families than at any time in our past. The difference between net worth and net financial assets also indicates that for average Americans housing wealth continues to be the largest reservoir of assets. In fact, for families in the middle three-fifths of America's net worth distribution, ranging from $1,650 to $153,000, equity in their principal residence represents 60 percent of their wealth.

While overall wealth has been increasing at this staggering rate, wealth inequality has been increasing since 1980. By 1998 it had reached its worse level since 1929. The richest 1 percent of families controls 38 percent of total household wealth, and the top 20 percent controls 84 percent. Financial wealth is even more lopsided: The richest 1 percent owns 47 percent of the value of stocks, bonds, real estate, businesses, and other financial instruments, and one-fifth of America's families controls 93 percent. In contrast, the top 20 percent receives about 42 percent of all income.

The financial wealth of the bottom two-fifths of the population actually falls into negative numbers; that is, family debts overshadow financial assets. Nearly three in ten households have zero or negative financial wealth. These figures illustrate the extreme concentration of wealth, and when we view American families' economic health through this wealth lens we see that it is more fragile than acknowledged previously.[4] Economic inequality increased markedly as the boom of the 1990s fizzled. The wealth of those in the top 10 percent of incomes surged much more than the wealth of those in any other group. The net worth of families in the top 10 percent jumped 69 percent from 1998 to 2001.[5]

These numbers present a staggering portrait of inequality in America, but, as aggregate statistics, they cannot show us what wealth means in people's lives. I will turn to one of the wealthiest families we interviewed to put financial assets into the concrete and human context of real families and to glimpse the organizing role that assets play in family life.

## The Doucette Family Story

In 1982, Jen and Sam Doucette bought a home on a quiet residential street in the Mar Vista section of West Los Angeles—bordered by Santa Monica to the north and Culver City to the east—from a friend who had moved away and was looking for someone to take over his mortgage. They had just married, and both held well-paying jobs they liked. Like the others in their immediate neighborhood, their home was a small, one-story, stucco tract home built right after World War II, probably for workers from the nearby Hughes and Douglas defense plants. They were the first on their block to add a second story, which not only doubled and modernized their living space but also began an upscaling of this neighborhood from working class to upper middle class. Their street is considerably west and south of what most call Mar Vista, but according to local real estate agents I spoke to, Mar Vista is becoming more a state of mind and status than a precise geographic area.

The Doucettes' part of Mar Vista is a section of Los Angeles that is increasing in value rapidly because it is only one mile to the ocean and because of its location on the affluent west side. Many homeowners have, like the Doucettes, recently expanded vertically to bring them more in tune with upper-middle-class urban lifestyles. The activity and newness of the construction brighten the neighborhood and give it a different air from the areas that surround it. Their block clearly has the sorts of amenities and new city services—like freshly painted crosswalks and curbs, neatly trimmed trees, buried electric lines—that herald up-and-coming neighborhoods. It sends out an air of rising property values.

In terms of financial wealth, the Doucettes are the wealthiest family we interviewed. Their net worth (including their house) of $1 million places them among the richest 1 percent of Americans. Sam is a corporate executive and makes more than $200,000 a year. Jen used to work at one of the motion picture studios but has been a homemaker since Blaine, their 5-year-old, was born. They possess an assortment of mutual funds, IRAs, 401(k)s, CDs, and pension plans that total about $450,000. Sam and Jen have access to over $700,000 in net financial assets tomorrow to take advantage of an opportunity, meet a crisis, or plan for their future.

In addition to their various savings plans, they bought another house in their neighborhood two years ago and fixed it up to rent as an investment property, and they feel very confident that it will rise in value with their neighborhood. They were able to put down about half of the purchase price for this investment property in cash. Several years ago on a vacation to Lake Arrowhead, they fell in love with the area and decided to buy a second home. Jen recalls,

*Homes could be had for a very reasonable price. I don't think we ever dreamed in a million years that we would have a vacation home this early in our lives. It fell into our lives, basically. We almost immediately decided that we wanted to buy up there.*

They found a three-bedroom, two-bath vacation home and bought it for $140,000, using $65,000 as a down payment. Both of their additional properties have appreciated considerably, adding another $100,000 or so in property to their wealth portfolio. At the time of our interview, their house was worth about $160,000 more than it had cost them, including the improvements.

This is a very prosperous family, and evidence of this prosperity came through throughout the interview. Like most Americans, though, Jen and Sam do not believe it is appropriate to disclose financial details. Jen was so guarded about family finances that I had to ask for details more than once. When asked to rank her family's wealth as compared to other American families, Jen guessed about the 80th percentile, though in fact they are about the 99th percentile. At the other end of the spectrum, we talked to families with zero or even negative assets who ranked themselves at 50 on this scale. It seems that the commonly held perception that all think of themselves as middle class is accurate. The Doucettes responded to questions about wealth with discomfort, even though they had been clearly informed beforehand that I would ask them. Interestingly, we rarely got this attitude from families with few assets, who had perhaps more embarrassing and less "successful" stories to tell.

Despite their initial reticence, the Doucettes told us that they treat their wealth as a special kind of money different from income. According to Jen, wealth "is definitely long term. We act as if it's not even there." She is expressing her sense of economic security grounded in wealth.

Like many wealthy city residents, the Doucettes live in a community that they like but feel trapped in a school jurisdiction in which they have no confidence. Mar Vista may be a state of mind, as the local real estate agents like to say, but it unambiguously falls within the boundaries of the Los Angeles Unified School District, notorious for weak schools, drug problems, and violence. Blaine is attending a Montessori preschool. I ask Jen what will happen when he is ready for kindergarten and decisions must be made. Jen is clear and adamant: "Our neighborhood school is not an option." Instead, they are looking into a couple of charter and magnet schools, and they plan to petition neighboring Culver City for admission since this city's schools have a very good reputation. These are backup plans because Pacifica Oaks, "the private school that we applied to, is our first choice." It is one of the most expensive private schools in Los Angeles; the cost of kindergarten for Blaine would start at $12,000.

The capacity of wealth is powerful in the Doucette family. It allowed them to buy a house in a desirable location and a vacation home that gets them out of Los Angeles in the hot and smoggy summer months and into Southern California's mountains and lakes. They can use their wealth to acquire the kind of educational environment and experience they think best for Blaine. At the end of the interview, I ask Jen if she has a sense of economic security: "Very much, yes." I then ask her to tell me a few things she is able to do because of her sense of security. "Take trips, buy additional property, make certain investments," Jen says. "We definitely have freedom to do things." The Doucettes are a delightful family and seem quite happy. We have no way of knowing how important money is to their happiness, but for this family wealth is important for homeownership, community, a vacation home, and shaping the life of their child.

## The Racial Wealth Gap

Surprisingly, household surveys did not begin collecting detailed information about wealth until the mid-1980s, when a couple of surveys began including questions about family assets. This information provides the basis for analyzing the racial wealth gap.[6] The charts below look at data from 1999. (See Figures 2.1 and 2.2.) The typical black household earns 59 cents for every dollar earned by the typical white household. This income comparison closely matches other national data and is the most widely used indicator of current racial and ethnic material inequality. However, changing the lens of analysis to wealth dramatically shifts the perspective. The net worth of typical white families is $81,000 compared to $8,000 for black families. This *baseline racial wealth gap*, then, shows that black families possess only 10 cents for every dollar of wealth held by white families. The issue is no longer how to think about closing the gap from 59 cents on the dollar to a figure approaching parity but how to think about going from 10 cents on the dollar to parity. In dollars, the baseline racial wealth gap is

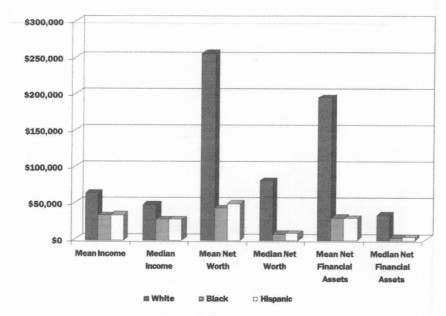

Source: PSID, 1999

**Figure 2.1  Family Income and Family Wealth**

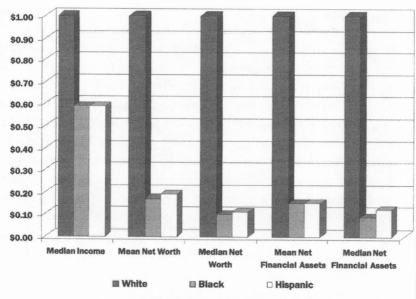

**Figure 2.2  Family Income and Family Wealth
Minority Cents-to-Dollar Values**

Source: PSID, 1999

robust: The typical white family's wealth is $73,450 more than the typical black family's. Even though both white and black families increased their net worth between 1988 and 1999, the black-white gap actually grew by $16,000 (in 1999 dollars).

The figures for net financial assets do not improve the picture. The typical black family possesses $3,000 in net financial assets compared to $33,500 for the typical white family. These figures represent wealth accumulation for both whites and blacks between 1988 and 1999, indicating that the typical white and black families had progressed financially. These figures also show a whopping $20,000 increase in the net financial asset gap. While families were doing better, inequality increased.

## The Connection Between Income and Wealth

Why does this huge racial wealth gap persist, and why is it getting worse? One alternative explanation that minimizes the significance of race argues that wealth is a product of income and savings; that is, as incomes rise, people save and invest more, which leads to greater wealth accumulation. This classical economic view attributes the racial wealth gap primarily to income differences between whites and blacks.[7] The explanation points to narrowing the income gap as the principal remedy for the racial wealth gap. In order to test this perspective, it is critically important to address whether the wealth of blacks is quite similar to that of whites with comparable incomes. In fact, while the evidence supports the importance of high salaries to wealth accumulation, the evidence also suggests that income is only part of a larger picture.

Table 2.1 shows that white households in every income quintile have significantly higher median wealth than similar-earning black households. In the lowest quintile, net worth for typical white households is $17,066, while black households in the same quintile possess only $2,400. Among highest-earning households, white median net worth is $133,607, while net worth for black households in the highest income group registers $43,806. The median net financial assets data is just as revealing: At the middle quintile, for example, typical net financial assets for white households are $6,800, which is markedly higher than for black households, $800.[8]

#### Table 2.1   Wealth by Income and Race

| | White | | Black | |
|---|---|---|---|---|
| | Net Worth | Net Financial Assets | Net Worth | Net Financial Assets |
| **Highest fifth median** | $133,607 | $40,465 | $43,806 | $7,448 |
| **Second highest fifth median** | $ 65,998 | $13,362 | $29,851 | $2,699 |
| **Middle fifth median** | $ 50,350 | $ 6,800 | $14,902 | $  800 |
| **Second lowest fifth median** | $ 39,908 | $ 3,599 | $ 6,879 | $  249 |
| **Lowest fifth median** | $ 17,066 | $ 7,400 | $ 2,400 | $  100 |

Source: PSID, 1999

It is important to observe that controlling for income in this manner does lessen significantly the white-to-black wealth ratios. The baseline median white-to-black net worth gap is a dime to a dollar overall but narrows when comparing white and black households in similar income quintiles. The gap, as expressed in black-to-white dollar ratios, stays about the same for people at the lower end but narrows to 30 cents on the dollar, 45 cents, and 33 cents, respectively, for people in the $25,000–$39,000, $39,001–$60,000, and highest earning ranges. In brief, as shown by this comparative procedure, controlling for income indeed narrows the gap, but a significantly large gap persists. This factual record does not support hypothetical propositions that whites and blacks at similar income levels possess similar wealth.[9]

No matter how much or how little you make, then, wealth is dramatically higher for white households. The evidence shows that higher incomes lead to high wealth accumulation, but the same evidence does not support the contention that the racial wealth gap derives principally from white-black income differences. This alternative explanation of the racial wealth gap lacks evidence. Lest my rejection of the income explanation sound too dismissive, let me be clear: The racial wealth gap does decline as incomes rise. At the same time, even when incomes are equal and high, a cavernous gap remains.

But aren't things improving for younger people? We might expect to find a more sizable racial wealth gap among older people than among younger people because of progress in other areas of racial inequality. As younger generations begin and go through life with more equal opportunities than previous generations, the wealth gap should narrow. And yet there is a consistent pattern. Further, the racial wealth gap is not simply a matter of starting at different places and then maintaining this constant gap; the gap widens as people advance through the life course. For whites and blacks who were 20–29 years old in 1984, the gap increased $23,926 by 1994. As white and black families progress through the life course, the different opportunities afforded by increasingly disparate financial resources continue to compound racial inequality and make it worse.[10]

Earlier in this chapter we detailed the extraordinary magnitudes of wealth inequality between whites and blacks that remain even when they are matched on key characteristics such as income. The research findings support my contention that a single source or even a few sources cannot account for the racial wealth gap. Rather, its roots run more deeply in contemporary American life.[11] A more informed and comprehensive analysis therefore needs to (1) identify which factors are most important in creating the wealth gulf; (2) explore how much of the racial wealth gap can be explained by a combination of key factors; and (3) assess the contribution of merit and nonmerit factors in creating the racial wealth gulf.

We now can use a statistical method called multiple regression to examine the relationship between wealth and the variables we think predict wealth, such as income, age, marital status, family size, region, job, and education. It allows us to see how changes in the various variables affect wealth. For example, multiple regression can give us a good understanding of how much wealth increases for each additional year of education completed net of changes in the other factors. The first step in regression analysis is to identify a set of variables that are expected to have an impact on wealth. Income? Education? Jobs? Age? Family? What combination of factors? I want to emphasize that this sort of analysis best identifies key factors and the contributions they make for the variance in wealth. Later, I will use our family interviews to assess the importance of head-start assets in launching a family's well-being.

The results in Table 2.2 show that in this survey income, inheritance, and having one full-time (highly paid) family worker are the most significant predictors of differences in net worth, followed by home ownership. When one has a college degree, the number of children in one's family, marital status, female-headed family, and full-time employment are less important. Income is the most important factor in net financial assets variation, followed by inheritance and one full-time family worker. Table 2.2 also allows us to observe the contribution each variable makes to wealth accumulation.

Income is the most important variable determining net worth. Each additional dollar of annual income generates $3.26 in net worth; thus the net worth difference between a family with a $30,000 income and a family families with $60,000 in earnings is nearly $100,000. This wealth disparity is built upon years of income difference. Owning a home returns about $56,000, which is another indication of how important home equity is for building wealth. For net financial assets, each additional income dollar generates $2.95, and middle-class occupation nets $31,000 in comparison to working-class jobs.[12]

The results just presented include all families, and thus they do not tell us about racial differences. Now we can investigate whether, for example, a college education rewards blacks as well as it does whites. Table 2.3 opposite presents separate analyses for blacks and whites.

### Table 2.2  What Accounts for Wealth Differences?

|  | Net Worth | Net Financial Assets |
|---|---|---|
| White | 32,509.00 | 24,503.00 |
| Age | 1,011.00 | 586.00 |
| Age Squared | 38.04 | 33.80 |
| Live in South | −3,121.00 | −4,782.00 |
| Education in Years | 5,695.00 | 3,693.00 |
| Bachelor's Degree | 54,398.00 + | 41,933.00 |
| Middle-Class Occupation | 26,108.00 | 31,748.00 |
| Number of Children | −15,161.00 + | −10,840.00 |
| Widowed | −73,541.00 | −73,333.00 + |
| Married | 12,353.00 | 45.86 |
| Female-Headed w/ Children | 62,509.00 | 43,993.00 |
| Experienced Unemployment | 7,902.00 | 5,575.00 |
| Employed Full-Time | −68,163.00 * | −55,476.00 * |
| Retired | 39,746.00 | 28,457.00 |
| Own Home | 56,238.00 * | 15,899.00 |
| Income $ | 3.26 *** | 2.95 *** |
| Inheritance $ | 0.13 ** | 0.10 ** |
| CONSTANT | −229,954.00 * | −171,773.00 + |
| N | 6367 | 6583 |
| R Squared | 0.174 | 0.139 |
| Adjusted R Squared | 0.171 | 0.137 |
| Total Model Significance | 0.00 | 0.00 |

+ < = .10; * < = .05; ** < = .01; *** < = .001
Source: PSID, 1999

Income translates, for example, into more wealth for whites than for blacks. Everything else being equal, blacks accrue only $1.98 in wealth for each additional dollar earned, in comparison to $3.25 for whites, so that, net of all other factors, the average black family earning $60,000 possesses $76,000 less wealth than the average white family with the same earnings. The most dramatic difference is the wealth effect of homeownership, which is worth about $60,000 more for whites than blacks. This evidence bolsters my core argument that the way homes are bought and sold, where they are located, and how the market values them provides a contemporary foundation for racial inequality.

These findings using 1999 data vividly show the continuing importance of race in the wealth accumulation process. We noted that demographic, achievement, and inheritance factors actually explain a small portion of the racial wealth gap. Examining wealth accumulation in 1999 in this way provides an excellent snapshot for the United States

**Table 2.3 What Accounts for Wealth Differences Among Blacks and Whites?**

| | Net Worth | | Net Financial Assets | |
|---|---|---|---|---|
| | **WHITE** | **BLACK** | **WHITE** | **BLACK** |
| **Age** | 3040 | −157 | 2041 | −101.576 |
| **Age Squared** | 26 | 8 | 28 | 2.479 |
| **Live in South** | −2908 | −1741 | −9376 | −2162.824 |
| **Education in Years** | 14170 | 1530 | 9484 − | 235.308 |
| **Bachelor's Degree** | 35654 | 5974 | 28176 | 15516.457 |
| **Middle-Class Occupation** | 36356 | 24682 | 42808 | 27125.477 + |
| **Number of Children** | −30210 + | 2564 | −25713+ | 6122.664 |
| **Widowed** | −78336 | −4211 | −85342 | −4756.381 |
| **Married** | 22051 | −12846 | 4329 | −17886.824 |
| **Female-Headed w/ Children** | 61031 | −1648 | 41959 | −9432.589 |
| **Experienced Unemployment** | −17216 | 16699 | −14752 | 1188.436 |
| **Employed Full-Time** | −81635 + | −22750 | −67562 | −19695.876 |
| **Retired** | 55255 | 6120 | 37753 | 3476.659 |
| **Own Home** | 86658 * | 27324 * | 39427 | 1467.46 |
| **Income $** | 3.250 *** | 1.974 *** | 2.951 *** | 1.938 *** |
| **Inheritance $** | 0.118 * | 0.141 | 0.093 * | 0.05208 |
| **CONSTANT** | −382,178.00 * | −50,836.00 | −277,028.50 + | 23670.359 |
| **N** | 3981 | 1859 | 4074 | 1963 |
| **R Squared** | 0.169 | 0.064 | 0.137 | 0.049 |
| **Adjusted R Squared** | 0.166 | 0.056 | 0.134 | 0.041 |
| **Total Model Significance** | *** | *** | *** | *** |

+ < = .10; * < = .05; ** < = .01; *** < = .001
Source: PSID, 1999

at one point in time and thus provides valuable insight into racial inequality. We can track families over time and examine their wealth accumulation and ask questions beyond the capabilities of cross-sectional data.[13] What distinguishes wealth-gaining families from families whose wealth does not change or from families whose wealth declines?[14] The first table in Appendix I (Table A.1) presents the results of factors that distinguish wealth-accumulating families from others between 1989 and 1999. Income, inheritance, and retirement during this period distinguish wealth-gaining families from those who did not gain much wealth. All the factors explain about 15 percent of the change in wealth between 1989 and 1999.

Change in family income is the most important factor in wealth changes. Each additional dollar in family income generates over $3.22 in net worth. Surprisingly, family educational status changing from no college graduates to college degrees is not important in distinguishing wealth-gainers from others. Becoming a homeowner during this period is not significant, in my view; homes do not rise in value very much in short time spans. However, homeownership will magnify differences over longer time periods. Finally, every dollar inherited between 1989 and 1999 created 60 cents in net worth.

Table A.2 shows changes in wealth from 1989 to 1999 separately for white and black households. One can note for each racial group how different factors are significant in distinguishing wealth-gainers from others. Change in family income, again, is the most important factor, but income once more translates into more wealth for whites than for blacks. Blacks accrue only $2.00 in net worth wealth for each additional dollar earned, in comparison to $3.22 for whites. Receiving an inheritance in this period is an important characteristic distinguishing white wealth-gainers, adding 59 cents in net worth for every dollar inherited.[15] Significantly, inheritance does not distinguish wealth-building among black families, perhaps because inheritance is so much more infrequent in black families and, when they do inherit, the amounts are small. I will pursue this key finding about the relative importance of inheritance in white and black families further in the next chapter.

To make our finding even more graphic we can look at what would happen if whites received the same returns as blacks on all factors. We know already, for instance, that whites receive $3.25 in additional wealth for each new dollar of income and that for blacks one additional income dollar generates only $1.98 in wealth. The idea here is to demonstrate the wealth effect of using blacks' wealth return for income instead of whites', and so on for every factor under analysis. We already know that a typical white family's mean net worth is $247,730, but what happens when we swap white functions for black ones? This method yields an easy way of projecting the cost of being African American. Swapping functions in this way lowers a family's net worth to $111,556. Thus the cost of being black amounts to $136,174. In net financial assets, the cost of being African American amounts to $94,426. These numbers present our best attempt to put a dollar figure on penalties African Americans pay.

In my view, it is equally important to explore the relationship between the hidden cost of being African American and the advantage of being white. This involves some tough reckoning. Do advantages in some areas translate into disadvantages for others? Is whites' well-being related to blacks' hardship? The white advantage in housing markets, as we have suggested already and will explore in detail later, seems to result in fewer homeownership opportunities and less built up in home equity for blacks. In later chapters, I will make a strong argument that advantages in education opportunity also come at the expense of disadvantaging others. In other areas, whites' advantage may not translate directly into blacks' disadvantage; instead, it may limit opportunities for minorities.

The idea of calculating white advantage is a good deal more threatening. The reason for this incongruity is that our national discourse typically frames racial discussions around why black Americans are not as successful as others are. Depending upon viewpoints, framing our national discussion on racial inequality this way puts the onus for black disadvantage on overt racism or on blacks themselves for not doing better. Both perspectives tend to see African Americans as victims. In my view, part of the power of dominant groups (in this case, whites) is their seeming invisibility and the fact that their status is often taken for granted, as if they are not active actors, agents, or benefactors in an unequal relationship. I believe we must begin to discuss white advantage and its direct impact on blacks. In the context of the next two chapters, which examine inheritance and middle-class achievements,

I develop more fully the relationship between white advantage and black disadvantage.

For now, however, the focus remains on placing an objective dollar figure on white advantage. Class enters the picture once again because the figures tell us about the average white family. In reality, many do not benefit at all while the dollar advantage to others far exceeds the average. The figures for the cost of being black are also—obversely—the dollar figures for white advantage: The hidden net worth advantage of being white also amounts to $136,173; similarly, the net financial assets advantage for being white is $94,426.

The Doucette family, described earlier in this chapter, gave us a glimpse at what wealth means to a very prosperous family. But what of families more firmly situated in the middle class and more like an "average" American family? In fact, the more typical case, as people's stories showed us repeatedly, is that addition or subtraction of a relatively small amount of assets can lead to radically changed lives. Take, for example, the Andrews family, a professional, middle-class family living in St. Louis.

## The Andrews Family

Judith Andrews is the kind of person who anchors a community—energetic, bright, and involved. She was 7 years old when her family moved from the public housing projects into their own home and became the first African American family on the block. Her father was a musician, and her mother was a seamstress. She was educated in the Catholic schools of Cleveland before becoming the first in her family to go to college. Using a combination of scholarships, working, and school loans, she earned her bachelor's degree at Cleveland State and then a master's degree in public affairs from Occidental College. After college, she moved to St. Louis for additional training in public affairs and started working as a planner at an agency focusing on housing for low- and moderate-income families.

Judith Andrews loves to tell the story of how she found and bought her home in 1982. Through her work in urban planning, she found a condemned house in the "dicey" but potentially up-and-coming Vandeventer neighborhood of north St. Louis. Just out of college, single, and with little in the way of savings, she took a calculated risk, bought a dilapidated house for $1,500, and completely rehabbed it from pipes in the ground to roof tiles. Fixing the roof was more expensive than the purchase price. Since first buying the house, she has put $30,000 into making the once-condemned property a comfortable home. In 1990, a few years after she bought her home, the average selling price for a single-family residence in this area was $32,000. In 2000 Vandeventer is 97 percent African American, 29 percent of the housing units are vacant, abandoned, or boarded up, and the poverty rate is high. When I ask why she chose her neighborhood, she says, "I kind of liked the urban pioneer spirit that St. Louis seemed to exhibit at that time." Judith particularly enjoys the liveliness of the nearby Central West End neighborhood, with its restaurants, shops, activity, and integrated feel.

In 1994 Judith married Steve, who works as a paralegal. The Andrewses' block fits sociologist Mary Patillo-McCoy's description of black middle-class neighborhoods in her book *Black Picket Fences.* More poverty, worse schools, higher crime, and fewer services than middle-class white neighborhoods characterize them. This results from the geography of residential segregation that typically situates black middle-class neighborhoods between poor black communities and whites. The Andrewses share space and public services with poor blacks, and thus the problems associated with poor black urban neighborhoods, while they serve as a buffer between the largely white, upscale West End they identify with and those same problems.

The street Judith lives on is a block north of a major thoroughfare that many consider the northern perimeter of the Central West End. As with the Doucettes defining themselves as a part of Mar Vista, it is important for Judith to identify as a Central West Ender, which supplies a middle-class persona that Vandeventer cannot. Her block is like many others in sections of St. Louis that are all black. Judith's home is a three-story brick house in good shape set back about 15 feet from the street with trimmed grass and plants in front. Trees provide much-needed shade on this block and some separation between houses that otherwise are close together. The houses on either side look like hers and add to the spruced-up, middle-class feel of her block, but across the street, and indeed interspersed every three or four houses, buildings are boarded up and broken windows and tall weeds designate obviously vacant homes. Turner Park, located near Judith's house, is a perfect example of the mixed economic condition of the Vandeventer neighborhood: At one corner there is a playground that could be the cornerstone of the surrounding blocks; at the other corner there is an unmaintained baseball diamond whose teams have long since moved from the neighborhood.

Judith enjoys seeing herself as a pioneer, but she also talks about needing to play frontier sheriff when drug activity increases and she must intensify her neighborhood commitments. She discusses her constant quest to "turn houses over to families who would make an investment in the neighborhood." She fears that many of the homes could be "wiped out overnight."

*Just wiped out. Like one year, the man across the street died. The man next door to him died. The man next door to me died. And two doors down across the street, the lady died. And they were all like in their eighties. . . . And those houses were all vacant. I mean, that's a scary thought. One day, they're occupied and fully functional; and then you wake up and they're vacant.*

Judith calls this the "scourge" of her community, which she and others regularly combat with constant vigilance and by marketing the area to prospective homeowners and small businesses.

Judith and Steven are successful in their professional careers, earning more than $80,000 between them. This urban-pioneer story is not just a tale about boldness and risk rewarded. It also is an asset success story. They live and find part of their urban identity in the "lively" Central West End. They probably could not afford to live within the traditional borders of the Central West End, where homes are far more expensive, but they are helping to stretch its boundary. The wealth accumulated in their home also means they do not have to shoulder the burden of poor urban public schools. Judith's 17-year-old son goes to an all-black parochial high school with excellent educational standards. Their young daughter will go to day care full-time until she reaches school age, when she too will go to private school, if she does not get into the city magnet school for gifted children. Their healthy incomes cannot pay the private school and day care bills, which total $18,000 annually. Judith and Steven have taken out a home equity loan to provide for their children's needs and other family expenses.

The house is worth about $70,000 in the current Vandeventer real estate market. We will analyze this in more detail in later chapters, but the real estate mantra of *location, location, location* clearly is evident here. Everything about this house—its architecture, its size, its condition, the way it feels—suggests that if we moved it to a more affluent community its value would rise significantly. Its Vandeventer location puts a racialized ceiling on its value because middle-class white families will not choose to move to this neighborhood. With the pool of potential buyers limited to blacks who can afford the Andrews house, the law of supply and demand values homes in black communities at considerably lower prices. Even though their home provides the Andrews about $40,000 in equity, if it were in a white middle-class community, the value of the house would be higher and their home equity would be much larger. This is one of the ways being black disadvantages even successful, hard-working, playing-by-the-rules, middle-class blacks. Several later chapters will pick up this theme and break down these dynamics in detail.

# 3

# Inheritance—"That Parent Thing"

## Parental Wealth and Head-Start Assets

SUCCESS IN AMERICA FEATURES SUCCESS in well-paying careers or businesses. Success results from education, skills, hard work, the kind of work one does, and perhaps a touch of luck. As success is based on merit, inequality is due to differences in ambition, ability, and effort. But the remarkable growth of wealth resulting from the post–World War II prosperity dramatically increased the number of people who inherit significant amounts of money. The baby boom generation, born between 1946 and 1964, marked a critical transformation in the American experience because a considerable number of them grew up in middle-class families that accumulated substantial wealth for the first time. Now adults with families of their own, since 1990 they have been collecting a $9 trillion bounty from their parents. And this in turn has allowed them to live in houses in neighborhoods that they simply could not have afforded without parental wealth. I do not begrudge an average family inheritance, but I am concerned about how weakened public commitments to children, families, schools, and communities encourage people to use inheritances for private advantage. How adult baby boomers use this unprecedented wealth transfer is crucial to under-standing racial inequality. Moreover, most families think they have earned everything and success is entirely of their own making, and this attitude makes progress toward equality more difficult.

A leading economic theory asserts that most people accumulate wealth from scratch each generation; wealth grows over one's working life and is spent by one's death. This is known as the life-cycle savings model of accumulation.[1] In recent years, the viewpoint that inheritance is inconsequential to how families accumulate wealth has come under empirical criticism, with some estimating that as much as 80 percent of family wealth derives not from savings but from transfers of money from generation to generation.[2] The academic debate entailed in these two positions is important because it highlights a question important to this study, the meritocracy-inheritance dilemma. The debate also has political ramifications for the estate tax issue. Expert estimates of the sources of an individual family's wealth weigh a variety of factors, including retirement, health care costs, age at death, wages, and portfolio growth rates. One recent study found that one-half of a family's net worth derives from handed-down, transformative assets.[3]

A core part of my argument is that family inheritances, especially financial resources, are the primary means of passing class and race advantages and disadvantages from one generation to another. Examining information about parental wealth is a good starting point to explore empirically the potential significance of legacies in perpetuating racial inequality. After all, if whites tend not to come from families with greater wealth accumulation than blacks, there are no financial advantages to pass along, and we can immediately reject a notion of racial legacy secured by family wealth. If whites do come from families with greater wealth, on the other hand, then it is important to examine the extent and effects of this disparity. This seems like a simple question but it is difficult to study because collection of data on parental wealth did not occur until 1988, when the Panel Study of Income Dynamics asked respondents how much wealth their living parents had. Further, parental wealth is not a proxy for future inheritance because we know nothing about individual parents' plans for their money, health care, or financial portfolios, or their ideas about giving, for that matter. Nonetheless, net worth is the single most important piece of information about the prospective *capacity of parents* to assist their adult children financially at critical times like buying a first home or paying for private schooling.

The parental-wealth measure captures the capacity of parents to give their children a head start in life. The parental-wealth charts (Figures 3.1 and 3.2, pages 63 and 64) below show the percentage of all American families whose living parents possess wealth. This includes 81 percent of all families, which seems like a healthy state of affairs but does not give any indication of how much wealth a family possesses. More than nine-tenths of white parents (91 percent) surveyed hold assets compared to fewer than two-thirds of black parents (64 percent).[4]

Of families reporting wealth, the typical family in this survey has parents with just under $150,000 in net worth. Among families who reported positive asset figures for their parents, average net worth skyrockets to over $400,000, with home equity representing the largest source of assets. The huge difference between the mean and median figures again illustrates the huge disparity between rich and poor; most of the respondents' parents have some wealth, but only a few have a great deal. Not surprisingly, among those with wealth, these data demonstrate large racial differences in parental wealth: The parental net worth for typical black families was $46,700, compared to almost $200,000 for white families. In other words, among families with positive assets, the financial capacities of the parents of white families are four times greater than those of the parents of black families. The dollar gap is the difference between parents' ability or lack thereof to buy an average house and a midsize station wagon. The average figures are even bigger, $503,800 to $93,000, or 5.4 times greater for white families than black families. These results pinpoint serious differences in wealth between previous generations of blacks and whites.

The important figures in these charts show that whites are about one and a half times more likely to come from families with assets than blacks and that an enormous racial wealth gap exists among families with these resources. In general, whites and blacks come from families with substantially different wealth capacities. What does this mean in practical terms? As a way of thinking about this question, I will describe the concept of *head-start assets* as a way of measuring what considerable financial assistance entails. Previously, we discussed the idea of transformative assets, meaning resources that can put a family on an economic and social path beyond the means of their salaries. We never quantified an amount, because this is a relative concept based on a family's starting point and the requirements for upward mobility. Going back to a family we met earlier will be instructive. Kathryn MacDonald told us in the first chapter about the various inheritances that allow her and Evan to live in a middle-income community and Evan to go to a school with middle-class peers, services, and amenities. She could not

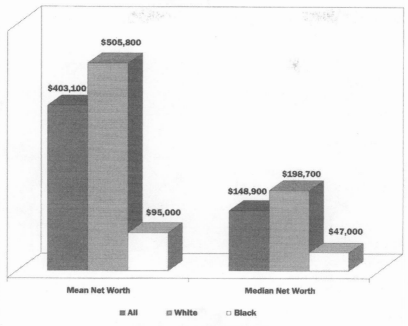

**Figure 3.1 Parental Wealth***

*1999 dollars
Source: PSID, 1988

afford to live in Florissant, Missouri, based on her $16,000 earnings. Transformative assets protect her family's well-being and class status.

How much wealth is needed by people like Kathryn MacDonald to gain middle-class status? We will look at head-start assets as the amount needed for the down payment and closing costs on the typical home in the United States. In 1999 the median-priced home in the United States sold for approximately $160,100, with typical downpayments ranging from at least 5 percent of the purchase price to about 10 percent. In addition, banks customarily charge a finance fee, usually 1 percent of the loan. At closing, then, a family buying this typical house needs between $9,600 and $17,600. We will use a figure three-quarters along this range to represent head-start assets in 1999—$14,000.

Figure 3.2 displays the percentage of families in the United States whose parents possess enough assets to help their child buy a typical house. This is a quick way of identifying families that might potentially receive large enough financial assistance to transform biographies, improve their class standing, and attain advantages for at least one child.

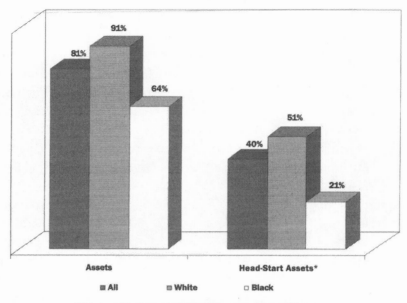

**Figure 3.2 Parental Wealth, Percent with Assets**

*$14,000 or more
Source: PSID, 1988

Among all American families, only two in five have this capacity. Breaking this down by race provides a key piece of evidence for my argument. Among those with living parents, half of all whites come from families with the ability to deliver head-start assistance versus only a fifth of blacks. White families are 2.4 times more likely than blacks to have parents with substantial wealth resources. Another way to think about this finding is that monetary support among whites is most likely to go from parents to adult children, whereas elderly blacks are more likely to need help themselves from their adult children.

## Inheritances

We commonly think of inheritance as limited to bequests at the death of a parent, and this sense of inheritance echoed throughout our interviews. When we asked people if they ever inherited money, they always responded with money received at the death of a parent. This notion of inheritance is quite restricting, because it does not include wealth given between living people, usually from parents to adult children. It omits major transfers like parental assistance for down payments for first-time homeowners or paying for college. These transfers are not inheritances in the traditional sense of the word, but they have critical short- and long-term impacts on the well-being of the receiver and his children. One study determined that 43 percent of wealth transfers occur between living relatives.[5] Therefore, to arrive at a reliable idea about the role of inheritance in passing advantages and disadvantages along from generation to generation, these kinds of wealth transfers must be included and evaluated.

Among the college-educated whites we interviewed, a majority received substantial assistance from their families for college. Paying for college is crucial because it is another way parents provide advantages to children.[6] Graduating college with large student loans versus with parents footing the bill is the difference between starting a family and career with debts versus lack of debts. It also is the difference between needing to pay off this debt monthly versus saving money. And it is the difference between mortgage lenders looking at a credit record already saddled with large monthly obligations versus few obligations. Other things being equal, for instance, a lender is less likely to approve a home mortgage application from a credit-constrained family and more likely to charge higher interest rates.[7] We will meet the Conway and Barzak families in a later chapter and see how this crucial difference—one couple had their college bills paid, while the other is still paying off $33,000 in student loans—reverberates throughout their lives.

In our interviews, not one white or black family even mentioned parental payment of college expenses as inheritance.[8] Almost all acknowledged the helpfulness of parental support; they just did not consider it part of an inheritance. We therefore asked who paid their college expenses and probed for an estimate of what portion came from parental assistance. I am convinced that omitting payment of college expenses from how we think about inheritances neglects a significant wealth accumulation dynamic, just as it renders comparing white and black savings rates highly suspect. Simply, college graduates without debts and college loans start their working lives with a huge head start over those who start their working lives having to pay back $50,000 or more in college loans. In this instance, the intergenerational transfer shows up not as accumulated wealth in the possession of families but rather as lack of debt. Of course, it also could be a decisive factor in thinking about going to college. In our interviews, 15 African American and 7 white families talked about still paying off student loans from college and technical schools, which they invariably called burdensome. Student loans weighed heavily on one person who told me her "student loan was going to follow me the rest of my life." Another person told me, "I have my student loans and I have bad credit. And we didn't even graduate!"

Cultural capital is yet another form of inheritance that allows families with ample assets to pass along nonmonetary benefits to their children that give them a competitive edge in school, the job market, and other areas. Cultural capital refers to an understanding of what gives a person advantages or disadvantages in school, business, and social situations; for example, knowing the work of the painter Jacob Lawrence signifies a particular knowledge of and taste in art and might add points on college entrance exams, reveal class standing in a business meeting, or provide a connection in a social setting. It also refers to other intangible preferences associated with different classes or groups that are important parts of inheritance and upbringing parents give to children. Educational sociologist Annette Lareau writes in *Home Advantage* that it is important to understand how standards of social institutions reflect the family life of privileged classes and dominant groups.[9] It is clear, for instance, that taking art lessons and going to museums influence achievement and aspirations because schools reward knowledge gained from those experiences. It is the difference between families and schools cultivating tastes and talents or allowing natural growth. Closing times, school sports schedules, and extracurricular activities in most upper-middle-class public and private schools typically assume that one parent who is not working will be available to drive children. A child whose family does not fit this standard sticks out. On an individual level, cultural capital may seem as silly as knowing a salad fork from a fish fork, but it often is the kind of informal knowledge that signals one's class—whether one "belongs" or not. Cultural capital is acquired through family life, formal education, informal educational experiences such as visiting museums and zoos, social connections, networks, friendships, proficiency with cultural codes and nuances, and community. Cultural capital is typically found where financial wealth is high.[10] The point here is that individuals inherit different opportunities for cultural capital, and lack of cultural capital can pose a significant impediment for advancement.

## Who Inherits?

I have attempted here to articulate a broad notion of inheritance linked to financial, cultural, social, and human capital. This topic is crucial to our larger argument about handing down racial inequality. Reliable data about family financial inheritance unfortunately also are scarce and elusive. However, we can develop a sense of who inherits and what it means to their lives with information from both the Panel Study of Income Dynamics and our interviews.

The first examinations of financial inheritances among normal American families appeared in the 1990s. Studies indicate that nearly 1 in 4 white families (.244) received an inheritance after the death of a parent, averaging $144,652. In stark contrast, about 1 in 20 African American families had inherited in this way, and their average inheritance amounted to $41,985. White families were four times as likely as blacks to benefit from a significant inheritance, and whites were much more likely to inherit considerably larger amounts, by a $102,167 disadvantage.[11]

Another recent study suggests that about one-third of baby boom whites in 1989 were due to receive future inheritances worth more than $25,000 ($34,718 in 2000 dollars), versus fewer than 1 in 20 blacks. Over the lifetime, whites' inheritances are on average seven times larger than blacks' inheritances. The study estimates that the white-black gap in the value of inheritances for baby boomers will be much larger than it is for those born before 1946. Black boomers will inherit 13 cents for every dollar inherited by white boomers. The mean white baby boomers' lifetime inheritance will be worth $125,000 (in 2000 dollars) at age 55, as compared to only $16,000 for black baby boomers. The preceding generation of whites inherited around $70,000. The black-white inherited gap is larger than the noninherited-wealth gap among baby boomers.[12]

We also know that about one in five families receives help from living relatives, averaging about $2,500.[13] Surprisingly, family assistance is just as common among poorer families as among wealthy families, though the amounts differ considerably. Black Americans were just as likely to receive this sort of family assistance as whites. The difference obviously was the largesse of the helping hand. The gift for the average white recipient was $2,824, compared to $805 for black families. Black families are just as willing to help their adult children, but their circumstances limit their ability to do so.[14]

Another study calculated the racial giving difference at $1,622.[15] For both whites and blacks, men and women living on their own are the most likely to receive money, followed by single mothers, married couples with children, and couples without children. Consistent with my argument, married couples receive the largest amounts, again among both whites and blacks.

Yet another study suggests that in a three-year period 5.3 percent of families received financial gifts from living relatives, averaging $14,860. Three-quarters of these financial gifts went to adult children, and 84 percent of gifts received originated from parents. Recipients of this wealthfare are younger, have higher incomes and net worth, are better educated, are more likely to be white, and expect to receive larger inheritance money in the future. Significantly, in this three-year window, they are about three times more likely to buy a first house as families that do not receive at least $3,000.[16] As we will see shortly, buying a first home, in fact, triggers large amounts of wealth-giving.

It is difficult to synthesize an agreed-upon set of facts from a review of inheritance studies because they use different data sources, measurements, and assumptions. A survey begun in 1984, which asked questions about inheritance at five-year intervals, allows us to pull together the trends associated with financial inheritance over a longer period. When the survey introduced the topic, families were asked if they had ever received an inheritance or large sum of money. The survey then catalogued family assets and liabilities at five-year intervals, in 1989, 1994, and 1999. Families were asked if they received any inheritances during the previous five years.[17] Access to inheritance information over a 15-year period like this is superior to one-time-only information because it allows us to track how families subsequently use the money and how it may change their lives.[18]

Table 3.1 compares families who inherit wealth with those who do not inherit or have not yet inherited. Inheritors can be distinguished from noninheritors in that they are older, have fewer children, are better

### Table 3.1  Who Inherits?

|                                       | Inheritors | Noninheritors |
|---------------------------------------|-----------:|--------------:|
| Mean Net Financial Assets             | $282,643   | $ 94,301      |
| Median Net Financial Assets           | $ 57,000   | $ 10,000      |
| Mean Net Worth                        | $361,907   | $129,800      |
| Median Net Worth                      | $129,236   | $ 28,700      |
| Median Income                         | $ 49,230   | $ 38,000      |
| Median Number of Children in Family   | 0.0        | 1.0           |
| Median Years of Education             | 13.0       | 12.0          |

Source: PSID, 1984–1999

educated, and are more likely to own their homes. One of every two families who inherited money works in upper-middle-class occupations, compared to fewer than one in three families (30 percent) who have not inherited wealth. Perhaps more fundamental, key resource differences separate families who have inherited from those who have not. Families with a financial inheritance report significantly higher incomes, $49,200 to $38,000. Net financial assets divulge the widest and most revealing breach between inheritors and noninheritors. Mean and median net financial assets among inheritors amount to $282,600 and $57,000, compared to $94,300 and $10,000 for families who have not inherited wealth.

This portrait of inheritance over 15 years allows us to break it down by race, as shown in Figure 3.3 (page 71). About one in five American families already has received an inheritance; the average inheritance was $47,878 while the typical family inheritance was $10,000. This information plays down the incidence of inheritance because the typical family who has not inherited money is headed by a 41-year-old, and most likely one or both parents are living, so the inheritance window is still open.[19]

The most dramatic findings concern the black-white inheritance gap. Twenty-eight percent of whites received bequests, compared to just 7.7 percent of black families. Three and a half times as many white families already have received an inheritance as black families. Even this wide disparity does not represent the full measure of inequality, because for whites the average inheritance amounted to $52,430, while for black Americans, it amounted to $21,796. Median inheritance figures registered $10,000 for white families and $798 for black families. Thus, among those fortunate enough to receive bequests, blacks received 8 cents of inheritance for every dollar inherited by whites.

Breaking down these inheritances by age further illuminates the connection between age and past discriminatory processes. Among all families, the incidence of bequests rises with the age of the family because parents are more likely to be deceased. The amounts received increase significantly between the under-45 age groups and those 45 to 65 years old and then decrease almost as significantly for those 65 and older. This pattern fits what we know about generational events since younger families (under 45) are more likely to have one or two living parents and therefore a smaller probability of already receiving money from both parents.[20]

Two sets of observations seem pertinent here. First, matching virtually all the other data we have presented on the racial wealth gap, whites receive inheritances at least three times larger than African Americans and up to 20 times greater (among 45–65-year-olds). Inherited money is the most obvious form of nonmerit wealth, and in this regard Figure 3.3 discloses a black-to-white inheritance ratio that is larger than the baseline racial wealth gap, 8 cents on the dollar of inherited wealth versus 10 cents on the dollar total wealth. This is prime evidence for our understanding that inheritances are reversing gains earned in schools and on jobs and making racial inequality worse

The difference between average and typical inheritance for black Americans is striking. The typical (median) inheritance is less than $1,000, which simply means that at least one-half of blacks who inherit receive less than $1,000. By way of comparison, more than one-half of all white inheritances amount to $10,000 or more.

Receiving an inheritance does not merely mean that bank accounts are fatter, even though they are; rather, these assets have the capacity to change significantly a family's trajectory. Evidence shows that this enhanced capacity translates into real advances because inheritors and those receiving helping hands are more likely to own homes, own their own businesses, be self-employed, and have higher incomes.[21]

In our interviews, families spoke about the advantages family assistance and inheritances—both when parents pass away and at important life events like graduation, marriage, and birth of children—give them in getting a head start in life. As we already suggested, and our interviews emphasize, the single event (other than parental death) that triggers by far the largest transfer of wealth between generations is the purchase of a first home. Homeownership provides the pathway to

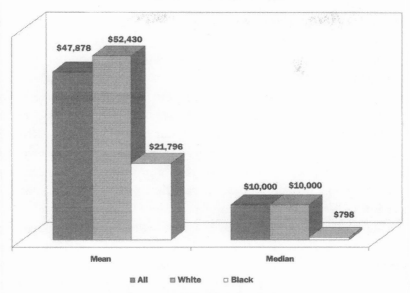

**Figure 3.3 Inheritance and Race**

*1999 dollars
Source: PSID, 1984–1999

community and schooling, and parental assistance in buying a first home is key to setting opportunities for their adult children and their families.

The families we interviewed correspond with the national studies, even as they furnish another layer of information. Only three black families out of 85 had received a head-start inheritance, at least $14,000, upon the death of a family member. In contrast, just about one in four white families already had received similar substantial inheritances. In our interviews, whites were seven times as likely to be given substantial inheritances.

Among white families who received an inheritance, the amount averages $76,000, compared to $31,000 for blacks. Among all black inheritors, half received less than $10,000; among all white inheritors, only five bequests fell below the $14,000 mark. Whites received about two and a half times as much money when they did inherit.

Beneath the numbers, the patterns and stories are revealing. The mention of grandparents in our interviews provides an interesting clue linking financial assistance to previous generations. Remember that we interviewed people who were mostly between 25 and 45 years old, when it is likely that one or both parents are still alive. Two black families mentioned receiving money from grandparents, and in both cases the amounts were quite small. More striking, however, is that 14 (out of 22) white inheritors mentioned wealth passed to them upon the death of grandparents. For the most part, the amounts are not staggering or even substantial. What the low level of inheritance from grandparents corroborates is that the legacy of grandparents of black baby boomers, who lived and toiled under harsh discrimination and glaringly different conditions, did not include financial resources. We see a glimpse of the racial reality of two generations ago continuing to impose and structure differences onto the present generation of young adults and a generation of children still coming up.

Passing wealth along to children or grandchildren apparently involves passing along class standing as well. The racial wealth gap is an important reason why black families have more difficulty passing along achieved middle-class status than white families do. A large proportion of families who were given inheritances could claim middle-class status. This is verifiable for both white and black inheritors, as only 2 of 8 black inheritors and 4 of 22 white inheritors are below middle-class standing, as measured by income, jobs, or education. Interestingly, if we think of people who inherit wealth but cannot sustain a middle-class existence as falling from middle-class grace, then those falling from grace are mostly women inheritors who subsequently experienced marital difficulties and women who were single mothers at the time we talked. The income consequences for divorced or separated women have been a cause for concern for some time.[22] Our interviews hint forebodingly at the devastating asset consequences for these women, their children, and the subsequent well-being of the family.

Another thematic difference between black and white inheritors involves the form of bequests. Several black inheritors talked about receiving insurance money upon the death of a family member, usually between $5,000 and $8,000. Mention of receiving money through the death of an insured relative was very limited in the white interviews.

## Transformed Lives, Deserved Inheritances

Americans believe in a strict form of meritocracy that mandates that we should only get what we earn through ability and effort. Listening to how families tell the story of inheriting wealth and the meaning they attach to this advantage in light of our meritocratic ideals provides valuable insights into understanding how families view success and reconcile conflicting values of inheritance and earned wealth.

Twenty miles from the Arch in downtown St. Louis, the Barrys and their three children moved in 1996 into a "real cute little house" on a bluff alongside the Mississippi River. Joe Barry is a computer specialist, and Briggette is a sign language interpreter who works part-time. Both earned college degrees, and their combined income is $70,000 a year. This is a solid middle-class family—educated suburban homeowners with professional jobs. They live close to Briggette's parents in a smallish white and gray vinyl-sided house, with a basketball hoop, surrounded by trees and open space. It looks like a picture-perfect place to raise kids. Their daughter attends parochial school; the two boys are still in day care. Joe and Briggette's parents enjoyed successful careers (one was a teacher, one a lawyer, another a school principal), and they accumulated considerable wealth during the post–World War II economic prosperity. This family is on track for the American Dream, but the road has not always been straight or smooth. They have relied upon parental financial assistance to maintain their success, middle-class lifestyles, and identities.

Our conversation about parental helping hands starts when I ask Briggette if they had any trouble coming up with the down payment for their new house. "Not at all," she said. "My parents gave it to me. So it was a real easy matter of depositing a check." Before her parents offered this money, she explains, it was not going quite so easily at all.

*We were trading in the kids' savings bonds. We were working two jobs each. We were working at night. We were working around the clock. We were saving every penny. We were having garage sales. And finally my mom said, "Well, this is stupid. We've got a lot of money here."*

When I ask if they encountered any unanticipated expenses with closing costs on the house or moving, Briggette remembers the difficulty they had because of two open Federal Housing Administration–insured loans. "We had to convert from an FHA loan on the new home to a conventional one," she says, "so we had to come up with an additional ten thousand dollars in closing costs within the span of seven days." For most families, coming up with an additional $10,000 within a week would throw a gigantic wrench into their plans. How did they do it? Briggette said to her mother, " 'Mom, we need more than we thought.' And my mom and dad gave it to us. They gave us a chunk; we had the whole chunk of money for furniture and other things. But instead we had to take ten thousand of the money they gave us and put it into the closing costs." All together, her parents gave Briggette and Joe $30,000, and her grandmother chipped in another $2,000 to help with the move.

When I ask about other kinds of financial assistance, Briggette says she probably has "bought a total of five outfits for my children," because "every season" her mother buys "a whole wardrobe for each of my three children." I ask if her parents help with day care. Briggette says, "Not on a daily basis. They're too old for that." This ubiquitous parental assistance must leave them lots of discretionary spending money in their $70,000 earnings, which could boost their savings rate, so I wonder how they spend their money. "Oh," Briggette says, "we piss it away on our kids."

> We go to movies. Oh, here I go. Because we are both full-time working parents, and we don't have, like, Mommy at home—I don't know about you, but when I was a kid, Mommy was home. In the summertime, every night, it's Discovery Zone or the swimming pool, or McDonald's or Raging Rivers or Six Flags. I mean, almost every night, unless we're just too tired to do anything. We spend our money on our children. We spend at Blockbuster Video. We spend a hell of a lot of money on groceries. My kids eat me out of house and home. Yeah, we spend a lot on day care and private school. But seriously, when I add it up, it's about fourteen thousand dollars a year. It's unbelievable. But it's worth it, you know? What are my choices? That's what I wanted. I wanted kids. You have to pay for them.

Parental help started much earlier in their marriage, when Briggette was pregnant with their first child.

> Early in our marriage, we had a lot of financial difficulty. When I was—let's see—when I was seven months' pregnant, Joe got laid off from his job. And then I had to go out on medical leave because I could no longer work. We almost went into financial disaster. We almost lost our home.

How did they save their home?

> *My mom and dad and his mom and dad chipped in and gave us the money.*
> Parents again. That parent thing [emphasis added]. *They gave us the*
> *money. And we turned all of our bills over to Consumer Credit.*

What about presents from family that help financially—or other
major gifts, like a television, car or dishwasher?

> *Sure. Lots. Yes to all of it. They've given us money for the down payment on*
> *the house. His father bought us two of our cars, and my parents bought us*
> *one of our cars. My parents bought us a washer and a dryer. My parents paid*
> *the tuition for my daughter's school, because it's the Catholic school and they*
> *just wanted her to be educated for that. Let's see. Yeah,* you name it, we get
> it [emphasis added]. *They paid our mortgage payment for two months,*
> *before my husband found his other job. They have set up trust funds for my*
> *children, for each of my children; so that when it's time for them to go to*
> *college, they will have money to do so. This isn't money they gave us, but they*
> *helped us set up financial plans for Joe and me for retirement.*

I ask Briggette to estimate the value of the help her parents give them
by buying clothes, household appliances, and other presents, taking
them out to dinner, and so on—things one normally does not count.
She is taken aback somewhat—"Oh, my God! Like I can really put a
price tag on it"—but manages an estimate: "Oh, Jesus, I would seriously
say fifty or sixty thousand dollars [since her marriage] ... maybe five
thousand a year."

Briggette Barry's memory seems accurate as she catalogues all sorts of
parental wealthfare with matching dollar figures. At various points in
our conversation, she expresses great appreciation and gratitude for this
familial help, commenting, "Gotta love parents." However, as soon as
the conversation turns to how she and her husband acquired assets like
their home, cars, and savings account, her attitude changes dramatically.
"As far as anything else [their assets], no," Briggette asserts, "we worked
our butts off for what we have." How did they acquire the cars?
"Worked our butts off to pay for them." How did they accumulate their
$3,000 savings account? "Worked for it. All worked for it." The $1,000
retirement account? "Yes. It's taken out of my check."

She is emphasizing an important point I heard from many other families. While acknowledging a generous parental helping hand and the loving bonds between generations, the Barrys—like other families we interviewed—adamantly maintain that they deserve the unearned wealth benefits that transform their lives and opportunities. The Barrys describe themselves as self-made, conveniently forgetting that they inherited much of what they own. I do not doubt how hard they work to improve their lives, and I am sure their hard work has improved their well-being, but hard work alone has not brought them to their current level. The flawed and uncritical attribution of success to hard work precludes coming to terms with their unearned advantages. It redefines what is fair and what is unfair in a way that puts the onus for lack of wealth on those without the same advantages. Simply, what a family inherits cannot be earned. The idea of deserving unearned things is very important to the Barrys and families like them in that deservedness and worthiness substitutes for earning and merit. I emphasize this because we so often confuse advantages and connections with ability.

Had their biographies been different, they would not be able to afford their suburban middle-class home, and their daughter probably would not be attending private school. Even with a $70,000 family income, with their bad credit histories, sizable credit card debt, and no savings available for a down payment, homeownership would be highly improbable. It is entirely possible, had they not come from prosperous and generous families, that they might have made different choices in the past to avoid the financial mess that necessitated parental bailouts. The point here is not to ponder counterfactual, hypothetical scenarios so much as to underscore the taken-for-granted sense of entitlement around deservedness we found in many of our interviews with white middle-class families. Presented with the Barrys' information without all the parental assistance, a mortgage officer most likely would advise them that their financial situation exceeds commonly used industry standards and might suggest that, although mortgage underwriters use discretion in approving loans for people who have large debts in relation to their income, it would be prudent to look for ways to lower their housing sights or change plans.

Many of the families we interviewed expressed similar thoughts about inherited money. They rationalize handed-down advantages as deserved by attributing success to their own endeavors and hard work. Sociologist

Heather Beth Johnson writes about a sense of entitlement among middle-class white families.[23] In her reading of these interviews, she describes an ideology of meritocracy: the idea that positions are earned through hard work and personal achievement and through no resources other than one's own. Families talking about "earning" their assets through hard work, a solid work ethic, and playing by the rules legitimize this entitlement. For many of these families, it is as if the effort of earning the reward is more important than actual accomplishments.

Glee and Barry Putnam, 36 and 38 years old, live in a suburban middle-class subdivision in South County St. Louis. Barry works as a computer network technician for a large Fortune 500 corporation, where he earns about $45,000. Glee takes care of their six children, who range in age from 3 months to 12 years. Their financial resources are typical of America's broad middle class, $56,000 in net worth and $26,300 in net financial assets. I ask them about the role of parental help in their lives.

> GLEE: *My family helps us, yes. . . . When we got married, our parents gave us some money* [about $5,000]. *When we came into this house, my mom gave us some money to help with the carpeting, and just things like that. My parents help out with my kids.*
>
> INT: *What gifts did they give you when you were married?*
>
> GLEE: *Well, my parents give us gifts all the time. I mean, they're both retired, so it's like "Let's help you out here." They'll come out here, they'll give us gifts. "Oh, let's buy dinner the entire week we're out here" or "Here's some extra money for gas since you're bringing us all around," you know. They'll do things like that.*
>
> INT: *When they helped with the home repairs when you first moved here, do you have an idea of how much they may have given you as a gift?*
>
> GLEE: *They didn't really help with the home repairs. . . . They wanted to help with the carpet, that was my mother's gift. "Here's some money, go out and buy carpets, carpet, whatever you can with this amount of money."*
>
> INT: *Okay, do you remember how much that was?*
>
> BARRY: *A thousand dollars.*
>
> INT: *Have you received financial help from your family, like did they help pay for college or help out with the purchase of a house or home repairs or any other kinds of assistance that you can think of?*
>
> GLEE: *Well, like, my parents helped me get my first house.*

BARRY: *Six thousand dollars.*
INT: *Was that a loan or a gift?*
BARRY: *A gift.*
GLEE: *It was a gift.*
INT: *That's fine. Any other gifts that you can recall over time?*
GLEE: *She gave us about $450 for the kitchen, didn't she?*
BARRY: *Just two years ago we redid the kitchen, and she gave us some money*
    *for that.*
GLEE: *My parents help us out all the time by just giving us money.*
BARRY: *Oh, they have flown everybody at some point or another out there*
    [Utah] *to vacation for a while.*

Glee and Barry have just catalogued how their parents gave them a
large cash gift as a wedding present, a $6,000 down payment to buy
their home, financial help in remodeling their kitchen, $1,000 for
carpet; in addition, their parents help pay for family vacations and give
them money regularly. In other parts of the interview they acknowledge
that they could not be living where they live and their children would
not be in the schools they are without parental help. Yet when I ask how
they acquired their assets, they put a different spin on it.

INT: *How did you acquire the different assets that you own, like the money in*
    *the savings account?*
BARRY: *We worked for it.*
INT: *That was just, like, from every paycheck?*
BARRY: *Yeah.*
INT: *And the stocks, that was from?*
BARRY: *Every paycheck.*
INT: *Okay, and the IRA?*
GLEE: *I worked for it, I saved from work.*
BARRY: *The same thing.*
INT: *Same with the home equity and—*
BARRY: *Um-hum, everything, overtime for that.*

Ambiguity and denial about inherited money provided poignant
moments in many of our interviews, affecting how families told their
stories as well as what they said. Loans became "gifts," as we will see

when we examine down-payment monies. Wives corrected husbands about amounts given by the wife's parents, and vice versa—in every case adjusting to a higher amount, as the original answer downplayed the importance of that gift in the couple's success. Precise answers in previous sections of the interview to questions like the class of the neighborhood they grew up in sometimes gave way to hesitation. The reason for this, I believe, is that these families were responding to the strongly held American belief of meritocracy, knowing that the advantages they were describing were not wholly earned. For many of these families, the language of deservedness had replaced the fact of achievement and merit.

The concept of transformative assets challenges this understanding and instead examines the ability of inherited wealth—nonearned assets—to structure class standing beyond a family's earnings. The test is simple: Are a family's life chances bettered sufficiently by their inherited assets to move them upward in class, community, and educational environment for their children? In the mosaic of America, there are no typical families, but we can look at lots of different pieces that make up the larger pattern. From our interviews, at least, we get a solid foundation for determining the validity of the concept of transformative assets and the frequency with which such assets are found in families. The interviews also give us an appreciation of the large number of ways in which assets influence life chances and change families' lives, including the way they think about themselves and their future.

Shauna and Shawn Ferguson, 44 and 50, are white and live in St. Louis with their two children. He is a lawyer, and she is a legal assistant. Financially, the Fergusons are doing very well: The family income is over $100,000, and their net worth exceeds $200,000. Both grew up in St. Louis; they have been married since Shawn was in law school. They inherited substantial money that helped to buy a home, pay off school loans, start college funds for their children, and provide a safety net. The conversation with Shauna Ferguson took over two and a half hours, and inheritance was a main topic throughout the interview. "Oh, I never got it all at once, but I tried to figure it out once," Shauna says when I ask her how much money she inherited. "It was probably eighty thousand dollars." Interestingly, it seems that every time we come back to the topic her answers become more and more expansive, even correcting earlier statements. "Well, my parents had died, so it wasn't [difficult]," Shauna says when I ask her if they had difficulty with the $14,000 down payment for their home. "My parents had died three years before. We were basically waiting to get out of law school. We had a very good situation. The rest of the inheritance was invested."

When I ask Shauna if their finances limited where they looked for a home, she begins talking about other ways they used the inherited money.

*Well, I would have liked to have been in a community where there were more young professionals like us. But Shawn got out of school with a forty-thousand-dollar debt, and he was only getting twenty-five thousand a year to start. Sallie Mae* [federally guaranteed student loan program] *wanted five hundred a week. And I was working basically in day care for Sallie Mae. And, you know, there was deprivation. I mean, not severe. It's not like we were living in Central America; but on the other hand, you know, I was not going to choose where I needed to live. You know? But I remember my parents struggling. And I just always felt like I had all this money in investments that I could use. And we did use the income from one to make our car payment. And we did use some to move during law school.*

*At various times we used the money. And I had siblings on the East Coast, weddings and stuff. And also, if you ran into trouble, you'd have that money to touch. We've used some to buy a computer. And I used some* [for] *one small school loan: two thousand dollars. And I paid that off. And I put a little money down on the car. I bought a baby crib, which was four hundred dollars. I took a trip to Russia.*

*Oh, I cannot tell you how much peace it gives me, just to know that if something happened. . . . Well, I have a stash of money that I don't touch. But* [our financial situation changed] *when my grandmother died. And since my mother had died previously, each of my siblings and I got her share. And I just put that money in the bank account. And I've added to it. And I have seven thousand dollars now. It's amazing . . . I mean, shoes, classes, braces. I mean, it's just—it's amazing. And that is my security blanket, because I have—you know, I have investments. You know, we both have 401(k)s, we have IRAs. But it's just like you can't touch any of that stuff.*

The savings account is from her grandmother; "most of that is from inheritance." The IRA and the retirement also are from inheritance:

"I inherited money, and I invested in bonds. Those are long-term bonds. Some of those are for college. . . . The IRAs, I got it from inheritance." More inheritance monies may be in their future as well: "When his mother dies, there'll be a little bit, but I'm not sure."

The Fergusons are accomplished professionals with a family income in the top 10 percent. But even with their $100,000 income, if it were all they had, Shauna and Shawn would not be close to the financial position and status they enjoy. Wealth accumulated over two generations assists the Ferguson family in living a good and secure life.

Nancy and Mark Hollings also are white and live with their daughter in Dorchester, an economically and racially diverse section of Boston with old but solid housing stock. The prices there seem low in the otherwise hot Boston real estate market because some sections of the community are poor and black. Nancy is an administrator in the nonprofit sector, and Mark is a teacher. Together their salaries are a very respectable $70,000. They bought their condominium just as the Boston housing market reached a low point, in 1995. In fact, they paid $55,000 for it, whereas the previous owner had paid twice that amount just a few years earlier. Most middle-class white families, and some black ones, see Dorchester as "iffy" due to its high level of class and race diversity and rapidly changing neighborhoods. The traditional valuing of location does not work well in such mixed communities, and families like the Hollingses feel that they have found good value for their money, as long as they are willing to take the risks. They were able to make a down payment of half of the purchase price with monies inherited from an uncle and a grandfather and a "loan against the inheritance" from Nancy's parents.

Financially, this family seems to be doing well, as represented by their good income, low living expenses, and over $100,000 in net worth. As is the case for most middle-income American families, their largest asset pool is their home equity; for the Hollingses, it represents one-half of their net worth. When I ask how they acquired their assets, Nancy says, "From working. I'd say at this point, most of the money represents earned income." In essence, their families gave them a large down payment for their condominium, so they had to take out only a small mortgage and therefore pay a relatively small amount in fixed monthly housing costs. Because of this, they are able to put money aside from their salaries and invest it. Since 1995 these assets from savings and investments have grown to about $50,000. Truly, then, Nancy is correct when she says that most of their assets come out of earnings. In another sense, however, one needs to recognize that this family's ability to save, invest, and accumulate $50,000 is highly structured by the large down payment, inherited or given by family, that fixes their housing costs at a small amount of their monthly income and leaves considerable discretionary income for investments at the end of each month.

What if there were no family inheritance? The point is to examine how they put their good fortune together. It would cast their choices about homeownership, community, and education in an entirely different light—the same light as many of the families we talked to who do not have assets. And this, in turn, would affect where they live and the schools their children attend. Because of their large down payment and relatively small mortgage, their current fixed monthly housing costs are $250, far below typical rental housing costs in Boston. With a solid income of $72,000, well above what most American families earn, they would qualify for a mortgage of about $170,000 and pay $1,500 monthly housing costs. The Hollingses, in fact, could buy the same house they live in now without family assistance, but the family finances would look very different. The current low monthly costs would rise considerably, by $1,250 in additional mortgage and interest payments. In this light, their ability to save, invest, and accumulate over $50,000 in financial assets is made possible directly by their inheritances. In essence, family inheritances give them an additional $1,250 in discretionary resources each month.

Later in the interview, I ask about future inheritance. Nancy, who grew up in a well-to-do Boston suburb, says, "It's kind of hard to say. My parents are sixty-five now. They are worth a fair amount of money, but they could also go through a lot of money if they end up moving into a retirement community, so I really don't know."

One young couple I interviewed burst out laughing when I asked them if they expected to receive an inheritance and if so, how much it would be. In explaining their laughter, they said their parents initiate numerous explicit and detailed discussions about severe illness, life support, and death, while the subject of family money is taboo. Although it is often an uncomfortable topic, most of the people we talked with had a solid indication of future prospects in this regard, even if the exact numbers are hazy. When I asked Frank and Suzanne Conway of Los Angeles if they expect to receive anything through inheritance, the following dialogue took place:

> FRANK: *The majority of the stocks that we personally own have been inherited stocks.*
> SUZANNE: *I don't remember how much more we are supposed to get.*
> FRANK: *That was all.*
> SUZANNE: *No, that was from our daughter's* [legacy] *estate.*
> FRANK: *And we are still getting more?*
> SUZANNE: *Yeah.*
> FRANK: *We are? All of the stocks we have were inherited.*
> SUZANNE: *We'll probably get some more from both of our parents, not in the near future, I hope.*
> FRANK: *My grandmother died just over a year ago, and we inherited ten thousand dollars from her. Five thousand dollars for Logan* [their daughter] *and five thousand for myself. She was like ninety-six, and she was ready.*

In the scheme of things, the way families gauge inheritances or receiving a large unexpected sum of money is entirely relative to their expectations and life circumstances. When I interviewed the Toppine family in Boston, Sherryl called out to her husband, who had left the room, "Hey, Dennis, how much did you get from your grandparents when they died? Did you get money from your grandparents when they died?" "Yeah. Gosh," Dennis answered, "it was like forty thousand or something." The casual reference may indicate a sense of entitlement; certainly it sounds like a taken-for-granted part of their lives.

American society is of two minds about inheritance, and we seem to want it both ways. We take pride in our accomplishments, often marking them in monetary terms, and see nothing wrong in passing on what we earned to our children. Indeed, part of the motivation for working hard and acquiring things includes bettering our family and our children for future generations. This notion, however, collides with the equally strongly held notion of meritocracy because inheritances are unearned, represent a different playing field entirely, and have precious little to do with merit, achievements, or accomplishments. We live with this duality, partly because we deny what inheritances represent, partly because we see it in individual and family terms, and partly because the current political balance heavily favors those with advantages and privileges.

The Barrys, Conways, Fergusons, and Hollingses are examples of families who undeniably have worked hard, capitalized on the resources and opportunities available to them, and achieved success. But they have done so in specific contexts, and it is these contexts they tend to ignore when talking about their successes.[24] We tend to look only at the result, not the path, of success. Noting this tendency in *Stacked Deck*, Lawrence Mitchell writes that this tendency to forget leads us to believe that our successes are due only to ourselves.

We need to recognize that inherited wealth can perpetuate inequality. The sociologist Georg Simmel called money a frightful leveler, but it might be more appropriate to understand inherited money as a frightful conveyor and transmitter of inequality. Inheritance is not an achievement, and we are conflicted by it. Asking how inheritance has affected our lives can deepen our understanding of inequality.

# Part II
# MAKING RACIAL INEQUALITY

# 4

# Middle Class in Black and White

## How Level Is the Playing Field?

THE GENIUS OF THE AMERICAN DREAM is the promise that those who work equally hard will reap roughly equal rewards, be it in wealth, lifestyle, or status. The question of equal opportunity frames our truncated national dialogue on race because we feel deeply that barriers blocking achievement based on race are unfair and deprive society of skills and talent. The dialogue on racial inequality often becomes a contentious debate about how level the playing field is, past injustice, and if or how the past affects the present. While not ceding the equal opportunity question, because the battle for equal opportunity is far from won, I am arguing that even black and white families with equal accomplishments are separated by a dramatic wealth gap.

## Middle Class

It is often observed that most Americans think of themselves as middle class. Traditionally, our definition of the middle class includes job, income, or educational achievement, but the level of each needed to qualify varies wildly depending on whom you ask. To define the middle class, we look first at income, marking families in the middle 60 percent as middle class, those earning between $17,000 and $79,000. This relative definition will always produce a middle class representing 60 percent of families. With regard to education, we can draw the middle-class line at families in which at least one adult has earned a bachelors' degree. The most commonly used method of determining middle-class status employs job rankings. This notion of the middle class includes professionals, technical workers, administrators, managers, supervisors, and clerical and sales workers. My own preference includes all of these criteria. Since the aim in this chapter is to compare white and black families with middle-class accomplishments, I will use the three definitions of the middle class as a way of making sure that my argument really does compare people of similar achievement. Looking at the middle class in different ways—by job ranking, income, and education—produces different boundaries for who attains middle-class status. This exercise allows us to examine the racial wealth gap among similarly accomplished families as well as to see whether it is contingent upon sociological definitions.

We know already that the wealth distribution is more unequal than the income distribution. It is also true that wealth links directly to class status. Wealth increases dramatically as one moves up the class ladder. Wealth matters for class, and class matters for wealth, and we need to appreciate the magnitude of this connection before examining wealth among white and black middle-class families. Figure 4.1 provides a stark reminder that class, as defined by the traditional sociological criterion of occupation, matters enormously for financial resources, well-being, and security. Lower white-collar workers have double the net worth of upper blue-collar workers, as typical net worth rises from $20,000 among skilled manual workers to $45,000 for secretaries and salespeople. Upper white-collar workers have twice as much wealth as lower white-collar workers, as typical median net worth rises to $90,000 for professionals, administrators, and technical workers. The upper-middle-class group of professionals has six times as much net worth as semiskilled and unskilled laborers and four and a half times as much as skilled workers. Class, at least as defined by occupation, matters greatly for wealth. Now we can examine whether race matters for wealth accumulation among the middle class.

We saw in Chapter 2 that in 1999 black families owned just 10 cents of wealth for every dollar owned by the typical white family. The baseline net financial asset deficit, which excludes wealth built up in homes, registered $30,500; white families owned a dollar for every 9 cents of wealth owned by the typical black family. Figures 4.2, 4.3, and 4.4 (pages 90 and 91) show the racial wealth gap among middle-class families. Remember that this compares families of similar achievements, so the racial wealth gap should be negligible if wealth is largely the product of accomplishments. When we use the income definition of middle class, we see a

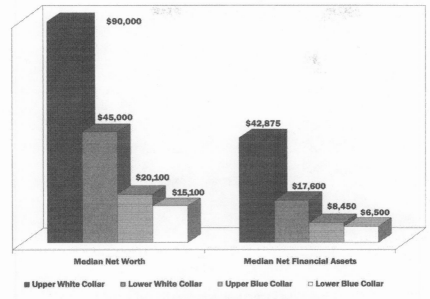

**Figure 4.1 Class and Financial Resources**

Source: PSID, 1999

reduction in the baseline racial net worth and net financial asset gaps to $44,500 and $17,000, respectively. Family income thus accounts for a large chunk of the racial wealth gap, though a huge disparity remains among white and black families earning similar incomes. We knew from the data analysis in Chapter 3 that this would be the case; yet looking at this through a lens of similar middle-class achievement helps us focus on the contributions of class and race factors in wealth accumulation.[1]

Interestingly, when we define middle-class status by jobs, the gap swells to $96,500 in net worth and $48,800 in net financial assets while blacks in middle class occupations possess 22 cents on the net worth dollar of similar whites. This brings up the conundrum of measuring equality by seeing the glass as half full or half empty. The gap between whites and blacks grows using the occupational definition of the middle class because it does not have an income ceiling and thus includes proportionally more well-to-do families, and highly paid professionals and executives tend to be white. Conversely, employees in lower-middle-class jobs—office workers, civil servants, and sales-people—are disproportionately black. In any case, this poses a classic

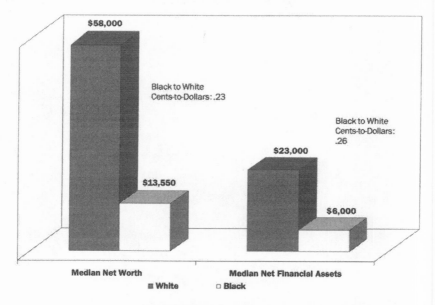

**Figure 4.2 "The Income Middle Class," Race and Wealth**

Source: PSID, 1999

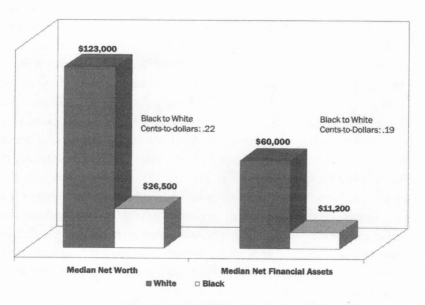

**Figure 4.3 "The Occupational Middle Class," Race and Wealth**

Source: PSID, 1999

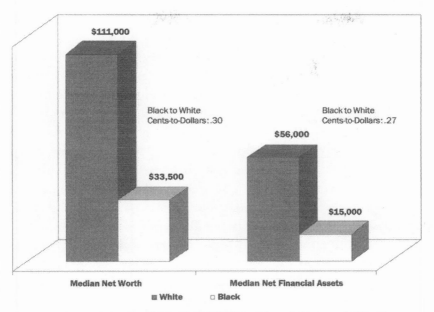

**Figure 4.4 "The Educational Middle Class," Race and Wealth**
Source: PSID, 1999

dilemma for notions of inequality in that middle-class blacks fare far better than working-class families and better than they did in the past, but if they compare themselves to their white professional equals, their wealth disadvantage grows.

This pattern repeats to some extent when college education is the marker of middle-class standing. In this instance, the income gap closes to 69 cents on the dollar, which is disappointing considering that this definition compares college-educated whites and blacks, and one needs to wonder why comparably qualified blacks do not receive commensurate jobs and incomes. The net worth disparity is $77,500, while the gap closes to 30 cents on the dollar. The net financial assets picture is similar: The absolute dollar difference grows to $41,000, and the cents-to-dollar gap closes to .27. The results of this middle-class exercise indicate that achievements do matter in the sense that middle-class status rewards families with wealth, no matter whether the family is white or black. That is the good news.

However, at the same time, white middle-class families possess between three and five times as much wealth as equally achieving black

middle-class families, no matter how one defines middle class. The definition of middle class apparently does not matter when examining
wealth, unless, of course, the definition includes wealth, in which case
black families headed by professionals like doctors and lawyers would
be in the same class as white families headed by blue-collar workers such
as coal miners.[2] Even when incomes of white and blacks are similar, an
enormous wealth gap of $50,000 remains. The black middle class that
emerged between the mid-1960s and early 1980s is a success story
written in education, occupation, and earnings. An asset perspective,
however, shows that the white middle class stands for the most part on
the two legs of good earnings and substantial assets while the black
middle class stands for the most part on the earnings leg alone. Middle-
class status is thus more precarious for blacks than it is for whites; blacks
are more susceptible to falling from middle-class grace, less capable of
cushioning hard times, and less able to retool careers or change direc-
tions. Consequently, because of this status and resource fragility, it is
more difficult for black middle-class families to translate accomplishments into status that they can pass along easily to their children.

## Middle Class in Black and White

Frank and Suzanne Conway are solidly middle class by any standard,
whether occupational, income, or educational measures are used. Their
annual income is around $70,000. Suzanne, 45, works as an operations
supervisor at a capital management company, and Frank, 38, worked at
a communications-marketing firm that laid him off six months before
our meeting in Los Angeles. Frank is going back to school to become
an elementary school teacher. They own a home in Jefferson Park, an
area of Los Angeles near the University of Southern California, and
their daughter, Logan, attends private school.

Richard and Kim Barzak, 41 and 43 years old, also are members of
America's middle class. Both are college graduates. Richard is a consul-
tant with his own business in telecommunications and real estate, and
Kim is a screenwriter. Together they bring in about $84,000. Their two
children, Zamian and Xavier, attend private school. The family lives in
a condominium in Fox Hills, a middle-class African American neighborhood in Culver City on the West Side of Los Angeles. Previously,

they lived in Compton, a largely black city with a high poverty rate, but moved to Culver City two years ago for many of same the reasons that most Americans move: safer communities, better schools, more job and business opportunities, and bettering themselves. Richard and Kim explain, "Coming from Compton to here was a chance to start fresh." I ask them to elaborate: "More business opportunities. Yeah, more business opportunities. More opportunities. Better neighborhood. Yeah, just job opportunities." The move also gave them access to "good schools," which was a concern because, Richard says, Compton has "the worst school district in the state. It's nothing to be proud of." In fact, Kim says the schools were a "huge, huge" factor in their decision to move to Culver City, and she does not mean just the good reputation of Culver City's public schools. Fox Hills was attractive because of the nearby private Montessori school. The Barzaks' plan is for Zamian and Xavier to stay in the Montessori school for a while and then continue with private school, if the family can afford it, or go to the public schools if they can get into a magnet school or program for gifted children.

The Conway and Barzak families both fit the American middle-class picture neatly: educated; good incomes; white collar, professional, or self-employed; and homeowners. Both have done well, although when we talked the Conways' middle class status appeared more tenuous because Frank was out of work and back in school. Indeed, both families sound like an all-American achievement story. The Conways are white, and the Barzaks are black. The conventional wisdom tells us that race does not matter here. Let us see how the asset perspective puts a different lens on these two equally achieving families and their capacities.

The Barzaks were only able to finance the down payment on their condominium by wiping out Richard's 401(k) retirement account, where he had stockpiled their savings while working for the telephone company. He angrily recalls how he "actually took the money out of my 401(k). Of course, the IRS still makes you pay a penalty. That still sticks in my craw. I had to give them ten percent on top of the taxes to borrow my own money." They did not have substantial nonretirement savings and did not own any stocks or bonds to use as a down payment, and their parents were not in a financial position to help them. When they were college students, Richard and Kim took out hefty student loans; they still owe over $30,000. The condominium has appreciated so that today they have accumulated about $35,000 in home equity, but their student loans practically nullify this asset. Their asset and liability balance sheet shows about $10,000, all of which is in home equity.

On the other hand, the Conways' abundance of assets allowed them to consider a completely different set of opportunities. The accomplishments of these white and black middle-class families are equivalent in virtually every other respect. The Conways have no debts left over from college because their parents paid their college bills. Frank's mother gave them $10,000 for the down payment on their Jefferson Park home. In addition, they have already inherited $95,000, and they expect to inherit more in the future. They have socked this money away in stocks and bonds, while another $53,000 keeps growing in retirement accounts. All together, their net worth is approximately $140,000, most of which is in financial instruments and not anchored in home equity. In addition, Frank explains, they have some nontraditional assets like vintage clothing, professional cameras, antiques, silver, and flatware, probably worth an additional $125,000.

I drove to the Conways' neighborhood fully expecting to find a white upper-middle-class neighborhood and was not surprised to find an enclave of large houses with well-kept lawns, gardens, and wide streets. For me, what was unexpected was that the neighborhood was overwhelmingly black. I became quite curious, because they did not fit patterns of other middle-class white families with young children whom I interviewed, and anticipated a good story. Where they live challenged my argument that white families with young children leave places like Jefferson Park for whiter and more affluent communities. How did this white family get here? Are they going to stay? What are their plans for the future? Does the presence of a young child such as Logan change the way they think about community?

As I pieced their narrative together, the answers to these questions turned out to be intriguing and insightful, not challenging my argument so much as providing a marvelous variation of my thesis. The Conways bought a house in Jefferson Park because of its proximity to downtown Los Angeles, where both worked. Housing prices in Jefferson Park were reasonable at the time they bought, especially compared to similar houses in white middle-class sections of West Los Angeles where their co-workers live. As long as they were childless and devoted most of their time to working long hours at their careers, the area's class or racial composition and the quality of its schools did not matter a great deal to them, and they were quite happy in Jefferson Park. Unlike most white families, the Conways seemed to place more importance on proximity and affordability than on class or race characteristics of their community.

The birth of their daughter, Logan, brought a profound change in their thinking about their community. Suzanne says they really like the neighborhood and want to stay, but "now we are considering possibly moving because of the school district." When I ask where they are thinking of moving, Suzanne says they are "very interested" in moving to South Pasadena because her mother lives there and

> *I think it has a really great school district. Additionally, it has a really old feel to it. The streets are lined with trees [that] create archways. It has a lot of old buildings, which I think are terrific old homes. . . . All in all, it has a real good community feel, and I think that is important. And old community charm.*

The "terrific old homes" that provide the community feel and charm are located in predominantly white sections of South Pasadena. Charm and old character come with a price. Old money lives here. In the pricey real estate market of 1999, one could expect to spend at least $600,000 for an intact period house in clean condition with original floor plans on a quiet street. However, such a house would probably require tens of thousands of dollars more in renovations. The town's exceptional school system ranks as one of the best in the state.

The Conways' annual income is typically about $70,000, but Frank's unemployment means that this year the family's income will be $35,000. Only the inheritances already received and expectations of hefty family financial assistance in the future can make this sort of upward mobility and access to great schools possible. Because they spoke positively about diversity in Jefferson Park, I asked Frank and Suzanne if they would miss it or felt they would lose something by moving to South Pasadena. They evaded my question and responded instead about South Pasadena's great architecture. The racial and ethnic composition of the section of South Pasadena they want to live in and the school

Logan would attend is dramatically different from Jefferson Park. The area they have in mind is largely white, and the local elementary school is 50 percent white and 26 percent Asian.

In financial terms, the differences between the Conways and the Barzaks in terms of how they bought their houses and what their plans for the future are provide powerful insight into the asset crossroads that families face. Some would have us believe that cultural differences are the primary factors in why some racial and ethnic groups save more money than other groups.[3] We hear about "poor future orientation," excess consumption, and lack of deferred gratification on the part of African Americans resulting in lower savings. The facts speak otherwise. It is not clear whether any deficit in the African American savings rate has played a role in the racial wealth gap. In fact, economists Francine Blau and John Graham reviewed the small number of studies on savings by race and found no evidence that African Americans have a lower savings rate than whites.[4] Even assuming whites saved more than blacks, for which there is no strong evidence, would it help explain the racial wealth gap? Economists Maury Gittleman and Edward Wolff examined savings rates and wealth accumulation among white and black families over a 10-year period. They found that the racial wealth gap would have narrowed had the share of income that African Americans devoted to savings been as high as whites. Importantly, however, much of this difference is attributable to the fact that saving rates rise with income and African Americans have lower incomes than whites, rather than whites having higher savings rates.[5]

Nationwide studies and books by sociologists Dalton Conley (*Being Black, Living in the Red*) and Lisa Keister (*Wealth in America*) show that the inheritance and asset accumulation histories of our interview subjects closely resemble the empirical reality for white and black families across the nation. We can learn larger patterns from their stories. The Conways received $10,000 toward their down payment from Suzanne's mother, while Richard Barzak was forced to wipe out his retirement plan (and had to pay a penalty on top of the taxes for early withdrawal) to come up with his down payment. The Conways' families paid the college bills, while the Barzaks still have $33,000 left on their burdensome college loans.

We know already that parental financial help, or lack thereof, is one of the great keys in determining a young family's starting point. Finding substantial differences in parental resource capacities between whites and blacks, we assumed for the most part that this parental wealth gap represented differing parental class positions and historic inequalities. Now I want to examine parental wealth information looking only at upper-middle-class families as another way of testing the argument that the racial wealth gap really is about class and not race. Using the common indicator of occupation to designate class status, we reexamined the national parental wealth data. More than nine-tenths of all upper-middle-class families, white and black, had parents with measurable wealth, with the typical family possessing $169,000 and the average over $400,000. Only 5 percent of white parents did not possess financial wealth, and among those with parents owning assets, the average was a whopping $459,000. The parents of most upper-middle-class black respondents also had wealth assets, although the proportion declined to 79 percent and average wealth was considerably less, $95,500. Figure 4.5 (page 98) reveals that even among upper-middle-class families whose living parents own property, the capacity of white parents to help, or to have helped already, their adult children financially is at least four times greater than that of black parents. Thus the road to middle class status may be quite different for white and blacks.

Examining upper-middle-class families in this chapter is a way of presenting a best-case family scenario of successful families. While these white and black families have earned their status, the data we just reviewed shows the importance of parental wealth. The idea of head-start wealth—the amount needed for the down payment and closing costs on the average house, $14,000—provides another way to investigate parental financial capacities among upper-middle-class whites and blacks. As shown in Figure 4.6 (page 98) the assets of 54 percent of the parents of upper-middle-class families reach this critical threshold. The parents of 57 percent of all upper-middle-class white families hold this amount of wealth resources, in contrast to only 36 percent of blacks. Among black and white upper-middle-class families, then, whites are 1.5 times as likely as blacks to call upon parents with head-start assets. These data, of course, do not tell us how many parents actually help out their adult children or the amount of any financial assistance, but it is nonetheless abundantly clear that the achievements of upper-middle-class African American families are earned with far less parental financial backup than those of their white counterparts.

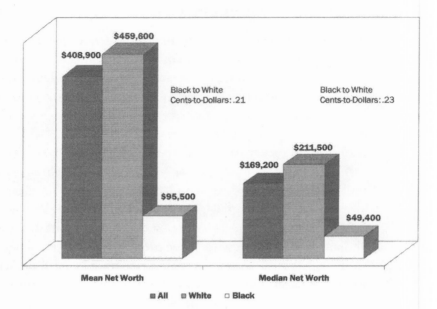

Black to White
Cents-to-Dollars: .21

Black to White
Cents-to-Dollars: .23

**Mean Net Worth**   **Median Net Worth**

■ All   ▨ White   □ Black

**Figure 4.5  Parental Wealth of Upper-Middle-Class Families\***

*1999 dollars
Source: PSID, 1988

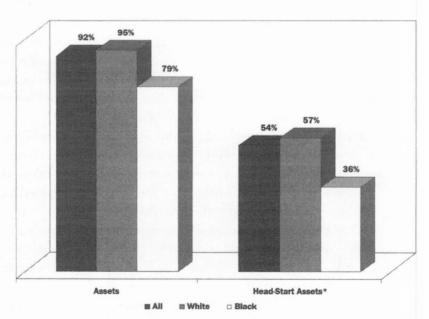

**Assets**   **Head-Start Assets\***

■ All   ▨ White   □ Black

**Figure 4.6  Parental Wealth of Upper Middle-Class Families\*: Percent with Assets**

*$14,000 or more
Source: PSID, 1988

We asked people if they ever offered financial help to their parents, relatives, or friends. Posing this question to middle-class families further facilitates an examination of the differences between white and black families in terms of their spending behavior and their attitude about wealth. In addition, it allows us to see what happens to the language of deservedness.

One salient theme emerged throughout our interviews distinguishing the giving and helping behavior of white and black families. Earlier in this chapter, we compared the so-called savings behavior of the Conway and Barzak families. Because of their striking differences in parental assistance and level of debt, these two families also have different savings and investing capabilities. Cultural explanations offer only feeble rationalizations for what look like highly divergent and structured circumstances. So, too, one needs to be wary of superficial cultural explanations concerning giving behavior. The pattern in behavior, however, is unmistakable: Less financially able middle-class black families consistently give more financial assistance to parents, relatives, and friends than their more capable white counterparts do. Glee and Barry Putnam provided a case in point. Immediately after hearing them talk about all the assistance they received from family, I asked if they ever helped out family financially. Glee started, "Well, we've had a hard enough time just getting by, so . . ." Her voice trailed off, never finishing the answer that will say no. Barry said he does things like help people move but gives no financial help.

We asked families about what kinds of assistance they provided relatives, friends, or others. Forty-seven families described helping others in some manner, most characteristically, though not always, involving giving money. Of those 47, 34 were black.[6] The response from Kevin and Donna Hays of Los Angeles is representative of a number of middle-class African American families. Donna is an account executive for a public utility, and Kevin is a manager for a large telecommunications company. "The bank of Kevin," Donna replies when I ask if they ever help relatives with money or other assistance, "the bank of Kevin. I can't think of anybody who has helped us, but he's always helping people. . . . Countless times, more times than I can remember. Just crazy amounts of money." Kevin fills in the blanks: "Family members still owe me three, four thousand dollars. A thousand dollars. Five hundred. Seven-fifty."

Donna says that they finally came to an agreement that they would never lend any more than they expect to get back, but Kevin laughs and says, "I broke it." Donna does not let him off the hook: "Yeah, you broke it." Kevin explains a situation involving his grandfather, a cousin, and a piece of property where he is still waiting settlement. That is not what is important to Kevin. "We've had good fortune come to us, just incredible good fortune, and it really overweighs what we have lost in being good-hearted. Absolutely."

I talked to one woman who helps pay college tuition for a waitress who befriended her mother; another helps her mother pay college tuition for her sister. Angela Slater is a senior financial analyst working for a health care company in Los Angeles. Her husband, Andrew, is president of a small company. I asked Angela if she helps people.

*Are you kidding me? Like all of them* [laughter], *all the time. Pretty much we've kind of been there for each other. . . . We have a younger sister who is a single parent, she is by herself. It's kind of, she doesn't really financially assist her son. So typically you kind of help her out because we all got help getting started. So when she wants to buy* [something important], *we all contribute to that. Some of us make wiser business decisions financially than others, you know.*

This attitude about giving is not limited to the black middle class. Elizabeth Turner is 41 years old, unemployed, raising three kids in Boston. She is an unlikely source of help, yet she furnishes a couple of examples.

*Well, my nephew was incarcerated, so I used to try to send him a little something. When he came out, I put a roof over his head and food in his mouth, which was not an easy thing. And he has got his own place now, his own job. I adopted my two nieces, my sister's kids. Kids. Kids. I mean, what more can you do? 'Cause everything is not based on the money value. I give these kids my love, affection, attention, that's about it, 24–7.*

In a perverse sense, middle-class black families have greater opportunity and broader windows for giving assistance: African American families tend to be larger, so chances are that relatives need assistance more, and reciprocities of extended kinships are more common.[7]

Financial resources tend to flow from parents to children in white families, while money flows from children to parents and other relatives and friends in black families. The greater needs of elderly black parents in comparison to white parents in our sample and the financial ability of their adult children could explain the greater giving behavior. Needs, resources, and expectations are critical, and we do not need to open the door solely to interpretations like cultural differences in family support.

## Possessive Advantage

In Chapter 3, we discussed how families justify inheritances and advantages as deserved. We now know that white middle-class families are far more likely than blacks to receive financial wealth from parents and other relatives. In this section, I build upon the notion of deserving inheritance to examine how families feel about their inherited wealth advantage. How do they justify privilege for themselves individually? What are the implications for the way they view racial inequality?

Thomas and Mary Edsall write in *Chain Reaction* that race in modern America affects a range of domestic issues, from death penalty debates to college admission standards, from minority set-aside programs to the decline in urban manufacturing jobs, from prison construction to the globalization of economic competition, from school reform to suburban zoning practices.[8] Most white Americans favor the principle of equality but oppose court-ordered, administrative, regulatory, or federally mandated solutions. Poll data and survey research reveal that Americans, at least on the record, have adopted the principles of racial equality.[9] As we know all too well, principles often differ from practice, and high levels of racial inequality endure in all arenas, public and private.

The sociologist Larry Bobo advances the idea of laissez-faire racism to explain how whites justify racial inequality. The appeal of this justification is that whites view African Americans as individuals just like themselves, using the same set of rules to compete for success in the marketplace, rather than as members of a group who were forced to play by rigged rules used historically to ensure their disadvantage and white domination. Overt bigotry, Jim Crow laws and policies, government-mandated discrimination, and the belief in black inferiority have virtually disappeared. Laissez-faire racism, instead, involves persistent negative stereotyping of African Americans, a tendency to blame blacks for their own conditions, appeals to meritocracy, and resistance to meaningful policy efforts to ameliorate America's racist social conditions and institutions. Government is formally race neutral and committed to antidiscrimination, and most white Americans prefer a more volitional and cultural, as opposed to inherent and biological, interpretation of blacks' disadvantaged status.[10]

Support for this theory comes from survey data and an instructive body of literature based on qualitative interviews with whites about their views on blacks and racial inequality.[11] Whites rely on a number of frames or explanations to account for racial inequality. Outright racist explanations are still evident, although they represent a minority.[12] Most whites explain black disadvantage in cultural, moral, and character terms. In these works, the majority of whites prescribe meritocracy and making it on one's own as the correct path to racial equality, as opposed to government assistance, set-asides, handouts, and preferential treatment. The focus of this work is, in essence, to get inside the heads of whites and discover what they really think about racial inequality and how it occurs. In this sense, the focus falls on explaining minority disadvantage from the majoritarian perspective—whites talking about the troubles of blacks. Recent surveys have shown repeatedly that nearly every social choice that white people make about where they live, what schools their children attend, what careers they pursue, and what policies they endorse is shaped by considerations involving race.[13] Our interviews picked up and confirmed this theme at different salient points, especially when we asked whether families consider race when choosing communities and schools, as we will see in later chapters.

Our interviews also investigated how whites explain advantage and privilege, that is, how the fortunate explain their advantage. Our point of reference in the interviews centered on their family's community and school decisions, not on principles of equality. We asked about concrete situations, choices, decisions and actions, and self. People ascribe their success to their own merit or personal characteristics. Families seek to justify their position, advantages, privileges, identities, and worth in the coin of meritocracy.

Historian George Lipsitz superbly described the notion of people's possessive investment in whiteness, by which he meant the rewards and benefits that many whites accrue from past and present racial inequality.[14] Many whites are born with advantages that come to families through profits made from housing secured in discriminatory markets, through the unequal educations allocated to children of different races, and through networks that channel employment opportunities and other benefits to relatives and friends. For many white families, these are the hidden advantages that simultaneously structure and reward decisions around community, schools, and jobs.

Lori and Dan Olsen and their three children live on what Lori calls "one of the most magical, beautiful streets" in suburban St. Louis. She is a homemaker, and Dan earns $60,000 a year as a plant manager for a chemical company. The three Olsen boys attend a Lutheran parochial school. When I talked to Lori and Dan, they had lived in their dream house for a year, largely using equity built up in their previous house for the down payment. Because they had not sold their previous house before closing on the new one, they needed a bridge loan. (A bridge loan is a loan that is used for a short time until permanent financing is put in place. Bridge loans are often used to facilitate timely real estate acquisitions because they allow purchasers to act quickly.) Dan's mother arranged the loan through her finance company. At the end of the interview, I asked Lori if she felt that their assets affect where they chose to live and where their kids go to school. Lori is conscious of her family's possessive advantages.

> Now it's not necessarily fair and it's not necessarily right, but I think certain neighborhoods are better, certain schools are better, and your children will have a better childhood and better educational background because of where they go. But it's not right. I don't think it's necessarily right, but I think everyone should have the same opportunities my children do, but they don't. . . . Okay, I'll rephrase that. I don't think it's right that my children get to go to a private school [parochial] and get to wear Adidas and there are other children living in the city who aren't even fed breakfast, who wear raggy, holey clothes, who have teachers who don't want to be there, and they get no educational benefits whatsoever.
>
> . . . I feel guilty because I'm not doing anything to make their [kids in inner-city schools] life better or try to help them. I'm hiding out here in my little nice neighborhood and my little private school and I'm like sticking my head in the sand and pretending like these problems don't exist. So I do have a sense of guilt over it.

Above all, advantages come to families through intergenerational transfers of inherited wealth that pass spoils of discrimination to succeeding generations. This structure of advantage provides many whites with resources, power, opportunities, enhanced capacities, and status. Advantaged groups not only control important resources and institutions, they attempt to make their advantages appear legitimate in their own eyes, as well as in the eyes of the disadvantaged.

I think that many white families defend these advantages when they attempt to legitimize unearned advantages. In Chapter 3, we catalogued the parental financial support Joe and Briggette Barry received. Despite facts to the contrary, possessive advantage is behind the Barrys' claim that they have worked their butts off for everything they own. Just as contrary to the evidence, as we also saw in Chapter 3, this also is what is at stake for Glee and Barry Putnam when they say everything they have is a result of hard work and saving. Legitimizing possessive advantage is hard work. The irony here, of course, is that language once reserved to explain class domination finds use in a new context: nonelite whites seeking legitimacy for their own advantages. Later chapters build upon possessive advantage to explore how whites hoard opportunities and capacities to maintain their advantaged position while passing competitive advantages along to their own children at critical moments.

# 5

# The Homeownership Crossroad

## At the Mortgage Table

THE ASSETS THAT YOUNG FAMILIES bring to the mortgage table in buying their first home represent a crucial institutional and biographical moment. Significant parental assistance at this critical stage in a family's life can advance the standing of their adult children beyond the merits of their own achievements, providing what I call transformative assets. Furthermore, the social reproduction of class and racial inequality moves into a third generation in this process because, among other things, homeownership sets the educational environment of children and the terms of success as well. Simply put, if I can buy a house in a better neighborhood, my kids will grow up there, make friends there, go to school there, and grow accustomed to its status.

Among the white middle-class families I interviewed, 48 of 56 already owned homes, and about 1 in 4 white working-class families did. Of the 41 black middle-class families interviewed, 22 were homeowners; of the 14 black working-class families, only 1 owned a home. In my interviews, 2 white middle-class families and 15 black middle-class families said they had plans for buying a home. Examining the plans and wishes of two of these families provides an analytic window into the contexts in which families buy homes and an understanding of the unique and diverse social circumstances that blacks and whites face in becoming homeowners.

Elaine and Bradford Johnson rent an apartment in Fox Hills, a middle-class African American section of Los Angeles. Elaine, a former schoolteacher, occasionally does some substitute teaching but mostly stays home and cares for 4-year-old Maya and 10-year-old Macy. Bradford is a television news reporter earning $117,000. The television news business is one of those occupations in which salaries are high but downtime between jobs is common. Indeed, this is the case for the Johnson family, as they had to cash $30,000 out of investments and pension and savings plans for living expenses when he was last between jobs. They are in the red because, like most American families, they have considerable credit card debt. When we talked, things were looking up and they looked forward to buying a house in the next half year.

What kind of house can they afford? How can they finance it? They are looking to buy a home in the $250,000 range in nearby Ladera Heights or Baldwin Hills, two of Los Angeles' better-known African American middle-class communities. With Bradford's high salary, they can qualify for a loan to buy the kind of home they want, but they have used up all their savings, which leaves them without any assets. Where will the down payment come from? Bradford says, "Well, my father is a real estate broker, so we'll try to work a deal with him, where he could use his commission as the down payment. So that we don't have to come up with any money up front, we just basically move in and take over the payment. I know it's going to take a while, but those kinds of deals are out there, so we're trying to find something we can get without a lot of down-payment money." They also will try to avoid other up-front costs, like points to originate and service the loan.

In the real estate market of early 2003, they can afford to finance a home valued at about $210,000. They will not pay any points, and Bradford's father will forgo his commission for the down payment of $10,000. This means that the Johnsons could qualify to borrow $200,000 at 5.75 percent interest for 30 years. Their monthly payments will be $1,167. But because the down payment they can afford is only about 5 percent of the purchase price, they will need to purchase private mortgage insurance. (Because lenders can lose a great deal of money on an unpaid mortgage, mortgage insurance is generally required for all loans with less than a 20 percent down payment, even if the borrower has a good credit rating.) Mortgage insurance will cost them another $112 per month, raising their monthly mortgage payments to $1,279.

Across the country in Boston, David and Kerri Scully also rent an apartment with their children, Emily and Josh, 12 and 14. David works for a neighborhood development agency in Boston, and Emily teaches preschool. Together their incomes bring in $70,000. They have been looking forward to buying a house.

The Scullys' earnings also qualify them to buy a home for $210,000, but they will finance it differently than the Johnsons. Kerri's father, who runs a successful business and who has helped them out before, will lend a hand by contributing a 20 percent down payment of $40,000. David and Kerri will dip into their savings, almost all of which came from earlier gifts from their parents, and pay 2 points, $3,400, on the loan in return for a lower interest rate of 5.25 percent and thus lower monthly mortgage payments. Thus they will borrow $170,000, and their monthly payments will be $939. The Johnsons and Scullys both qualify to buy a $210,000 home, but because of the financing arrangements the Johnsons will pay $340 more per month, or $4,080 per year, or $122,400 more over the 30-year mortgage.

The Johnsons and Scullys seem to have roughly similar qualifications, but each brings a family legacy as a silent partner to the mortgage table. The loan transaction cements past inequality into present mortgage terms, which contracts inequality for another 30 years.

## Housing, Real Estate, and Financial Markets

Most Americans accumulate assets through homeownership. Home equity accounts for roughly 44 percent of total measured net worth.[1] Wealth built up in one's home is by far the most important financial reserve for middle-class families. In fact, home wealth accounts for 60 percent of the total wealth among America's middle-class.[2] We pride ourselves that America has the highest homeownership rate in the world, with about two-thirds of Americans owning homes. A set of federal policies that started in the 1930s has made this high homeownership rate possible. The Federal Housing Administration, the Veterans Administration, and the GI Bill, for a previous generation, have been instrumental in guaranteeing long-term, low-interest mortgages, which put the American dream of homeownership within reach of most families. The tax status of home mortgages and tax treatment of profits from home sales, both of which I address later in detail, are indispensable in keeping homes affordable. The vast growth of suburbs, where most new housing is built, is only possible with transportation policies that subsidize transporting people to residential suburbs in automobiles. However, the same federal housing, tax, and transportation policies that have been so successful in making America a land of homeowners also have traditionally reinforced neighborhood segregation by favoring economically and racially uniform communities over integrated ones. [3]

Table 5.1 shows the homeownership rate for blacks to be 25 percent less than it is for whites. This difference is not merely the result of income differences; rather, it results from historical legacies of residential segregation, federal housing, tax, and transportation policies, and discrimination in real estate and lending markets.[4] The effect is racial redlining, whereby mortgage lenders fail to make mortgage loans available to minority communities. Racial redlining encompasses declining to lend in minority neighborhoods, discouraging mortgage loan applications from minority areas, and marketing policies that exclude such areas. Racial redlining reduces housing finance options for borrowers in minority neighborhoods and weakens competition in the mortgage market, which often results in higher mortgage costs and less favorable loan terms.

Continuing residential segregation has an enduring effect on black families' ability to buy and sell homes and on their asset accumulation. Judith Andrews illustrates this racial dynamic well. In Chapter 2 we saw that her home value is limited because the market for it is restricted only to black families who can afford it. Whites will not buy a home in her black neighborhood.

There are three major phases in the homeownership process fraught with discrimination and major consequences for wealth accumulation. Access to credit is important because whom banks deem creditworthy affects who can buy a house. Is it more difficult for equally creditworthy black families to qualify for mortgages than it is for whites? We need to understand this process because discrimination in securing financing has lasting consequences for gatekeeping who can buy homes and build up wealth through home equity.

The second area of potential discrimination concerns the price of credit or interest rates attached to loans. It costs black Americans more to become homeowners. Later in this chapter, I will show that blacks typically pay higher interest rates on home mortgages and analyze the

**Table 5.1 Homeownership and Race**

| | Percent Homeowners | Average Mortgage Rate | Mean Home Equity | Median Home Equity |
|---|---|---|---|---|
| **White** | 74.2 | 8.12 | $74,859 | $58,000 |
| **Black** | 48.2 | 8.44 | $46,254 | $40,000 |
| **Difference** | 25.8 | 0.32 | $28,605 | $18,000 |

Sources: Joint Center for Housing Studies, 2002; Bureau of the Census, 1998; SIPP, 1994

reasons why. Paying more in monthly payments to banks means less discretionary income, home equity, and savings.

As is well known, housing values climbed steeply during the 1970s and 1980s, far outstripping inflation and creating a large pool of assets for people who owed homes. In the last five years of the 1990s, housing prices climbed by one-third. Did all communities and homeowners share equally in the appreciation of housing values, or is housing inflation—and the wealth it creates—color-coded?

## Who Qualifies?

Anyone who has bought a home knows that families must first qualify for a mortgage. Banks play the key role in this process by creating a list of "risk" factors they use to evaluate each prospective homeowner. This list of criteria by which banks evaluate families typically includes past credit history, job history, family income, and family wealth.[5] Economists point out that what matters about the way bankers look at risk is the ability to pay back a loan, or creditworthiness.[6] The lender examines past credit history to evaluate how promptly bills are paid, income, job stability, previous homeownership, bank accounts, and assets. Bankers set the bar at a very high level because it is their business to lower their risk as much as possible.

Studies using matching white and black couples with identical job, income, and credit information consistently reveal discrimination by real estate agents and banks.[7] Based on legally mandated release of mortgage data, the Federal Reserve Board investigates the controversial issue of redlining and mortgage discrimination. The most comprehensive Federal Reserve Board study, the Boston Fed Study, examined outcomes from all loan applications mandated by federal legislation and demonstrated that lending institutions rejected blacks for home loans 80 percent more often than equally qualified white families.[8] "Equally qualified" here includes meeting the stringent creditworthiness test.[9] Thus, no matter how egregious past segregation and redlining may have been in real estate, grave levels of racial discrimination are still alive in financial mortgage markets. In *The Color of Credit*, Stephen Ross and John Yinger examine the phenomenal and unprecedented amount of criticism showered on the Boston Fed Study. While cautioning against overstating discrimination, in the most exhaustive treatment yet published of mortgage discrimination that weighs evidence and critics, Ross and Yinger uphold the report's major conclusion concerning differences in minority and white approval and rejection rates.

In the face of heated criticism by community, housing, and civil rights activists, financial industry professionals testified before Congress in 1993–94 and claimed that no smoking gun exists to prove discrimination in mortgage markets. Many responded that studies like the Boston Fed Study are statistical and based on averages and that discrimination is hard to document by examining specific loan applications. A small number of banks started looking for ways to remedy potential discrimination and encourage applications from minorities. This is a heated and politically charged issue because by law banks must be fair and equal opportunity lenders. As a result, they are sensitive to charges about mortgage discrimination, predatory lending, and redlining.

In the last decade or two, several striking changes have occurred in mortgage markets. We have seen a dramatic growth in home loans originating from mortgage companies as opposed to banks. These are lending institutions that usually do not hold any deposits; thus they act as loan originators by bundling a large number of loans together, which they then sell to financial companies and banks. The growth of mortgage companies may have ramifications for low-asset families because the companies like to bundle uniform, standard loans that will be attractive to larger financial investors and thus tend to discourage loans tailored to individual circumstances. Automated underwriting is another development since the Boston Fed Study. This involves a uniform application form that is scored automatically, leaving less room for considering unique circumstances or understanding family situations.

Some argue that these two developments will make mortgage lending less discriminatory, while others worry that they will result in more mortgage discrimination.[10]

Predatory lending—lending practices in poor, minority, and immigrant communities that rely on consumer ignorance, deceptive marketing, lack of lending choices and, occasionally, fraud—is on the rise. Government enforcement agencies have forced several banks and lending companies to cease the most flagrant practices and to set aside millions for consumer redress.[11] As government agencies slow down some of the most egregious practices, new forms of predatory lending in mortgages, home equity loans, and home repair financing have arisen.

## Down Payment Help

Once a lending institution approves a family for a home loan, they decide upon a mortgage package. Interest rates on home mortgages are tied closely to rates set by the Federal Reserve Board. When the Federal Reserve Board raises or lowers interest rates, banks customarily follow suit. As we will see shortly, interest rates can vary somewhat according to the size of the down payment, the length of the loan, and the number of points paid. On average, African Americans pay mortgage interest rates about a third of a percent higher than whites.[12] A third of a percentage point may not sound like much, but let's consider how this affects the typical home purchase. In 1999 the median home purchase price was $161,000. If one had bought a house then, putting down 10 percent, leaving a mortgage of $145,000 on a typical 30-year loan, this difference amounts to "only" $32.65 a month. On the typical house, then, over the loan period the average African American homebuyer will pay $11,756 more in interest to financial institutions than the average white homebuyer.

In the course of the research project that undergirds this book, we had the opportunity to present these results before all kinds of groups, including housing and Federal Reserve conferences attended by bankers and loan officers. They adamantly insisted that they do not discriminate by charging different rates for black and white customers. However, the practice of offering different interest rates stems not from overt discrimination but from invisibly seating racial legacies at the mortgage table. Banks charge fees to process loan applications and subsequent administrative and clerical services over the life of the loan. These "points" on a loan are usually set at 1 percent of the loan amount. In addition, down payments considerably higher than 10 percent can lower interest rates. Whites typically bring more assets to the table, use them to lower the amount of the loan or to pay up-front points on the loan, and consequently receive a lower interest rate on their mortgage. The more financial assets one brings to the mortgage table, the lower the interest rate. This is one reason why African Americans pay higher interest rates.

People who must pay higher interest rates because of little family savings, inheritance, or wealth must usually also buy private mortgage insurance. This is generally required for loans with less than a 20 percent down payment, even if the borrower has a good credit rating. It costs about three-quarters of 1 percent of the loan, or over $1,000 a year for a family buying a median-price house with a small down payment. In *The Color of Credit*, the foremost experts in mortgage discrimination caution that the trend in the mortgage market is clearly toward more choices in loan packages and greater variation in loan pricing, and this should be of special attention for those concerned about fair lending. We can now more fully appreciate the importance of head-start assets for homeownership and wealth accumulation. They mean more than the money itself because they can leverage lower interest rates and thus lower monthly mortgage payments as well as eliminate private mortgage insurance costs.

For young families, financial help from parents can make the difference between being able to buy a home and having to continue as renters. Research from the Joint Center for Housing Studies suggests that as many as one-fifth of first-time homebuyers receive significant parental help, averaging more than half of the down payment amount.[13] Many young families continue receiving financial help for mortgage payments for several years. A key finding in the center's *State of the Nation's Housing 2002* is that parental assistance "gives young white adults a significant head start that enables them to acquire better first homes and to do so earlier."[14]

People who bought homes between 1991 and 1995, for example, provide another key piece of evidence (see Figure 5.1) by identifying the immediate source of their down payments: entirely from their own savings, assistance from family, or assistance from other sources? Only 54 percent of whites said their down payments came entirely from their own savings. We have good reason to think this figure might be too high: This survey did not distinguish between saved money and money inherited or received as a gift at some prior point, so "own savings" could mean inherited money. In any case, 46 percent got their down payments from family, other sources, or some combination.

While income criteria are a key part of conventional mortgage underwriting standards, wealth constraints may be at least as important in the way bankers assess mortgage applicants.[15] Another important study, for instance, reports no racial differences in homeownership among households with enough accumulated wealth to meet standard down payment and closing cost requirements. Among similarly wealth-poor families, those whose assets are not sufficient to meet typical down payment and closing costs, 59 percent more whites own houses than minorities. One study demonstrated that wealth-poor whites are roughly twice as likely to own homes as similarly wealth-constrained minorities.[16] The authors

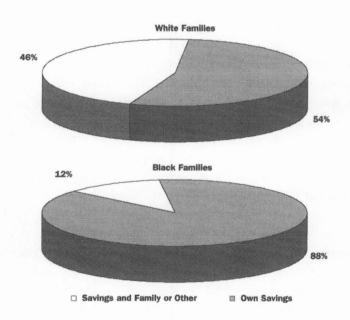

**Figure 5.1 Sources of Down Payment**

Source: PSID, 1996

of this study suggest that wealth-constrained white families come from wealthier parents and hence are more likely to receive parental financial assistance for down payment and closing cost requirements. Indeed, this parental disparity may well help account for a higher home mortgage rejection rate for blacks; one study shows that applicants with a gift or grant are less likely to be rejected for a home mortgage, controlling for other relevant application information.[17] In effect, young white families possess an advantage in housing markets and homeownership because their parents' economic livelihoods and ability to accumulate wealth were untrammeled by race in previous generations.

Blacks who bought homes told a contrasting story. Nearly 9 in 10 said their down payments came entirely out of their own savings. Only 1 in 20 relied entirely on family financial assistance. Black families typically do it themselves. Whites count on parents more than three times as often for down payment money. Given what we know about the greater wealth capability of white parents, the actual difference in how whites and blacks buy homes is not surprising but confirms how capacity translates into tangible disparity. This means that young white and black families approach the questions of when a home is affordable and what kind of home is affordable in what neighborhood from different perspectives. This understanding also helps to explain why the black homeownership rate lags behind that of whites with similar incomes.

The figures showing that over half of whites and 88 percent of African American families use their own assets for down payment money starkly highlight the racial differences in homeownership and financial assistance in acquiring that home. Through our interviews, we examined parental help in purchasing first homes in more depth than almost any other topic. Our interviews provide a wellspring of relevant information about the ways in which whites think about money, property, and neighborhoods and about family.

We met the Barrys in Chapter 3—the white family who told us they deserve everything they have because they have worked their butts off. The story of how they bought their home is similar to the stories of other white couples, although the details vary. In the life of the Barry family, the timing of abundant down payment money from Briggette's parents is crucial to buying the house they wanted and changing their lives. Briggette says:

*We lived childless for two years* [in another part of St. Louis]. *And then our first daughter, Elizabeth, was born.* [Then Joe's] *father died and so did his mother. And so we really didn't need to live in that area anymore. Then our son Alex came along, and it was getting to the time where we were going to have to start making choices for school, for Elizabeth. She was getting to kindergarten age. We didn't like the choices of schools that were in our area. The public school was in a not-so-good neighborhood, and the private schools didn't have the diverse education that we wanted her to have. It didn't have all the services that we felt that she could get in other areas . . .*

*And also, our neighborhood was starting to decline, in that there were more and more gangs of kids out at all hours of the night walking the streets. We had a friend who was a police officer in the neighborhood, and heard more and more of him responding to fights and kids wielding weapons in the elementary school. And we really weren't comfortable with that. . . . We looked in all kinds of neighborhoods.*

How did they choose a place to move? Bridgette identifies schools as an important factor.

*The choices of schools were much better. The school district, the public school district in our* [new] *area is very good. And the Catholic school in our area* [is] *very good. It offers a lot of services, if my kids need them, special services, as well as classes in computers and advanced classes and things that the Catholic schools in my* [old] *area didn't offer. So we found a real cute little house in that area and moved there about two years ago. And in that time, we've had our third child. And we're just real set there. We feel real at home. And my kids can ride their bikes down the street and I know Mrs. Woolworth is going to know that they're down there. I feel very attached to the community. And so it feels good. And that's the reason we wanted to be in that area.*

I ask how difficult it was to come up with the $30,000 down payment and closing costs. Briggette responds, "Not at all. My parents gave it to me." The stumbling block of large credit card debt, bad credit histories, and no savings dissolved for the Barrys with a generous parental helping hand. "Yeah, my parents told me they were going to give me thirty thousand dollars to move into our house. And we about died." The rest was "the real easy matter of depositing a check." As we will see in detail in a later chapter, parental help in buying a house is frequently a down payment on enhanced class and school status.

Maybe because it is so quintessentially bound up in the American Dream, people relish telling the story of how they acquired their homes, and everybody has a story to tell. Among the 53 white home-owners we talked to, 33 purchased their homes with financial assistance from their families. This familial helping hand was substantial enough that it enabled all but 6 of these 33 families to move to communities and houses they otherwise could not have afforded. This is the funda-mental nature of transformative assets. They allow you to move to a better house in a better neighborhood with better schools.

Asked how difficult it was to come up with the down payment, Amanda Parnet, a white single mother of two who lives in St. Louis, replied simply, "Daddy." In three of every four cases, the financial assis-tance was substantial, that is, amounting to $14,000 or more. The commonality of these gifts is as notable as the hefty amounts involved. This kind of direct family help averaged out to $18,000 among the white homeowners we spoke to.

Gift-giving between parents and children is subtle and complicated in unspoken ways that often characterize parent-child relationships. For instance, several families referred to assistance for down payment and closing costs as "loans" from family. Among whites, these loans often seemed to segue slowly over time into gifts, which was not the case for blacks. Elizabeth and Vance Cotter of Boston are a typical example. In this section of our conversation, Elizabeth says, "His mother gave us some of the money [for the down payment]" but Vance interrupts, "Well, it was originally structured as a loan with interest, and eventually the interest was waived." This was five years ago, so I ask if some or all of the loan has been paid back. "No, nope, it's still sitting there . . . oh, fifteen thousand dollars, something like that." Another woman told us that her family got down payment money from her mother, so I asked if it was a loan. The answer from this white middle-class Bostonian is typical, I think, of the way people view these kinds of familial "loans": "It's a loan. You know, I haven't paid it back yet. You know, when you get around to it. Like, it's not a loan, but I consider it a loan." This kind of reasoning suggests some tacit entitlement to a home on the part of young couples and some unspoken obligation on the part of their parents.

A combination of parental gifts, loans, and an installment on an inheritance eased this difficulty for Christine Perkins and Peter Kiley. They live in the Jamaica Plain section of Boston, an economically and racially diverse community, with their two children, ages 2 and 7. They moved five years ago from a triple-decker and bought their home. Knowing the steep real estate prices in Jamaica Plain, I asked Christine if they had needed any down payment help.

> *Yeah, it was a loan against—my grandmother was still alive at the time. And they said, "In your grandmother's will, she's leaving you X amount of money." It wasn't an amount of money, it was a percentage of her total. "And then you can pay us back when that money comes your way." That's exactly what happened.* [My parents] *loaned us forty thousand dollars, which they understood we would be able to pay back out of what I inherited from my grandmother.*

Debbie and Bill Payne live in St. Louis with their daughter and son. Debbie is a part-time child care worker, and Bill is a housepainter; their combined family income is $25,000. When I asked if it was difficult for them to come up with down payment and closing costs, Debbie explained, "Oh, no. Bill's parents helped us with that ... down payment and closing costs." I asked if they paid all of it.

> *I think they did. They knew that we needed to be in a house, and I think that his dad knew that he was sick and had cancer, and my mother-in-law wanted him to see us in a house before it got too bad for him to see it, for their grandkids. I think they did it mainly for their grandkids.*

Sometimes it takes an extended family to buy a house. The assets flew in from all sorts of relatives and circumstances to help Nancy and Mark Hollings, who are white, settle in the Dorchester section of Boston, where the housing costs are not as high as in nearby Boston communities. Nancy explains where the down payment, closing costs, and fix-it-up money came from.

*Well, actually we both had savings, that's part of it. But we both had inherited a little bit of money. Mark from his great uncle and me from my grandfather. . . . Actually, [Mark's] parents gave us some money, and my parents—no, actually, what it was, [his] parents gave us money, I think seventy-five hundred dollars. My parents kind of gave us a loan against the inheritance. They knew that that was going to be coming, so they gave us that money. . . . I think that we got that money after we moved into the house, though, so now I'm thinking we used that money to fix the house up. I think it was about twenty-five thousand dollars. I think that money was spent fixing the house up. So the main money was the seventy-five hundred that we had. And my parents must have given us a couple thousand or something, but I can't remember.*

Our interviews showed parental helping hands among African American families to be emphatically different than among whites in several important ways. To start with, in contrast to young white families, where 5 of 8 receive family financial assistance, only 9 out of 25 African American homeowners told us about receiving similar helping hands. This pattern also is consistent with information from national surveys.

Within this fundamental difference, the nature of assistance blacks receive also looks quite different from assistance whites obtain. Only four black families received direct financial help—as opposed to indirect help such as offering free rent, which allows families to save money—in contrast to two-thirds of whites. When the assistance is direct, the amount received by blacks also is considerably lower: The average runs between $3,000 and $5,000, which contrasts with the approximately $18,000 received by whites.

We identified another form of family assistance consistent with a tradition of extended family networks in the African American community. The author Carol Stack argues in *All Our Kin* that intense family loyalties and intricate trading systems evolved within African American communities to combat grinding poverty and help families survive. Black families without wealth to share are more likely to use other, indirect ways to help their adult children. Three families we met bought homes using money expressly saved while they lived with their parents and did not have to pay rent. In each of these cases, adult children with their own families who had been living on their own moved back with their parents to save money for their own houses. Joyce and Bruce Dove of St. Louis told me how this worked for them. Joyce said, "While I was living at home I saved money. We all had the opportunity to rent the upstairs, to save money so that we could buy a house." Faye Millen is a single mother of a 9-year-old and a 5-year-old living in Los Angeles who told me about moving back in with her parents after separating from her husband. Faye saved money at her parents' home and put herself through school to become an X-ray technician. I asked Faye if it was hard to save money to buy a house.

*In some ways yes, because after I finished school, I started at my current job. It was more money, and it was easy to just spend. I didn't have to pay rent . . . so it was easier to just go out and just spend money. So I started saving it. So it wasn't that hard, it was just I couldn't eat out every day. I couldn't just— when you see something you just can't go buy it. So it wasn't that hard. It would have been harder if I would have had to pay her more, pay rent, and everything else.*

African Americans have developed these strategies out of necessity and a tradition of relatives supporting the survival needs and mobility aspirations of one another. Many of these strategies are creative and apparently effective. However, while they allow some mobility, they do not provide the same opportunities for mobility typically used by young white families, where financial support is more crucial.

## Property and Values

This brings us to home equity. Information on home equity shows that buying homes typically increases wealth.[18] At the time of the interviews, most white families we talked to were living in their first house. Some talked to us in the second or third home they owned. In each of these cases, the family had moved up to a larger house in a better-off community. Given the general upward trend in housing markets and real estate appreciation during the 1990s, these families pointed to equity taken out of previous houses as key to buying bigger homes in better communities. They talked about using "savings" to buy their present homes, but when we pressed them about how they got down payment monies for their first homes, they invariably cited parental help in giving them a head start. Their parents supplied assets that leveraged subsequent moves up to bigger homes and into better-off communities. It is reasonable to assume that many of our first-time homebuyers will follow a similar path. For example, the Toppines of St. Louis were living in their third home, moving up each time, and I inquired if they needed help for the down payment on their first.

SHERRYL: *Yes.*

DENNIS: *Well, we did. Yeah, we did. We got a little family loan thing to help set us up on that one.*

SHERRYL: *Well, the down payment on our first house, they* [my parents] *helped with that*

INT: *How much?*

SHERRYL: *It was five thousand dollars.*

INT: *Was that a gift or a loan?*

SHERRYL: *I would say it was a loan.*

INT: *Did you pay it back?*

SHERRYL: *We've been working on it for eleven years. Basically. So it's a gift/loan.*

Alan and Marry Thurber, who live in the Jamaica Plain area of Boston, relate a different kind of family help that allowed them to buy their home five years ago. "My mother was looking to get rid of her house," Marry explains. "Real estate in Jamaica Plain was going up again, and so when we saw what people were asking, compared to what my mother was asking, we said, 'Let's do it, it's the right time.' When I asked how much they paid for it, she replied "a hundred and thirty-five thousand." What is it worth now? "Definitely twice that," Marry said. "We could probably get at least twice that."

The valuing of homes and home equity is color-coded. The value of the typical home owned by white families increases $28,605 more than the rise in value of homes owned by blacks. Moreover, there is strong evidence that region, length of ownership, purchase price, and date of purchase do not explain the racial differential in home equity.[19] This $28,000 difference is a compelling index of bias in housing markets that costs blacks dearly. My analysis includes only those currently still paying off home mortgages, excluding families who have paid off their mortgages entirely. My estimate is therefore very conservative because it excludes wealth built by home equity among all those who own their homes free and clear.

Our research finding that home equity is color coded corroborates recent research using different methods that calculates that homes lose at least 16 percent of their value when located in neighborhoods that are more than 10 percent black. Furthermore, homeowners require much steeper compensation for living in neighborhoods more heavily black. The dynamic of property values decreasing as black families move in and white flight takes hold is a common part of the American real estate story. A 2001 Brookings study reported that home values for black homeowners were 18 percent less than values for white homeowners. For every dollar of income, white homeowners owned $2.64 worth of house. By contrast, black homeowners owned only $2.16 worth of house. Black homeowners, according to this study, pay an 18 percent "segregation tax," and residential segregation is the culprit.[20] The segregation tax visits black homeowners in depressed home values and reduced home equity in highly segregated neighborhoods. The Brookings study found that the higher the segregation, the wider the black-white home value gap; that lower levels of residential segregation produce narrower gaps. The only prudent conclusion from these studies is that residential segregation costs African American homeowners enormous amounts of money by suppressing their home equity in comparison to that of white homeowners. The inescapable corollary is that residential segregation benefits white homeowners with greater home equity wealth accumulation.

Many homeowners know that another value of homeownership is that families may borrow money against equity built up by rising property values and regular monthly mortgage payments. The more a house increases in value, the larger the size of a potential home equity loan. The interest charged on home equity loans is tax deductible, as opposed to interest charges on personal loans and credit card debt.

Why do homes in African American communities not rise in value as much as homes in white communities? The explanation lies in how residential segregation affects housing markets. Only market forces—that is, economic affordability—limit a white family attempting to sell their house in a predominantly white community. A similar African American family attempting to sell their home in a community that is more than 20 percent nonwhite faces normal market limits as well as a racial "surcharge." The pool of potential buyers is no longer 100 percent of the affordable market, because for all practical purposes potential white buyers shun such neighborhoods.[21] The potential buyers are now mainly other black Americans who can afford the home and possibly other minorities. This economic detour shows how the marketplace for whites is the entire society while the marketplace for blacks has geographic and product restrictions. In turn, this helps explain why housing values do not rise nearly as quickly or as high in predominantly African American communities or even in communities more than 20 percent nonwhite. The Andrews family reminds us again that the comparatively low value of their home results from its location in an African American section of St. Louis. This is an example of the "segregation tax" extracted from black homeowners.

White flight from integrating communities has been going on since the passage of fair housing laws in the 1960s. In justifying their moves, whites commonly cite declining property values, deteriorating schools, and fear of crime. Our interviews expose an uneasy connection between racist attitudes and self-interest, which is to say, the reasons whites find not to live with blacks are commonly rooted in their perceived self-interest, whether their concerns are real or not. Patricia and James Keady are 38 and 44 years old and have two children, ages 6 and 3. Patricia describes herself as a homemaker, and James is a construction laborer and a union member. They are white and have been married for nine years. Patricia grew up in Maplewood, Missouri, in a working-class family—her father worked in construction as a pipefitter, and her mother was a homemaker. When he died three years ago, Patricia's father left them $50,000 and a coin collection worth another $40,000. James grew up in Shrewsbury just a couple of blocks from where they now live. His father worked in construction and then later went into the life insurance business. His mother was a secretary.

Although their neighborhood is predominantly white, they are worried about the possibility of "too many black families" moving in. They already have decided to leave if this happens, because they want to "get out" before property values go down. They reason that if they move out before it's too late they will not lose as much equity or even take a loss on their house investment. In other parts of our conversation, James and Patricia express overtly racist attitudes, but we can also see here that their thinking about community choice takes place in a context that ultimately "rewards" them for acting on those attitudes. They think that the only way they can retain the money they have built up in their home is to sell—and sell quickly before the neighborhood becomes integrated and whites will no longer move in. While it is fair for families to worry about losing value, assuming that black neighbors lower property values and acting as if it were true makes it more likely to happen. This comes out when I ask them if there is anything about the neighborhood that concerns them. Patricia says, "Just that there are a lot of homes going for sale, a lot of homes." When I ask what concerns them about that, she replies, "Who might move in." James picks up the conversation when I ask who they are concerned about.

> *Well, the blacks in the city are slowly moving to south St. Louis. The whites move out, the blacks move in, it turns into a pretty rough neighborhood. Deteriorates and so on. You know the old story. It seems to be moving in this direction. We're concerned how fast it's going to get here. Nothing against blacks, I work with them. The ones that I work with are telling me that "we can screw up a neighborhood."*

I ask if they really say that. "They admit it, yeah," James replies. I then ask if their neighborhood is declining.

> *JAMES: Don't ask me. I'm getting out before it gets bad. . . . I think people need to kind of stay where they're in place.*
> *INT: You mean like stay with the same incomes, same races?*
> *JAMES: Oh, yeah. . . . I'm telling you, if there's too many black families on the street, when you go to sell this house, you're not going to get what you think, you know? I mean, they don't do anything for property values. . . . You know, we try to stay with our own type of people.*

After the interview, I drove through their neighborhood expecting to see black neighbors and plenty of For Sale signs. I did not. I returned to this neighborhood three times since our interview and did not observe much change. On my last visit, in the fall of 2002, I systematically crisscrossed their neighborhood several times, noticing one For Sale sign, and did not see any African American neighbors. The Keadys live a half block away from a large, well-kept park equipped with several soccer fields and baseball diamonds, batting cages, and children's play structures. On a bright, sunny, clear fall Saturday morning, I did not observe any African Americans at the park. U.S. Census Information for 2000 confirms my observations: Whites comprise 97 percent of the Shrewsbury census tract they live in, and less than 2 percent of the neighbors on their block and the surrounding ones are blacks. It seems that the Keadys' alarm comes more from what they have heard or fear than from what is actually happening. This combination of attitude and behavior is a driving force in residential segregation.[22]

Charlene and Andrew Quinlin and their teenage son live in a white working-class part of Dorchester, a section of Boston. She is a homemaker, and he is unemployed; their income this year is about $15,000. Charlene explains why African Americans moving into their part of Dorchester concerns them.

*There's a lot of blacks that moved in. That I was starting to worry about, because I was afraid it was going to go down. I'm not prejudiced, but it's just that once a certain type comes in, that's it! My concern when a lot of blacks started moving in was with the drugs, the pushing of the drugs on your kids. Maybe getting stabbed or something. Or shot. A lot of people did move out because of that. . . . I'm just worried about it going down more. . . . I know a lot of whites moved out because of that problem—"I'm moving out, the blacks are moving in"—you know? All of them I met, they started selling their house.*

Mary and Tony Kruger, a well-educated middle-class couple from St. Louis, worry about the "type" of people moving into Maplewood, Missouri. Mary is a yoga instructor, and Tony is a criminal investigator; their combined income is $46,000. They say their neighborhood is "on the edge," and it may "slip" at any moment because people of "different values" are moving in. Mary says:

*We wouldn't mind people that move in that have education or a little bit of money, or some sort of value system. I'll tell you quite frankly what I would look for is more people who look—regular. Because I go to the shopping centers, and there's just a lot of people there that I probably wouldn't end up relating to. I feel a little bit sometimes like a fish out of water, like when I'm in the shopping center, I feel like I'm more in an inner-city slum.*

I don't know whether their concerns are reasonable or not, but in the context of St. Louis, moving to a community where people have education, a little bit of money, and similar values and look regular will lead them to an all-white middle-class suburb.

Our interviews underscore the gap between whites' general attitudes on race and whites' behavior in the specific context of homeownership and community. The explanations just given by the Keadys, Quinlins, and Krugers help us understand the thinking, actions, and interests behind white flight. The rationale is like a Dutch auction of race: The logic is that the first sellers receive the highest price for their homes, while waiting only ensures that property values will continue to fall. As a result, just when neighborhoods need stability, moving brings instability and perpetuates residential segregation.

Homeownership is a crossroads that separates owners from renters as it sorts owners into racially and economically segregated communities. For young families in particular, head-start assets are crucial to home-ownership aspirations. Within the current context of pressures around homeownership, opportunities for homeownership, and concern about race, the way we acquire homes and anxieties about property values exacerbate community racial divisions, racial disparities in family well-being and education, and the racial wealth gap.

# Part III
# LEVERAGING ASSETS

# 6

# Where People "Choose" to Live

U NDERSTANDING WHY PEOPLE CHOOSE TO LIVE WHERE THEY DO
is crucial to understanding racial inequality. Most particularly, we
need to understand the significant consequences of these private family
decisions for residential segregation, school segregation, and school
quality.

Kim and Mike Brown live in a white working-class section of south
St. Louis characterized by small clapboard homes cramped closely
together. Homes sell for about $80,000, and family incomes are below
the national average. Marketing firms that profile communities identify
this as a "rustbelt neighborhood" typical of older, industrialized
Midwest cities. The Browns call their community "Hoosierville"
throughout the interview; the area is 83 percent white and 9 percent
African American, according to the 2000 Census. The immediate blocks
around their home are all white, and their community is predominantly
white, but they feel that blacks are steadily encroaching into their neighborhood and that the closest St. Louis public schools are all black. They
told me that race was their main reason for sending their son to a
parochial school instead of the neighboring public school. The way they
think about race is not confined to school concerns.

> KIM: *Do you know we don't even go to eat around here? We go out to South
> County to eat dinner. There is no place to eat around here. The one
> place, we had a Ponderosa, it was absolutely the filthiest thing you've
> ever seen in your life.*
> MIKE: *Yeah, and I guess if you want to talk about race at all, I'd have to say
> that the racial aspect of it keeps us out of the restaurants around here
> because*—[he is interrupted by Kim]

*KIM: It's on a bus line, if that tells you anything.*

*MIKE: It's on a bus line. They* [only] *have Chinese restaurants up north, that's it. Chinese and fried chicken, that's it. We'd go to the Ponderosa, it was round the corner, and it was always very, very loud. It was predominately black and very, very loud. They tend to speak at high-volume voices; we couldn't hear ourselves. We couldn't tolerate it. So the restaurants, as far as eating out, we'd probably go to the county.*

I returned to their neighborhood a year after the interview and was not surprised to discover that the Browns had moved to a far more spacious neighborhood just beyond the city limits into St. Louis County, where schools are predominantly white and buses carrying African Americans across segregated neighborhoods do not stop.

Why did Jacki Frohmer, a social worker involved in Missouri's welfare reform program, move from University City to Ladue? She was not happy where she lived:

*Because I work for the Department of Social Services, when I'm not at work, I don't want to see, hear, or smell a welfare recipient. And when I moved into these condos* [in University City] *they assured me that there were no welfare recipients living there, but if these people are not welfare recipients, they're really close.*

For some Americans, *welfare* is a code word for poor blacks. Jacki also sneers at her Russian immigrant and "Mexican" neighbors. I do not know whether it is the sight or smell of poor blacks specifically or of poor people in general that upsets Jacki, but when she explains why she moved, it sounds as if she means blacks.

*I investigated the school* [in University City] *and discovered that they have this large population of welfare recipients . . . . When James* [her son] *was three, this other little boy across the street pushed my son and said, "I'm gonna bust you up, punk." . . . And so I thought, "Well, we gotta get into Ladue school district somehow," and that's how we moved.*

Ladue schools have excellent reputations. They draw from one of the wealthiest communities in Missouri, where four out of five families are homeowners, which leaves little room for renters, and 88 percent of the population is white and 7 percent African American.

## "Moving Up" and "Falling Behind"

The residential moves of Jacki Frohmer and the Browns are not unusual, because America is a nation of movers. Fifty million American move each year, with the typical adult making 13 moves in her or his lifetime. As families succeed economically, their options for housing and locations expand. We change residences once every five years on average. The moving pattern in 1999–2000 was not the same for all Americans: Younger people are more likely to move; blacks and Latinos are more likely to move; renters are more than three times as likely to move as owners. In *Restless Nation*, sociologist James Jasper makes the case that Americans move to solve problems, such as wanting better jobs, schools, security, or status. The main reason Americans move is to find work. Less pragmatically, Americans also move in order to better themselves in all kinds of ways, for family ties, or to get away from what they feel constrains them or what they fear. Jasper argues that we Americans identify with those above us in status because that is how we want to see ourselves, and that moving up is a peculiarly American way of acquiring status. He captures the American ethos that equates moving with upward mobility this way: "If we aren't moving up, we feel we are falling behind."[1] We will see how for most families we interviewed "moving up" invariably means moving to less diverse and wealthier communities with better schools, leaving behind problems often associated with race, lower classes, and cities.

Moving may be a fundamental part of our national psyche, but character is not the only reason we move. Housing policies like those of the Federal Housing Administration and tax policies relating to homes, which I will discuss in more depth shortly, along with residential segregation and rising home values, encourage movement. America's communities are highly stratified by income, and in most affluent and upper-middle-class communities, homeownership is necessary for residence; that is, there are very few rental properties available, especially for moderate- and low-income families. Homeownership in wealthier communities also is the way families gain access to important civic services such as good public schools, which are only available to residents. Harvard, Massachusetts's, public schools had the best test scores statewide in 2000 before slipping a few notches in 2001. How does one gain access to this top-notch public school system? It is not as simple as reading the results in the newspaper and deciding to move there. According to Census data, one must be a Harvard homeowner: 91 percent of residents own homes. Further, the typical home price in 1999 was $377,000. A conventional 30-year mortgage, with a 10 percent down payment, on this typical Harvard home costs at least $3,500 a month, including taxes and insurance. A family's annual income needs to be at least $120,000 to qualify for this home loan, according to standard mortgage guidelines. Finally, an income in this bracket places a family among the nation's top earners, so it is not much of a stretch to understand why this outstanding school system is available only to a fortunate few. This example is not an exception; a list of schools with the highest test scores in Massachusetts shows that, in fact, most of the other cities on the list (Weston, Wellesley, Winchester, Wayland) also effectively require homeownership and are even more expensive to live in than Harvard. The Massachusetts pattern linking highest-testing schools to a community's wealth is the same in most states. Residential segregation by economics and race is the principal reason for unequal educational resources.

Over a long period, federal policies, programs, and practices promoted residential segregation. Since its inception in 1935, the Federal Housing Administration (FHA) has assisted about 28 million families in becoming homeowners. The FHA created the opportunity for a majority of Americans to become homeowners by enabling people to buy homes with small down payments at reasonable rates over long periods. The FHA has done, and continues to do, much good—and much harm. It promotes new housing over repairing existing housing, suburbs over central cities, private vehicles over public transportation, and uniform communities—in terms of class, race, and ethnicity—over diverse ones. These federal policies and practices provide the foundation for ghettoes and maintaining residential segregation in the United States.[2] Henry Cisneros ended a four-year tenure as secretary of Housing and Urban Development (HUD) in 1996 with important reforms in the areas of residential segregation, spreading homeownership and equity, the FHA, and public housing. The reforms he passionately championed at HUD have not endured into the Bush administration. Over a period of 65 years, a host of housing and tax policies has shaped the way we think about community and our means of achieving it.

America's tax laws regarding owner-occupied housing affect many families' daily lives and important decisions on community, homeownership, and education. Homeowners get five different federal tax breaks that 40 million American families who rent their homes do not. In the best known of these breaks, the Internal Revenue Service (IRS) allows homeowners to deduct interest paid on mortgages for principal residences and vacation homes on federal tax returns. The higher a family's tax bracket, the more the deduction is worth, even for the same house. On the hypothetical average home in 1999 ($161,000 price, $16,000 down payment, and $145,000 30-year mortgage at 6.5 percent), a family reporting a healthy middle-class income falls into the 28 percent tax bracket while a top-end income of more than $288,000 pays the nominal 39.6 percent tax rate. If their mortgages were the same, then, the first-year mortgage interest for an average home amounts to $11,556. The tax benefit for the middle-income family is $3,236 compared to $4,576 for the wealthy family on the same house. Less than one-half of homeowners claimed the mortgage interest deduction in 1994, probably because most nonwealthy taxpayers do not itemize their deductions.

Home mortgage interest deduction is not the only way public policy rewards ownership. The 1997 tax law gave a tremendous windfall to the American homeowner. On the sale of principal residences they have lived in for at least two years, couples can exempt up to $500,000, avoiding capital gains tax on the profitable sale of homes. Homeowners can also deduct state and local property taxes on their federal income tax returns, which saves homeowners about $16.1 billion a year in federal taxes. Homeowners borrowing money against their home equity can deduct interest payments on these loans. The advantage here is that a family can consolidate credit card debt, on which interest cannot be deducted, and take out an interest-deductible home equity loan. Of course, one must be a homeowner to take advantage of these breaks.[3] The mortgage interest and property tax

deductions reduce homeownership costs compared to other investments, encourage homeownership and higher housing consumption,
and perhaps even encourage families to buy homes that are too expensive. In the bargain, federal housing subsidies increase house prices,
encourage suburbanization, and reward moving. The tax treatment
also favors high-income families and supports purchasing expensive
houses.[4]

The biggest tax break for most middle-class Americans is the home
mortgage interest deduction, which also encourages moving because
the tax break on interest paid is largest during the first few years of
the loan and decreases as the loan principal goes down. One study estimates the gross value of all housing-related tax benefits for the United
States in 1989 at $164 billion. Sixty-two percent derives from untaxed
return on home equity, mostly families selling homes and reinvesting
their housing equity into large down payments on newer, bigger, and
more expensive homes. Mortgage interest deduction accounted for
another $43 billion, and deduction of local property taxes accounted
for the remaining $20 billion.[5] Christopher Howard's book *The
Hidden Welfare State* reports that the 1995 figures for home mortgage
interest deduction alone rose to $54 billion. Putting this into perspec-
tive, Howard notes that hidden welfare-state subsidies for housing are
more than twice the direct federal expenditures for rental housing
subsidies and low-income housing. Yet, if we ask Americans what the
national housing policy is, most say helping low-income families with
subsidized rent or public housing. This is a measure of how ingrained
and taken for granted homeowner subsidies have become, as opposed
to the intense annual scrutiny programs assisting needy families
receive. The middle-class passion for costly homeowner breaks indicates the special entitlement accorded to homeownership in face of the
generally held view that taxes should be lower.

If one looks at budgets, subsidies, and expenditures as more indica-
tive of policy priorities than official pronouncements, language, or
rhetoric, then subsidizing middle-class homeownership is the most
significant housing priority in the United States. Although one might
debate the desirability of this on principle, it is hard to argue with the
effectiveness of this public policy, as research confirms that homeownership brings greater stability to families and communities.[6] I am

convinced that assisting homeownership is indeed good policy, but we need to do it in a much more equitable way.

The tax-break figures give us the big picture about federal home-ownership subsidies, but they do not break down the distribution of benefits, nor do they help us understand what tax incentives mean for individual families. As we have seen, public investment in private homes is huge, and wealthier families receive the lion's share of the benefits. In fact, each owner-occupied house received about $2,800 in 1990 tax subsidies, and this homeownership grant recurs annually.[7] Given what we know about how tax subsidies work—larger propor-tions of tax benefits go to top-bracket earners—it should not be too surprising to learn that housing subsidies are not distributed evenly among homeowners. The top 10 percent of owners receives one-third of all housing benefits and the top 25 percent receives 59 percent of all benefits. High-income households, those earning over $100,000, received 44 percent of home mortgage interest subsidies in 1994.[8] Homeowners' tax breaks amounted to $26 billion for families with incomes above $100,000.[9] The authors of one study on housing subsi-dies wonder what chance legislation proposing $26 billion in subsidies to wealthy families would stand if introduced in Congress as a spending bill. Of course, these tax breaks are not direct congressional expenditures; they are etched into our tax code, and provisions are called *deductions* and *exemptions* rather than *subsidies*.

These statistics show that the wealthy benefit disproportionately from homeownership status, but Amanda Adams, a middle-class African American Boston homeowner, needs no statistics to know that owning a home is a good deal. She simply says the "tax breaks" helped her and her husband decide to buy their first home. When I asked Susan and Daniel Molloy, also black first-time homeowners, what made them decide to buy instead of rent, Susan gave an answer that speaks for many: "Well, I thought it would be a good investment and, at the time, it's a good tax break. And I wanted to own one day." Lori and Dan Olsen, who are white, have an income about the same as the Molloys' but they are living in their third home; in fact, Lori tells me they have never rented. I asked Lori why they feel so strongly about homeownership. "I just feel like renting you don't get any tax break. I can't fix it up and improve it and get any money out of it. I've always been very much into homes, as a vehicle for savings and making money." These three middle-class families earn between $50,000 and $60,000, they live in modest homes, and their home loans are not large. Families with incomes in this range usually use the standard deduction on their tax forms, so I wonder about the ability of the Adams, Molloy, and Olsen families to take full advantage of the tax breaks they cite, which would require itemizing deductions on a separate tax schedule. Whether they take full advantage or not, their responses highlight the important role that public policy and potential tax breaks play in the thought process of American families in deciding whether to rent or buy homes. These structures and policies clearly reward moving and ownership.

Once a family decides to move, thinking about where to buy property involves more personal reasoning, as demonstrated by Lori Olsen when I asked why she picked the St. Louis suburb she did: "Most important reason, I guess, was because I was snobby and I wanted a snobbier neighborhood. And I'm ashamed to admit that, but I guess that's the truth. Since it's just you and me, I'll tell the truth." A "snobbier neighborhood," no doubt, means that she wants to identify with higher-status, more affluent neighbors, which, in the context of St. Louis suburbs, as in most suburbs, means a neighborhood that most likely has few minorities.

I talked in considerable depth to families about moving. I was most eager to talk to families with young children approaching school age, because I wanted to capture how families were thinking about assets and family moves at critical points in their lives. Having young children is typically a pivotal point in a family's history, when they face growing space needs and become concerned about their children's neighborhood peers and imminent schooling issues. Overall, our interviews show the extent to which families think about residential moves as a way to better themselves by becoming neighbors with the kinds of people they aspire to identify with and upgrading their social networks. I did not expect, however, the deep passions and the extent to which families use their financial resources to deliberately move away from community social problems they most often associated with race or class. Choices, resources, and limits shape how families act on these deeply felt convictions.

## Mobility Patterns

The last section linked homeownership and moving to government policies that reward them. I have suggested that families face pivotal
moments in which they make decisions that have far-reaching ramifications for the rest of their lives. Furthermore, I have argued that families
use accumulated wealth at pivotal moments to improve their lives
through moves to wealthier and educationally advantaged communities.
Now I need to investigate the residential decisions of families with
young children to examine the kind of communities they leave behind
and the kind they move to.

Surveys and polls have tracked white Americans' attitudes about the
kind of neighborhoods they would be willing to live in since *Brown v.
Board of Education* in 1954 and the first open housing laws. The
number of those saying they would live only in all-white areas declined
by about one-half between 1976 and 1994 (28 percent to 13 percent),
while the proportion saying they would live only in "mostly white"
neighborhoods hardly changed (30 to 34 percent).[10] Whites are less
willing to insist on complete racial segregation; a large majority of
whites want to live in mostly white areas; and an increasing number of
whites say they want a mixed area. These attitudes may or may not
correspond to actual decisions families make concerning where to live,
because this is a racially sensitive topic, and a gap exists between general
attitudes about neighborhoods where people say they will live and where
they actually do live. One study looked at moving between white and
black neighborhoods.[11] Remembering that about 50 million Americans
move every year, 984 out of 1,000 whites stay in predominantly white
areas or move to them yearly. Whites move out of integrated communities and avoid moving into them. Blacks are much less likely to move
away from racially mixed or predominantly black areas into white
census tracts.

This moving pattern is suggestive,[12] but it includes all families and
does not necessarily reflect the pattern of the families that are of most
interest to us, those with young children. In this section, to evaluate our
argument that families with young children move to wealthier white
communities, we will examine such families' moves over a long period
and the income and racial profile of the communities they move into.[13]

Table 6.1 presents data on family moves between predominantly white (meaning 91 percent or more white), racially mixed (between 10 percent and 89 percent black), and predominantly black (more than 89 percent black) census tracts from 1984 to 1994. In these 10 years, nearly 7 out of 10 (69 percent) families with school-age children moved.[14] In 1984, 82.5 percent of white families with school-age children lived in predominantly white neighborhoods, which shows the high degree of residential segregation. Ten years later, this figure increased to 85.9 percent. I am most interested in the residential patterns of young white families because it will allow us to examine if they are moving to more or less diverse communities and schools. Almost all white families with children—96 percent—who lived in predominantly white neighborhoods in 1984 continued living there or had moved to similar communities ten years later.

Of young white families living in racially mixed neighborhoods in 1984, 59 percent remained in integrated communities 10 years later, but

**Table 6.1 Where Do Families of Children Move?***
**1984–1994, By Race of Neighborhood**

| 1984 Residence | 1994 Residence | | | |
| --- | --- | --- | --- | --- |
| | Predominantly White Area+ | Racially Mixed Area+ | Predominantly Black Area+ | Total |
| | (n) | (n) | (n) | (n) |
| **WHITE FAMILIES** | | | | |
| Predominantly White Area | 95.6% | 4.4% | – | 100.0% (456) |
| Racially Mixed Area | 40.2% | 58.8% | 1.0% | 100.0% (97) |
| Predominantly Black Area | – | – | – | 100.0% – |
| **TOTAL** | 85.9% (475) | 13.9% (77) | 0.2% (1) | **100.0% (553)** |
| **BLACK FAMILIES** | | | | |
| Predominantly White Area | 66.7% | 33.3% | – | 100.0% (21) |
| Racially Mixed Area | 6.5% | 79.0% | 14.5% | 100.0% (214) |
| Predominantly Black Area | 8.5% | 56.4% | 66.3% | 100.0% (166) |
| **TOTAL** | 8.5% (34) | 56.4% (226) | 35.2% (141) | **100.0% (401)** |

Source: PSID, 1984–1994
*Census data, 1984–1994
+Predominantly White = 91% or more white; Racially Mixed = 10%–89% black;
 Predominantly Black = 89% or more black

incredibly almost all other families moved to predominantly white areas. White families with school-age children are obviously moving to or staying in white neighborhoods. In contrast to whites' more liberal attitude about race and community, the vast majority of white families with children live in predominantly white communities, move away from integrated communities, and stay away from predominantly black areas. This is powerful evidence that whites stay away or move away from diversity.

In contrast, over three-quarters of blacks living in racially mixed areas in 1984 remained in similar communities 10 years later. Young black families are twice as likely to move to predominantly black areas as they are to move to predominantly white areas, unlike whites, who move to predominantly white neighborhoods. Either because the areas they live in change and become less integrated or because families move to more segregated areas, the data tell us that young white and black families live and attend schools in highly segregated communities.

Like racial residential segregation, community economic segregation carries momentous consequences for school resources, quality, and performance. Three out of four white families with children remain in high-income areas. From 1984 to 1994, 70 percent of white families remained in or moved to similar upper-middle-income neighborhoods. Of those who moved out of upper-middle-income areas, families split roughly evenly between moving up and moving down (with slightly more moving to to lower-middle-income tracts). One in four white families living in poverty neighborhoods in 1984 moved to higher income areas 10 years later.[15]

The pattern for black families is different again. When black families with children moved out of upper-middle-income neighborhoods, most moved to lower-income communities: Four times as many moved "down" as moved up. Some stayed in the same place but their community declined. Over one-half of black families with school-age children who lived in lower-middle-income areas in 1984 lived in similar areas 10 years later. Movers closely split between moving to better-off and worse-off areas (with slightly more ending up in worse-off areas). More black children lived in poorer communities in 1994 than they did in 1984. In contrast, from 1984 to 1994, the vast majority of white children either stayed in upper- and upper-middle-income communities or moved to them. (See Table A.3 in Appendix I.)

The major implication is that whites' upward residential mobility typically places them into better-off communities with more educational resources and thereby improves their educational advantage. The fact that most whites live in homogeneous and financially viable communities during the years they have school-age children ensures white children greater access to higher-quality education.

Most black families are, then, sending their children to schools in predominantly black or racially mixed areas. Black families are living in communities where income is significantly lower than that of whites, implying that their children are attending different kinds of schools. The lack of resources, increased complexity in educating these children, and the utter double standard are likely to yield inferior educational opportunities compared to those whites have.

We saw in Chapter 3 how important parental financial assistance is in helping young families buy homes and getting a good start in life. We also noted how family assistance places many young families into better-off communities than they can afford with their paychecks. From this information, we can see that parental down payment backing is critical in helping families move to wealthier white communities. There probably is no clearer example of the power of transformative assets than this, that they enable young families to move into communities and educational environments they could not afford based on their achievements and income alone, securing advantages for their children that others do not have.

## Residential Segregation

Blacks and whites continue living in separate neighborhoods long after the end of official segregation, the passage of major civil rights, fair housing, and lending laws, and the growth of a black middle class. In fact, our analysis of family moves strengthens what some scholars call "American apartheid." Our data also highlight how powerful economic segregation is in sorting families into communities. In *Poverty and Place*, sociologist Paul Jargowsky details the importance of both racial and economic segregation in determining inner-city poverty, noting a trend of increasing economic segregation alongside decreasing racial segregation. In 2000 three-quarters of blacks lived in highly segregated communities.[16] Residential segregation persists at high levels, and it remains a powerful force undermining the well-being of blacks, who are concentrated in communities with weak public services like hospitals, transportation, police and fire protection, with decreased housing appreciation, and with inferior schools.

We saw how federal housing, tax, and transportation policies helped to shape communities so that they would be highly segregated racially and economically. We also detailed how mortgage discrimination, redlining, and predatory lending practices reinforce residential segregation. And we saw how racism remains a driving force behind community preference and white flight. Finally, deliberate acts of racial avoidance, violence and the threat of violence against minorities, local zoning decisions, and the isolation of public housing help to keep neighborhoods highly segregated.

In the 20 largest metropolitan areas, where 36 percent of all African Americans live, segregation pervades basic dimensions of community life. The residential color line means that blacks have greater difficulty overcoming problems associated with poor communities, especially crime, violence, housing abandonment, unstable families, poorer health and higher mortality, environmental degradation, and failing schools. No other group experiences segregation to the extent that blacks do. In many geographical areas, two decades of rising income inequality and budget cuts have produced a concentration of poverty that further compounds problems of segregation. Poor black neighborhoods are crowded, highly concentrated, and isolated far more severely than neighborhoods where poor whites, Latinos, or Asians live.

The residential color line is the key feature distinguishing African Americans from all other groups in the United States. In *Black Identities*, Mary Waters argues that African American segregation, especially in ghetto neighborhoods, is unlike geographic separation that ethnic and immigrant groups face. For children, it is far more encompassing, leading to higher school dropout rates, lower college attendance, higher unemployment and lower earning, and higher teenage pregnancy rates. Furthermore, effects of segregation are not limited to poor blacks but extend to middle-class blacks as well.[17] Since middle-class black families tend to share neighborhoods with more poor people than white middle-class families do, and since they more often live near and share schools with lower-class blacks, middle-class black students continue to face educational disadvantages.[18]

Just how segregated residential America is can be seen by looking at the typical metropolitan area in 1990, which was 13 percent black. To achieve a hypothetical semblance of integration where 13 percent of one's neighbors are African American, almost two-thirds (64 percent) of black residents would have to move out of segregated communities to white ones.[19] The evidence strongly suggests that segregation persists because of ongoing racial discrimination in real estate and mortgage markets, the persistence of white prejudice, and the discriminatory impact of public policies like local zoning decisions and the isolation of public housing.[20] I will review key parts of this case, present new evidence, and examine how families use their assets to leverage advantage within this structuring of choice and place.

Residential segregation is the linchpin of American race relations because so much else flows through community dynamics. We know from Chapter 5 that rising home values are color-coded by community. We learned that one immediate consequence is that homes in white communities increase $28,600 more over a 30-year mortgage period than comparable homes in black communities. A community's racial composition appears to be the most salient feature determining home values. Homes lose at least 16 percent of their value when located in neighborhoods that are more than 10 percent black. Furthermore, property values decrease more steeply in neighborhoods with larger percentages of blacks.[21] While white flight is a taken-for-granted social process, it is not just something that happens but is propelled by family actions, as the Keady family in the last chapter illustrates; some families drive white flight forward, and white flight rewards those in a position to move. The Keadys' social and economic fears about blacks moving into their neighborhood created a crisis that did not exist in reality.

Another way of understanding residential segregation, white flight, and institutionalized discrimination—less academic and more highly charged—is that they benefit white homeowners and enrich them at the expense of African Americans and other minorities. As a result of incentives, rewards, and patterns—what some call structure—whites do not need to be overtly racist or to personally drive white flight or to engage in discriminatory acts in order to benefit from nicer communities, better schools, and higher property values.

## Educational Segregation and Weak Schools

Arguably the most important aspect of living in segregated neighborhoods is the local schools. Schooling has always been seen as the path to upward mobility, especially for minorities, the disadvantaged, and immigrants, but one can argue that stakes are even higher now because the technological literacy and skills necessary for success today are set at high levels. Racial segregation experienced by black Americans, writes Mary Waters, "concentrates poverty and its effects, and subjects all ghetto residents to the cultural and structural effects of such poverty."[22] Residential segregation puts black children at risk from the start.

Racial segregation of minority schoolchildren is on the rise. In 1968, 77 percent of black students attended majority nonwhite schools. Segregated schooling reached a low point—down to 62 percent—in the 1980s, because of community and judicial efforts. But this progress reversed with rising residential segregation and as courts lost interest; school segregation intensified throughout the 1990s. By 1999 the percentage of black students in segregated schools had rebounded to 70 percent.[23]

A recent study on school segregation reports that "white students are by far the most segregated in schools dominated by their own group." Whites on average go to schools where 80 percent of the students are white. In comparison, blacks and Latinos attend schools where a little over half of the students are black or Latino.[24] The reasons behind white student isolation are quite different from why blacks and Latinos attend segregated schools. The interviews presented already powerfully suggest that white isolation is more purposeful, intended among other things to boost whites' competitive educational advantage. Later in this chapter, and in the next one as well, I present more family stories emphasizing other aspects of this compelling pattern.

The appalling school segregation picture underrepresents the segregated classroom experience of America's children. Evidence strongly suggests that even in schools that look integrated, whites and blacks who enter through the same school door walk down different corridors and learn in dissimilar classrooms. While African Americans, Hispanics, and children from poverty families may be less prepared from the start, a growing body of evidence suggests that students learn better in classrooms with peers of mixed ability than in classrooms of so-called grouped ability. In addition, compelling evidence from segregation cases and educational experts shows that schools often base ability grouping not on hard test scores but on softer criteria like student characteristics.[25] The effect of these practices magnifies the unequal classroom experience of African American students.

Although most white Americans now favor school integration in principle, resistance to remedies has kept educational inequality intact. In some cases, as we have seen, racism impedes educational equality. At least as important, as we will examine, the current system of choices and incentives commonly rewards whites for community and school decisions that advantage them at the expense of black Americans.

Student achievement, school success, and educational failure closely track class and race. While no set of statistics can tell this complex story, the fact that students from wealthier families are seven times more likely to finish college than students from poor families illustrates how prevalent educational stratification is in the United States. The difficulties expand when one considers that high school dropout rates for poor students are nearly 10 times higher than dropout rates for students from top-income families. Failure in school is a modern-day scarlet letter that practically ensures other lack of success, such as lower employment rates and earnings, troubles with the law, and jail. Young people who do poorly in school or drop out are more likely to land in juvenile court or in an adult jail. The average age of the children in the juvenile justice system is 15, but more than one-third of them read at the level of 9- and 10-year-olds. In the adult criminal system, 82 percent of prison inmates are high school dropouts.[26]

Disadvantaged children start school with significantly lower cognitive skills than other children. Given this, one might think that poor children, those from black and Hispanic families and from families where parents are less educated, need high-quality schools. Instead, they get just the opposite. In *Inequality at the Starting Gate*, educational researchers Valerie Lee and David Burkam provide forceful and persuasive empirical evidence substantiating that disadvantaged children begin school in systematically lower quality schools than other children. No matter how school quality is measured, whether by class size, teacher credentials, teacher salaries, computers, or curriculum, minority children begin learning in lower-quality schools than white children. The authors draw a sobering conclusion: "The children who need the best schooling actually start their education in the worst public schools."[27] This cements inequalities formed even before children reach school age, and the schooling process most likely magnifies them further.

Understanding inequality in learning climates that results from the distribution of educational resources is an essential part of understanding educational inequality. Students in high-poverty schools are less likely to have opportunities for extended-day, gifted, or talented programs than other students. They are more likely to learn math and sciences like chemistry and physics from teachers who did not major or minor in those subjects. High-poverty schools are least likely to have access to technology, computers, and the "information highway." Teacher salaries are higher in schools with little poverty and low in high-poverty ones. Schools in better-off districts spend more money per student than schools in lower-income areas. In terms of capital investment alone, schools in low-income areas (less than $20,000 median household income) spend 31 percent less than schools in higher income areas ($35,000 or more median household income). In actual dollars spent per pupil for educational expenses, the richest school districts spend 56 percent more per student than the nation's poorest districts.[28] All this means that family income and wealth of the community correlate strongly with the presence of high-quality schools. Less than 1 percent of children from families with annual income less than $33,000 attend high-performing schools, in contrast to 46 percent of children from families earning at least $55,000. Low-performance schools are spread a little more evenly, especially among middle-income families, but only 1 percent of children from families earning over $65,000 attend low-performing schools.[29]

Researchers have suggested that class size in the first few years of primary education is critical for student achievement. Smaller is clearly better for students, teachers, and the learning process, with researchers suggesting that the desirable range lies between 13 and 20 students. How does this optimal learning situation compare with classrooms across the country? In 1997 nearly 47 percent of elementary classes had 25 or more students, and in 1998 the average was 23 students. The majority of elementary students are beginning their important formative school years under adverse conditions in classes with too many children. Class sizes are not random. Black, Hispanic, and Asian children are enrolled in schools with larger kindergarten classes than white children. Poor children also attend schools with larger kindergarten classes. Children in urban schools generally attend schools with larger kindergarten classes.[30]

School segregation shortchanges minority children. What does this mean for individual student and local school performance? The *St. Louis Post Dispatch* newspaper reports that students receiving free or reduced-price lunches scored between 18 and 31 points lower on Missouri's statewide test, depending on the grade and subject.[31] Local elementary schools with the lowest scores on Missouri's test had more than five times as many low-income students as did elementary schools with the highest test scores. Illinois schools with the lowest test scores had 6 to 10 times as many low-income students as did schools with the highest test scores. Several schools with large numbers of low-income students in Missouri and Illinois performed well, demonstrating that educating poor children is a complex but achievable project. The Missouri and Illinois results illustrate a national pattern linking the distribution of educational resources by community wealth to specific and devastating consequences for student achievement in minority and poverty neighborhoods.

We have seen how residential segregation restricts minority households' access to quality schools. Unequal schooling leads to all sorts of educational disparities that generally provide competitive educational disadvantages for blacks, minorities, and the poor, as it maintains advantages for families with ample financial resources. Educational segregation connects to educational resources, achievement, and other vital outcomes. Mounting evidence shows that blacks who attend desegregated schools are more likely to achieve at higher rates and have higher aspirations than those from similar families who attend segregated schools, and these students are more likely to go on to college and secure high-status jobs. One controlled study showed that black students who moved to predominantly white neighborhoods were more likely to take college prep courses in high school, to attend college, and to select a four-year college than black students who remained in majority black neighborhoods.[32] Learning in integrated classrooms both improves test scores and changes lives.[33]

## Why People Move

We now know what moving patterns look like, and we have surveyed some consequences resulting from residential and educational segregation and school inequality. Our interviews were designed so that families could tell us in their own words why they move, and this provides a rich opportunity to explore the reasoning behind larger moving patterns. In asking why they moved, people most often cited type of neighborhood as the main reason for moving. Among the 68 families that framed their moves by referring to type of neighborhood, when pressed about what they meant, most talked about lifestyles, values, standards, peers, and atmosphere. Race and class often featured prominently when the interviews explored, in turn, what they meant by these motivations.

In Chapter 1, we met the Ackermans, who said that it did not matter if the neighbors were white or black, "as long as they had the same standards we had." They did not specify what they meant by "standards" in this context. Moments earlier, however, they were describing areas they were considering moving to, rejecting one city neighborhood because, "we just thought, the mix of the group and then all of these people going to the same school, it did not fit with what we wanted for our family." Given the residential segregation patterns discussed in this chapter, it seems reasonable to conclude that when families talk about values, standards, and lifestyle, they are really talking about race and class.

Angela Slater is a senior financial analyst for a health care firm, and her husband, Andrew, owns a thriving business in Los Angeles. Their income and wealth are in the upper echelons, placing them among L.A.'s new African American millionaires. Their eldest daughter attends a private Catholic school. I ask if the private school allows them to control who she is around, which is a concern Angela had expressed earlier in our conversation. Angela's answer is a clear-cut declaration of using financial resources to define community in an exclusionary way.

*To a certain degree. To a certain degree. You can control the element by who can afford to go there. You know, for example, ten to fifteen thousand dollars a year for children to go to elementary school.* So there is only a certain element there is going to be there. You know what I'm saying? So yeah, it is controlled by that [emphasis added]. *Most of the students are Catholic.*

*You don't have a lot of other, so there is a lot of likeness at the school. So they have a lot of the same interests. They are all going through the communions together. They all [have] that common, that commonality in terms of the family beliefs, the family structures, you know. The church on Sundays. It's really kind of just like one little community. One family, you know, the entire school. So that makes it socially, you know, controllable too.*

Even though Angela Slater is talking about a parochial school community in this part of our conversation, her desire to "socially control" a "certain element" touches a broader theme found throughout many of our interviews with white and black upper-middle-class families, although it is more prevalent among white families. Angela provides a straightforward illustration of the way in which families with resources define community in race or class terms that elevates their status by excluding others.

Forty-seven families discussed wanting more safety and security as the primary reason they moved. Many poorer families spoke about living too close to crime, drugs, and gangs and expressed apprehension for their children. Concerns about crime, security, and personal safety are real. Sometimes, however, safety and security concerns were expressions of race and class fears, and our interviews reveal this persuasively and colorfully. For example, when Jacki Frohmer related that another little boy said "I'm gonna bust you up, punk" to her 3-year-old, or when Mary Masterson talks (in the next chapter) about an "edgy attitude" she saw among her daughters' African American schoolmates, it is reasonable to think that they had race on their minds. Schools are the next most frequently cited reason for moving, which is the focus of the next chapter. Families also told us they move for other reasons, such as to be closer to friends, family, and church, for location, for more space, and affordability.

Sometimes families talked about overt racial themes as the reasons behind the choices of where they live or want to live. Duane and Merilyn Fisher and their daughter, Sarah, live in Afton, Missouri. They both work, and the family income is $35,000. Duane works several part-time jobs, fixing motorcycles, cutting meat, and acting as a sign language interpreter; Merilyn does clerical work at a chemical plant. Race and prejudice had come up several times in our interview, so when we were nearly finished, I asked then to describe their feelings on race and how these feelings affect where they live. Duane starts:

*Yeah, I, I struggle with it. I try to believe that I'm not prejudiced; everybody is to a certain point. I think I try to take a person one on one, but first impression is always there, needless to say, and my first impression of somebody is probably going to be the color of the skin. It goes down to where I'm not going to let that color of the skin affect how I feel about that person. It's just there. Then I go [by] how they act, what kind of character they have. Usually it's a group. I hate to say it, but that's the issue, um, one on one, it's different. But as a group, it's really, it's really a confusing thing because I don't like to sound negative. I mean, I don't believe I am a bigot, but I mean, in a lot of ways I gotta be because the first thing I think of is, you know, um, type. Typecast, I guess.*

When I ask Duane what he means by "typecast," Merilyn picks up the conversation,

*It's hard not to look at someplace like East St. Louis [Illinois] and say, "Well, you know, it's a black community," and people know what you mean when you say that. It means that, um, maybe it's a little run down and the crime rate's a little higher and it's not a very desirable place to even drive through. At the same time, it's not really fair to stereotype it.*

Earlier in our conversation, the Fishers talked to each other about race.

DUANE: *Oh, people that, you know, "Pity me, I'm Black" or "Pity me, I'm Indian" or "Pity me, I'm. . . ."*

MERILYN: *Let themselves be a victim.*

DUANE: *Yeah.*

MERILYN: *You know, "It's not my fault, it's because my group has been oppressed."*

DUANE: *Yeah, and then they want to blame it on me because my ancestors did this.*

Interrupting, I asked if they were looking for more of a white community, to which Duane simply said, "Yeah."

Most people do not typecast as readily or consistently as the Fishers, and even fewer act on it. The community the Fischers live in is white. Nonetheless, this interview demonstrates the power of racist thinking in defining community preference.

In Chapter 3, the Barrys told us buying a house was an easy matter because her parents wrote a $30,000 down payment check. Joe Barry tells a long story comparing their new neighborhood with the concerns they had about their previous neighborhood, where they felt as if they were becoming a minority:

> *We don't accept prejudice in our children, so I'm not going to be subject to that and say, "Well, we need to take it because we've oppressed black people for many years and we deserve it." Bullshit. Discrimination is discrimination. And I will not tolerate reverse discrimination anymore. And it just so happens that the neighborhood that we live in is predominantly white. That was not the reason we chose it.*

When I ask if they would live in an integrated community, Briggette says yes, "if it had had realistically good schools, and if my parents lived in that neighborhood, absolutely." Even though they insist that race was not a factor, their conditions effectively preclude integrated communities.

One does not need to contend that racism motivates all family moves, although it clearly does in some cases like those we have just seen. Families with children make important life decisions in the context of attaching increasing importance to high-quality education as a way for their kids to succeed. In this context, a highly stratified educational system and middle-class social apprehension combine to produce an environment where parents feel compelled to gain opportunities and advantages for their children. While moving for the schools is not new, it is now occurring in a rapidly changing and more highly charged context with high stakes for students. Parents make individual, rational decisions that make the most sense to them. The rewards include home equity, community services, higher-quality schools, and educational advantage. Larger racial consequences result from these family decisions. Unfortunately, the effects include residential and school segregation and huge educational disparities that disadvantaged families left behind.

Jan and Steve Hadley are white and live in the unincorporated Sappington-Concord area of St. Louis. They have been married for 12 years and have four children. Both are research technicians; their salaries give the family an annual income of $77,000. With $5,000 in down payment help from Jan's parents, one year into their marriage they moved from an apartment in the city and bought a starter home in the suburbs. They lived in their starter home until the birth of their third child, when they needed a bigger house and had to think about schools. Their friends convinced them that the Lindbergh School District, which services the unincorporated Sappington-Concord area, had good schools, so this is where they decided to look for a new home. Using $27,000 equity built up in their starter home, they were able to find a bigger house in a new development that had a yard for the kids. In Sappington-Concord, 95 percent of the homes were built after 1950, and 80 percent of residents are homeowners. In 2000 median home value in the zip code area they live in was roughly $150,000, and median family incomes were close to $60,000. In a metropolitan area where black Americans constitute 20 percent of the population, their new home is located in an area where less than 1 percent of neighbors are African American.

In our conversation they say they chose their community based on the school district's reputation and the recommendation of friends and because it is very close to their church. Their two older children, however, attend private school, and they plan to send the younger ones there when they are ready for school. Jan explains why they chose a community largely for its public schools even though their children go to an unaccredited parochial school.

*Even though we moved here for the Lindbergh School District, our kids belong, go to a parochial school right now. . . . But we knew that if at some point we couldn't afford the parochial school system we wanted to be in a good public school system, and that's one of the reasons we chose Lindbergh.*

I ask what they like about the school.

*JAN: It's a Christian school, which is our number one priority.*
*STEVE: It's a small school. Everybody knows everyone pretty well.*

JAN: *Fairly similar backgrounds.*
STEVE: *Yeah.*

In what ways, I ask.

JAN: *White, middle class.*
STEVE: *That is a point. There is not one black in that school, is there?*
JAN: *No, but there are some . . . like Lee's friend Kayla, I mean she's Oriental, and there are a couple, but as far as, um, African American, no, there aren't any, so.*
INT: *Is that something that was intentional?*
STEVE: *No, I mean, it just happened.*
JAN: *No, it's just, it's based on the churches, you know, the four churches that own the school and—*
STEVE: *Yeah, and they're from the South County area also, and for South County there aren't many blacks.*
JAN: *Unless they are part of the busing program, and you will find that in the public school system, but not in the private sector. And that's, I mean, that's not a problem as far as I'm—see, we have black friends, but it just happens to work out that way.*

At the end of our conversation, I ask Jan and Steve if there is anything they want to add to make sure I got the big picture. Of his own accord, Steve offers this realization.

STEVE: *Um, uh, I don't know, all of a sudden, going through, walking through this, I've gotten to feel like I'm one of the little, not an individual, but kind of [in] a mainstream middle class, you know, depending on where you work, not where you work, but how much you make. You have a house in the suburbs, in our case, live in a white neighborhood, and go to a white school system. I didn't really look at it like that before. But I guess it just kind of fits, I want to say mainstream of what's, um, we fit right into a very large class of people. But it didn't start out to be that way. I mean, we didn't consciously think of it that way, but we certainly did fit the mold.*
JAN: *Well, it's the background that we grew up in, too. I mean it's very similar to that.*

STEVE: *Yeah. So, um, I don't know.*

JAN: *It shouldn't be a shock to you, dear.*

STEVE: *Well, no, it's not a shock, it just, uh, I hadn't really thought of that before, and the reason that I pointed that out is because where I work at, in the labs, there is a very large ethnic diversity there. I mean, not just from the United States, from regions, but nationalities from everywhere. And it's actually, I think, interesting to get other national perspectives on things. That's not always—our way of thinking is not always, I'll say correct. If you look at it at a different angle, you may not be correct. So I guess my overall theme is that I like more of a diverse, I want to see more of a diverse education or experience as opposed to such a narrow one that I had when I was growing up with less exposure.*

Segregation "just happened" not only for the Hadleys but also for many other families. This way of seeing residential and school segregation makes highly racialized matters seem natural, therefore acceptable, and hardly ever questioned. The silent and invisible way race is built into our logic and structures is part of modern American life. There are no actors, no one benefits, and no one is disadvantaged. The Hadleys built a good life for their family. Without planning it, without decisions knowingly based on race, indeed without even realizing it, Steve Hadley's family is in the American "mainstream." The incentives, rewards, patterns, expectations—indeed, the structure—led his family into an all-white world, rational decision by rational decision. The extraordinary part is Steve's recognition of this taken-for-granted social reality. Whether or not he or anyone else is willing and able to do anything about it is a different question.

The issue is not that some innate, unalterable racism drives neighborhood and school segregation but that better-off white families reap benefits from segregated schools and communities whether they acknowledge it or not, and people of color, especially children, pay the steepest price. Residential segregation and institutionalized discrimination have enriched white homeowners at the expense of African Americans and others. Educational segregation and school policies favor white children at the same time they hurt children from minority and poor families. White neighborhoods and schools are better in part because black neighborhoods and schools are worse.

Our interviews highlight the importance of place, what real estate agents benignly call location. Homeownership has been an underpinning of the American Dream, signifying property ownership, mobility, pride, and prosperity. I think we are experiencing a change in what the dream means because homeownership increasingly is about identifying with a community's class, racial, and educational status as both sign of and road to success. For many of the families interviewed, homeownership means identifying with neighbors and characteristics of the place in which the home is located. As our interviews also clearly reveal, a powerful attraction of a new community is that it represents moving away from race- and class-related problems of the old place. When parents talk about their hopes for their children, it is clear from our interviews that they are disclosing deep-seated class and racial anxieties. The paradox here is that, in the present context of residential segregation and uneven educational systems, parents' choosing what is best for their children reinforces inequality.

# 7

# "Getting a Decent Middle-Class American Education"

## Pursuing Advantage in Schools

### Moving for the Schools—The Kirkwood Question

MILES FROM THE CITY, Kirkwood, Missouri, is a classic midwestern suburban neighborhood with tree-lined streets and small turn-of-the century homes. Closely mirroring the national average, its median income is $45,000 and the average house is valued at $111,000 in a community where 80 percent of families are homeowners. Mary Masterson owns a small brick house with yellow lattice. The headquarters of the Lutheran Church Missouri Synod is two blocks away, on a major thoroughfare. One cannot help but notice the large number of churches in her immediate neighborhood. In other sections of Kirkwood, some houses are newer and larger, as the community aspires to contemporary middle-class sensibilities. A chiropractor and a store selling ice hockey equipment and in-line skates are the visible commercial presence in Mary Masterson's neighborhood. Many homes in her neighborhood look alike, but they are dressed up individually; the yellow lattice distinguishes hers.

Mary Masterson, a 42-year-old divorcée, lives with her two daughters, Nora and Alexis, ages 7 and 12. She works as a child care center administrator. Her income is $18,480, her net worth is $98,000, and her net financial assets total $24,900. Mary grew up in a white middle-class family and continues to receive financial support from her parents. These inherited, transformative assets give her school choices she could not afford on her income.

Mary and her daughters used to live closer to the city in racially and socioeconomically integrated University City. But Mary started to worry about what she called an "edgy attitude" from the girls' African

American classmates, and she began to feel that she "needed to be out of University City" because she wanted to get her daughters out of this school district. "It just feels like there's an edgy sort of attitude problem," she says. "The kids that were causing me the most concern were the kids who had the huge egos and the huge attitudes, and I just sensed danger." Parental concern about violence and peers as these affect their children in middle school years is a recurring theme in our interviews. Mary wanted to get her daughters out of the University City schools before her older daughter reached junior high school because she was particularly worried about crime and violence in the junior high and high schools. With financial help from her parents, Mary moved out of University City and bought a house in a safer haven, Kirkwood— a white middle-class suburban neighborhood of St. Louis.

Mary chose Kirkwood because she thinks its schools are excellent and it is closer to her church. When asked what makes Kirkwood schools excellent she says she likes the class of people living there, and from other parts of the interview it is clear she means its white middle-class character. Whiteness and affluence of communities and schools are markers of school quality for Mary. She says she is happy with Kirkwood schools because of "the reputation and economic class of this area," adding that she is glad to have escaped city problems. She is clear about moving her daughters to a whiter, more affluent area so that they could go to school with kids from middle-class families. She succeeded in this goal. Her children now attend a suburban public school with a largely white middle-class student population. In reflecting on her move, Mary says, "I'm glad they had the multicultural exposure in University City, but I'm sure they're getting a decent middle-class American education now."

Mary based her decision on the reputation and economic class of Kirkwood in the assurance that her daughters would receive a decent middle-class education. She did not base her decision on whether class size, teacher credentials, computers and technology, resources, advanced placement classes, or curriculum in Kirkwood schools were significantly better than in University City's. She is not alone. In this chapter, we will see many other families base important life moves on reputation. Sometimes parents' perception of reputation is right on target, and sometimes it is off base. As with Mary Masterson, race and class concerns often undergird reputation.

The personal irony here is that her escape from University City schools for the good reputation of the Kirkwood schools is not working out as smoothly as planned. She is worried because Nora and Alexis are miserable. They miss their friends and do not like their new school. Both are experiencing academic and social-behavioral problems. Still, Mary Masterson hopes she made the right choice and that her daughters' unhappiness and school problems will soon fade.

Latoya Milton is 23 years old, makes $14,000 managing a dry-cleaning establishment, lives in a poor black section of St. Louis, and dreams of sending her daughter, Daphne, to Kirkwood schools, too. In talking about her aspirations for Daphne, this African American mother also thinks about the kind of sacrifices it would take to move to better schools.

> *I would have to make way more money. . . . I would sacrifice a lot to send her there. Like, I would not be able to have a telephone, and I would not be able to take car insurance probably, which is a law. . . . But I would have to sacrifice those things. And I probably would never have a big house like I want, but I would do it for her education. I'd do anything for her.*

Due more to their class and race status than their achievements, Latoya Milton's dream is Mary Masterson's reality. With parental financial assistance, the Masterson family moved from an integrated community and schools to predominantly white ones, while the Miltons will have great difficulty moving out of their impoverished African American neighborhood and its substandard, segregated schools.

This chapter explores how moving for the schools is the most direct and effective avenue for pursing advantage and passing inequality along. Many families move or seek to move for the schools, yet we will see that moving for the schools has different meanings for different families depending upon class and race. We will see from our interviews that when families move for the schools, class and race considerations are paramount.

In *Home Advantage*, Annette Lareau examines how social class affects parents' ability to pass advantages to their children. She details how middle-class parents use their social and cultural advantages, which are unavailable to working-class parents, to maximize their children's educational opportunities. *Home Advantage* is a wonderful account of how parents with ample resources exercise influence in schools and help their children succeed by maneuvering the system in a narrow, self-interested way to provide better resources for them.[1] My interviews complement her findings even as I take the family-schooling connection in a new direction. While Lareau focuses on what happens inside schools, an asset perspective emphasizing homeownership and community facilitates an examination of how children get matched to schools in the first place. It is far from random assignment because, as we shall see, community wealth largely determines school quality.

Academics write, lecture, and debate over education reform; politicians argue, posture, and legislate over it. For parents, the debate over how to improve schooling was resolved long ago and there is little to deliberate: They are moving or striving to move to better-off communities in the certain knowledge that moving up is the ticket to better schools. A lot of time, energy, emotional investment, and money go into this quest. There is no question either among parents or from numerous academic studies about the importance of education to a child's future. Parents understand that education has tremendous economic payoffs in terms of jobs, salary, and wealth. The story of the lengths to which parents will go to provide their children better opportunities is simultaneously heartening and revealing of how families use education to pass advantages to their children. Knowledge about what children learn in families and differences in family life on things like transmitting cultural capital and parenting styles has increased dramatically in recent decades.[2]

Our interviews reveal why families consciously look for homes according to school jurisdictions and school reputations, as well as the lengths to which they will go to get their kids into sought-after schools. The Yorrand family, for instance, enjoys living in highly diversified Mar Vista, a section of Los Angeles, but they bought a condominium in neighboring Santa Monica, moved childless relatives into it, and use that address to send their children to Santa Monica schools. The father's approving laughter came through a broad and satisfying smile as he told me, "It's like buying into a private school."

David and Vanessa Anzalone explain how they left nothing to chance when they moved to Monrovia, a suburb of Los Angeles. They had thoroughly researched Monrovia and neighborhoods within it, right down to targeting the school they wanted their children to attend.

DAVID: *I did research for six months.*

VANESSA: *We kept doing research until we found a house to buy.*

DAVID: *Well, I knew this was a good town when I picked it in 1995, and like a year later, it won the All-America City Award in like '97 or '96. Within Monrovia, some areas are nicer than others. We started looking around for a house and chose living north of Foothill Boulevard, which seems like a nice, safer area than some of the areas south. Also, it's part of the better school district, for the elementary school.*

VANESSA: *That is the strategy, like, if you are on this block, you go to a better school* [Franklin].

DAVID: *Two blocks* [south], *you would go to the other school, that is, your kids are with* a whole different world [emphasis added]. . . . *As in the school that they go to wouldn't be as good, or the parents aren't* [as] *involved in the school. . . .*

INT: *So two blocks away, what is different about the neighborhoods two blocks south?*

DAVID: *I'd say more rentals, and there's more problems. . . . It's just not as nice. Smaller houses.*

INT: *Two blocks south, what school district is it?*

DAVID: *Well, it's all Monrovia Unified. But the children would go to a different elementary school.*

INT: *About how far away is the school your kids attend from your home?*

DAVID: *Oh, I guess a mile.*

INT: *And the other school for the kids who live two blocks south?*

VANESSA: *It's actually closer, uh. . . . Yeah, it's actually closer.*

INT: *So when you bought this house you were conscientious about which blocks attend which elementary school, or did you know at the time?*

DAVID: *Not really, we kind of knew.*

VANESSA: *We asked the Realtor lady because we knew we wanted to attend Franklin School.*

INT: *So you had already decided on that school?*

VANESSA: *Yes.*

With the help of a real estate agent, they demographically targeted a house so their children could attend Franklin because children of high-status families go there. They did not visit Franklin or any other Monrovia school, nor did they know much about its curriculum, class size, or instruction, but they knew that children from nicer houses and higher status families went to Franklin.

While ample financial assets allowed the Yorrand and the Anzalone families to chart their children's educational path, many families without monetary assets attempt to use other means to get their children into better schools. For instance, one parent in several families we interviewed did volunteer work in school districts they wanted their children to attend. This volunteer status qualified them as school employees, and their children gained admission. One mother volunteered to work lunch hours in the school cafeteria; a father offered his carpentry skills for school projects; one mother did part-time clerical work in the Santa Monica schools. Several families we interviewed outright lied about their addresses to gain entrance to more desired school districts or a better school within a district. One Los Angeles mother puts her daughters on public buses for two hours each way to gain educational opportunities for them at a school that accepted them because a relative worked there. What motivates the expenditure of so much resources, energy, time, and emotion?

## Education and the American Dream

Educational preparation is a central issue for families with school-age children. In our conversations with families, the most heartfelt, some-times emotional, and often inspiring moments came when parents talked about the hopes they have for their children's education. People express similar aspirations and race and class do not seem to matter. For example, an African American mother from Boston said:

> *I monitor everything that goes on with my son's education.* [The teachers and administrators] *know me, my name, when I come to the door they know who I am, and I monitor everything about his education. When my son gets home, we sit down and we do homework, so I can know if he understands what he's going through, and I'm very picky about his teachers. If I know a*

*teacher has a bad reputation, I will ask for him to be moved to another class, which has happened in the past.*

Kim, a middle-class white Los Angelano, told us that

*the biggest thing, in my mind, is to get my children an education. To have them be respectful and have an education.*

Karen, who is raising her kids alone in Los Angeles because her husband is in jail, captures a strong working-class slant on education and mobility.

*The way that I was raised, you don't put much emphasis on material owner-ship. You don't. It comes and it goes so fast. It could be gone in a heartbeat, but education is, it's the only way the kids are going to make it. That's it. Without that, they will end up with the same exact life that my mother and I had. We can't have that! My husband is incarcerated.*

This working-class Bostonian echoes a similar theme.

*So always I'm going to be the working-class poor. I'm never going to be above and I'm never going to be below, and that's why I'm focusing a lot of my money on my children's education. Because I want them to go above. Not get stuck in the middle where I am.*

Especially for poor, working-class, and minority families, educational dreams often go hand-in-hand with family sacrifices. Many families talked about sacrifices they make, but these conversations were not complaints; rather, they highlighted the high value families place on education. In this respect Regina and Arthur Boyles of St. Louis are typical of working-class families who invest high hopes in their chil-dren's education.

*We just make sacrifices. And it's worth it, you know, to see that your child gets a decent education; where they can at least come out of school and have a decent job, with a decent income, where you know they can make it for them-selves. Yeah, it's worth the sacrifice at that point.*

I ask them what they sacrifice to send their child to parochial school.

> *We have to sacrifice maybe not driving the cars we want to drive; not shop-*
> *ping as often as maybe we used to shop; not buying clothes as often as you*
> *used to buy clothes; not eating the food, not eating out as often; maybe not*
> *being able to buy a new couch or a new bedroom set, if I decide that's what*
> *I wanted. So I'd have to let that go, so that I know his tuition could be paid,*
> *'cause that's what's important.*

Melissa, a 24-year-old working-class Bostonian, told me why education is so important to her:

> *Because if you don't know anything, you won't go nowhere. You won't. And*
> *I want my son to do something with his life. I don't want him to—I mean,*
> *I know it's his choice which road he chooses; but if I can try and show him*
> *what I mean, that he can make it by going the right way, then maybe, maybe*
> *he'll, you know . . .*

Lisa, a black working-class Bostonian, put it this way:

> *Knowledge is power. Without education, you'd have nothing. With educa-*
> *tion, you can do and say whatever you want, but you need to understand this*
> *society out here. That's the bottom line. Have knowledge. And as long as they*
> *are getting that, and I feel they're getting it, I don't have a problem with the*
> *school.*

Does she think education will pay off?

> *Definitely, definitely. Without that education, that's the struggle. Unfortu-*
> *nately, I was not able to go to college and increase my knowledge, but I do the*
> *best I can for my children. I count my blessings. For them I want better.*

Working-class, low-income, and minority families told me consistently about their high hopes that education would launch social
mobility and a better life for their children. Invariably, they express
dissatisfaction and frustration with available local options. Their educational aspirations are virtually indistinguishable from those of

middle-class families we interviewed, but the lack of financial assets makes a world of difference. For families struggling for a better life and social mobility, finding schools that will produce opportunities for their children is a challenge. The role of education in the context of the American Dream takes on a distinct language and meaning for these families. We heard them say education is important because they want their children to make it, to go above them, to do something with their lives, to get decent jobs, to earn decent salaries; in sum, they want better for their children. Their mission is to navigate poor school choices to give their kids an opportunity to build a better future. Lacking financial assets, poor families rely on other kinds of nonfinancial resources, like knowledge, contacts, resourcefulness, perseverance, enduring hardships, occasional schemes, and even lies.

The Lupi family of Venice, California, is a white working-class family whose educational concerns and aspirations are typical among families we interviewed, although the solutions they attempt are not exactly customary. Clarisse Lupi, 31, her husband, Dennis, 32, and her three children, ages 16, 7, and 3, rent a tiny house, which looks even smaller because it is wedged between a new three-story stucco apartment building and a large remodeled three-story house and is partly concealed by a neighbor's huge tree. Theirs is one of the few original small, working-class homes left in this rapidly gentrifying part of Venice. Clarisse and Dennis grew up in the area, and the children have lived in nearby locations almost their entire lives. In a sense, they are out of place in their gentrifying neighborhood, but this is not new for Clarisse, who grew up in neighboring Santa Monica. She explains, "We grew up in a neighborhood we didn't belong in. It was kind of in a part of town where people had money to live there, and we didn't have the money to live there, so it was a little tough."

Clarisse dropped out of school in the eighth grade. Two children and several jobs later, she went back to school and got her GED, and she is now enrolled in a nursing program. Three years ago she married Dennis, who had also dropped out of school and earned a GED; he is an auto mechanic earning $28,000. Not including $5,000 an uncle left in a dedicated account for her older children, the Lupi family has no financial resources, and, as Clarisse puts it, they live "paycheck to paycheck." They are living under the cloud of their school loans, totaling about

$7,000 and growing. Maybe because Clarisse grew up and attended school in an affluent part of nearby Santa Monica, maybe because she did not make the most of her opportunities, maybe because of school loans, she wants better schooling for her kids, and this struggle is a constant theme in her life.

Her oldest, Jimmy, 16, has "gone to school everywhere. . . . He has been in a lot of different schools. Now he is starting high school . . . and I don't like the L.A. district schools at all. There's a big difference between schools and between the districts." I asked her to explain the difference:

*In every way; academically, with just everything. The teachers, just the unity of the schools, there's a big difference. [Jimmy] was able to slip through the cracks during elementary school, because he was quiet. . . . And he really fell behind in school, because they just don't care in L.A.*

Things changed dramatically when Jimmy switched schools.

*I had got him into Lincoln [a middle school in Santa Monica] for the sixth and seventh grade, which was a tremendous help. You could tell. When he went to Lincoln, was when he really started getting a lot of help. He got tested, and they got him in tutoring and brought his grades back up. And then you can just tell that the school took him, you know, they took a more firsthand approach with him.*

However, Lincoln Middle School is not a Los Angeles school—it is in Santa Monica. How did Jimmy get into it?

*We okey-doked it [used a false address] it for the two years . . . [then] they caught us. I used his grandma's address. It was just a real hard thing. We even went as far as to let him live with his grandpa during the week, so he [could] stay in the school; but the district just wouldn't let us do it. . . .*

*I'm really grateful for the two years that I got out of Santa Monica, because they cared enough about him at that time. And they really, really helped as far as his education. They brought him back up to where he was supposed to be, and it really helped. I think that if he hadn't had gotten those two years, we'd be in a lot of trouble right now. . . . I think it really made a big difference in his life.*

Banished from Santa Monica schools, Jimmy was sent back to Los Angeles schools and started high school at Venice High, a notoriously tough school with gang and drug problems where only 26 percent of tenth graders test at the national norm for reading and 39 percent for math. Clarisse can only hope that it works out. She has no other viable choices.

Jasmine Lupi is in third grade, and Clarisse is quite satisfied with her education so far.

> *Actually, this is the only school that I do like. But it's in the L.A. district. . . . It's a great school. It's primarily run by women. But it's really a tight-knit community. There's a lot of community support, and there's a lot of parent support. . . . She's doing really well there.*

I ask if Jasmine is enrolled in her neighborhood school. "Actually, it's not her neighborhood school," Clarisse says, "We are on [the southeast] side of Venice, so she would probably go to Westminister. And it's a terrible, terrible school. And so I use my friend's address for over there." Clarisse talks about Jasmine's future education and says she hopes to get her into Santa Monica High.

Why don't they move? "We'd love to stay in this neighborhood. We'd love to stay on this block." The community is a big pull. Her ideal solution, Santa Monica, is not an option because of costly housing and rental markets. "It's harder to get a place in Santa Monica," Clarisse explains, "especially because there's five of us. So we need a big place. And it's hard."

At the conclusion of the interview, I ask Clarisse if she thinks that Santa Monica children have an advantage. Without any hesitation, her answer is clear: "Definitely, yeah." I then ask how this makes her feel. Clarisse, who has responded without hesitation to other questions, pauses and takes a full 10 seconds gathering herself before saying, "I don't know. I suppose that I am glad they have the opportunity to be educated in that way. They should [be glad], really. And I don't think they realize how lucky they really are."

The Lupis go to extraordinary lengths seeking educational opportunities for their children. Middle-class families we interviewed, when faced with similar educational dilemmas, use their assets either to move to communities with better schools or place their children in private schools. For Clarisse Lupi, and asset-poor families like her, moving to better schools or paying private fees is not a viable option. Unable to rent or purchase a home that would give them access to better schools, the schools where her children thrive, they are stuck within working-class borders. Among working-class and low-income families we interviewed, this family's heartfelt concern about education is typical, even if their solution is not normal. Clarisse is very conscious about how "lucky" others are.

Educational aspiration cuts across both race and class in our interviews, even if it seems that working-class and black families express it most fervently and eloquently. Critical differences appear, however, in decisive areas. First, as we have seen repeatedly, ability to make educational aspirations a reality for children clearly differs for working- and middle-class families, as it differs for white and black families. Second, what educational aspiration actually means and how families pursue it is different for middle-class families and working-class families. It is part of the classic American Dream for working-class families as they struggle for educational opportunities so their children can have it better than they did. In my interviews, middle-class families' focus extended to acquiring educational advantages for their children so they can be more in charge of their world. Economically successful families, in particular, were determined to give their children the best education possible so that they will have competitive advantages. Middle-class families use assets as they try to leverage advantage for their children. This difference corresponds to sociologist Annette Lareau's observation that working-class parents look for safe havens to guide their children's natural growth while middle-class families strive to cultivate and foster talents in their children.[3] This distinction may sound subtle, but it is the difference between struggling to find a place where children can learn and positioning them on the road to success. I will return to these critical differences at various points in this chapter.

Using Clarisse Lupi's phrase, we shall see middle-class families who not only know exactly how lucky they are but who consciously pursue and leverage advantages for their children. Unfortunately, in the context of educational inequality, high-quality schools are a scarce resource, and in the competition for these valued opportunities there are winners and losers.

## School Choice in the Real World

Educational quality results primarily from where children live and the resources their parents can provide. Fundamentally, opportunity results from the ways families utilize private resources. As we have seen, quality schools and substandard schools are not distributed randomly; schools commonly reflect a community's wealth and class and race composition. Politicians and educational experts continue to debate the effect of this dispersion of educational opportunity while low-income and black families act to gain access to better schools and middle-class families pursue schools that give their children an edge.

A simple way to begin grasping this difference is to look at who goes to private school. Among children attending private schools, 1 in 10 whites currently attends private school compared to 1 in 25 blacks. Private school choice also starkly reveal the class dimension of choice: Five times as many families with incomes over $50,000 opt for private school as against those with incomes of $15,000 or less (16 percent versus 3 percent).[4] Nearly 20 percent of families with children have sent a child to private school—22.3 percent of white families and 14.8 percent of black families. When we ask who goes to private school, the answers are more revealing. Nearly one in three families earning more than $75,000 has placed a child in private school. In contrast, 21.6 percent of children from middle-income families ($21,000–$75,000), and only 9.8 percent of the children from families with incomes less than $21,000 go to private schools. Examining the wealth of families that have sent children to private school compared to those who have not provides another perspective. Here, we find a disturbing stratification pattern: Families that send children to private schools possess $50,900 net worth compared to $22,950 net worth among families that have only used public schools. The net financial assets differential is even starker, $20,000 compared to $7,000.[5]

While it is obvious that wealthy families can pay for private school, this information also includes reasonably priced parochial schooling. Secular private schools generally provide greater educational resources and higher-quality learning environments than public schools, as measured by smaller class size, teacher qualifications, and computers. The private school option, then, places valued educational resources at the disposal of families who can afford it. Some families can pursue private remedies to weak public services.

When parents talk about their hopes for their children, their aspirations focus on education, but deep-seated class and racial anxieties lurk beneath the surface. As in the case of residential choices, our interviews reveal the symbiotic ways in which race and class inequality and individual family decisions profoundly affect each other.

This chapter opened with Mary Masterson's decision to move her family to Kirkwood. She moved from a community that was about half white and half black, but the schools were predominantly minority. Besides moving up in class terms, her daughters now live in an almost entirely white community. Her move to a middle-class suburb effectively removed African Americans from her daughers' school and peer circle. She is not alone or extraordinary in defining good schools with class and race characteristics. In interview after interview, a clear pattern among white middle-class parents emerges. When it is possible, they use financial clout to place their children in whiter, wealthier, and less diverse school environments. In our interviews with families having access to assets, I do not recall even one family move that did not fit this pattern, a pattern reinforced by our analysis of moving data.

Prosperous families we interviewed often viewed schooling choices as if they were buying a product or acquiring a service. Financial resources make this attitude and choice possible. It is worth recalling Elizabeth Wainwright Cummings' comment from the first chapter about the local public school, "We knew we weren't using the school district." Several affluent parents employed verbs like "use" when referring to local public schools, signifying a commodity perspective on public services and their viable option of purchasing private services. This is evidence of the increasing importance of a privatized notion of citizenship where families opt out of the social infrastructure that provides the common good. Many of the families I talked to said they do this because the public schools have failed them. In any case, the effect undercuts public education.

Just under 10 percent of schoolchildren attend private schools in the United States. Among the families we interviewed, 32 parents sent their children to private schools, with most of these (21) attending parochial schools. For many families with children in private school, we noted a distinct pattern of parents who were very fond of their communities but did not trust their local public schools. In particular, we talked to a number of middle-class black families who feel caught in a vise of weak schools and strong commitments to a black community. Their children often attend private schools.

Alice and Bob Bryant live in a part of Mattapan, a community in Boston populated mainly by African American professionals. Their son, Alan, is 4 years old. Alice works as an upper-level administrative assistant for a local corporation. Bob is a freelance photographer. Their combined annual income is $51,500 and their net worth is $17,000, but their net financial assets are in the red at minus $5,000. Alice and Bob cannot rely on their parents for financial help; in fact, the opposite is true, as they often help their parents financially.

Alice and Bob, who had been living in a poorer part of Boston, wanted to move to a suburban school district with good schools after Alan was born, but they could not afford to. Instead, they found that they could only afford neighborhoods with "halfway decent schools." The Mattapan neighborhood they moved into is part of a larger working-class area where schools are not as well funded as in districts that are more affluent. Alice says, "I didn't have enough money to buy where I would really like to be." She explains some consequences she sees resulting from this: "Alan will not get the best education, not what most people would call the best education. He is going to get the best that we can afford to give him. There are schools that probably will give a lot better education, but we can't afford to send him there."

Alice and Bob have done the best they can for Alan, but they cannot compete with advantages like the parental support Mary Masterson, for example, has. Our interviews with black families and families with few financial resources show stark contrasts to families with more advantage.

Families say that school quality is their biggest concern and that they are looking for "good schools." For us, this raises the question of what parents consider a "good school." How do parents define school quality when they are making choices about where to send their children to school?

## What Is a Quality School?

We need to understand what experts consider quality schools before examining whether parents' actions match this definition or whether race and class anxieties lurk beneath the surface of their actions. In December 2000 the U.S. Department of Education identified 13 key indicators of school quality having the largest influence on student learning and performance. The indicators defined in this report included school leadership, school goals, professional community, discipline, academic environment, teacher academic skills, teaching assignment, teacher experience, professional development, course content, pedagogy, technology, and class size.[6] Educational experts have identified these characteristics as distinguishing good schools from bad.

Some of the parents I interviewed mentioned taking into account school characteristics similar to these when choosing schools for their children. One white middle-class mother explained what kind of school she and her husband had looked for in a school for their daughters:

> *Smaller classrooms, a lot of parent involvement in the schools, I think that makes a big difference in the quality of education, the staff, the look and feel of the campuses, what kind of extracurricular things they have in the classroom. Computers, music, PE, the things that I would consider basic. . . . That is what I was looking for.*

Another middle-class white parent said:

> *I want small classrooms. I guess number one, I want good teachers. I think that is the most important thing. I want it to be safe. I want them to have good equipment.*

For these parents and a few others, characteristics such as class size, curriculum, instruction, and technology resources help determine what is a good school, but these parents are a small minority of those I interviewed. Overwhelmingly, parents we interviewed—especially white parents—did not note school-related characteristics such as those identified by the Department of Education when they talked about deciding where to send their kids to school. My analysis of the interviews strongly suggests that other considerations overshadow educational indicators and are much more on the minds of parents when they make real school choices for their children.

Repeatedly parents identified school reputation as the most important factor in where they send their kids. Families with resources often moved to particular residential areas based solely on the local school district's reputation. I asked a physician why he moved from Boston to Brookline. His answer was direct: "Well, generally Brookline schools have a better reputation than Boston, which is why we moved here in the first place." He is correct. Brookline has demonstratively higher-quality schools in terms of things experts consider crucial. And its schools are mixed. My point here is that Alice and Bob Bryant would love to make the same move but cannot because of lack of resources.

White middle-class parents we interviewed often explained that they choose schools by prestige or reputation. What in the minds of these parents contributes to a good reputation? Upon close examination, our interviews reveal that what parents mean by school reputation is usually quite different from the Department of Education's school quality indicators. Parents often directly tie school reputation to the school's race and class profile. More often than not, choosing a school district or a specific school within a district is driven by a strong need to avoid other schools—particularly urban public schools with minority or poor students. From my conversations with parents, wanting to escape or avoid bad schools is at least as important as finding good schools. One Los Angeles white parent expressed it this way:

> We specifically avoided the city because we did not want to have to deal with public education in the city. We avoided Hancock Park Elementary School for the same thing, not that the education was any worse but that the, um, people that my children would have to associate with were not, um, up to par, as far as I'm concerned. It's like, city, um, lower-class people.

Hancock Park Elementary School is indeed an urban school, but it is also one of the most highly regarded urban schools in California because of its exceptional test scores. One-fourth of the children attending Hancock Park receive free or reduced-price lunches because their families are low-income, a percentage that is considerably lower than nearby schools. Whites make up 26 percent of the school's students, 10 percent are African American, half are Asian, 12 percent are Latino, and the test scores are great. While it is true that urban schools with minority or poor students are most likely low-performing schools, this parent saw lower-class kids and missed exceptional-performing students.

Many white parents, as well as some black ones, determine school quality not by academic excellence, teacher skills, or classroom curriculum but by who sits next to and who will associate with their child. Shauna Ferguson, a mother of two from St. Louis, says: "You wouldn't want to send a child to the neighborhood schools." When I ask why, Shauna says, "The kids aren't getting great educations," because "anybody and everybody goes there." Other schools, though, she explains, are different. They are better if they are more exclusive, because not just "anybody and everybody goes there." In her mind, public schools in "nicer areas" and private schools are considered good schools. Unfortunately, Shauna's equation of nice areas and private schools with good schools is accurate too often. She is reminding us that not everyone has the choice of affording nice areas or private schools.

Parents define good schools as those where children from high-status families go to school. Class and racial composition becomes a proxy for school quality in the minds of parents as they actively seek out schools for their children. Avoiding city schools and those that have citylike demographics seems to be specifically an attempt to avoid urban populations, fears, and problems while accessing high-quality schools. Because of their financial resources, most of these examples come from middle-class families, yet the experience is not limited to middle-class families. Mike and Kim Brown are a white working-class St. Louis couple who moved out of the city because they did not want to live near African Americans. They send their two young children to parochial schools because "neither one of us wanted the kids to go to city schools." Mike Brown says:

It's not about the race, it's about the— it may even be the financial aspect of the people. The fact that they are in the projects. It's all subsidized housing, things like that. . . . So, like I say, while race may be an underlying factor,

*the Patrick Henry School, with the ten-foot fences with the barbed wire on*
*top, that just doesn't sit well with me.*

I do not imagine that Patrick Henry is the kind of school that sits well
with parents, certainly none I interviewed; yet schools like it exist in
urban areas I studied. Only those without choice, or without resources,
or without power to bring about change, or without hope send their
children to this kind of school.

Ginny and Matt Stayman explained why they moved their daughter,
Amy, out of a Los Angeles school they thought was excellent because of
their racial concerns.

> GINNY: *Well, Baldwin Hills School was African American.*
> MATT: *But I think that was actually a better school than Westside in terms of*
>        *what they were demanding.*
> GINNY: *Academically, right, it was.*

Even though they agree that Amy's old school was academically better
and more demanding, and they did not think any racial problems
existed at the school, they maneuvered Amy to a school where she was
not in the minority. I think most parents would make the same decision. But if the situation were reversed—imagine black parents
sacrificing school quality so their children can be with other black
kids—I suspect society would be quick to question their parental values.

Many parents define school quality by school address and student
profile. A father from Los Angeles discusses how he determines a good
school:

> *Actually the public elementary school is almost as good or better than some of*
> *the private schools in the L.A. area, because it's such a nice area. The parents*
> *care, and some of the real rich people that live farther up the mountain, their*
> *kids go there, and* [a] *city councilman's kids go to that school. So if it's good*
> *enough for him, it's a good school. The concern would be once they get out of*
> *the elementary school into the middle school, and especially the high school.*
> *Everyone* [goes to] *one high school, so everyone from the whole town mixes*
> *together in high school, which is the bad elements of everywhere. So he would*
> *be exposed to more undesirable things and people.*

I ask him to elaborate on "undesirable things."

> *Oh, probably some of the kids that are in gangs. Drugs. From the areas of South Monrovia where they have had drug problems, and you see graffiti, and you see old junker cars leaking oil in the street and trash all over and beer cans on the grass. Whoever those people are, if they are going to the same high school, it makes you concerned, wonder if the kids are exposed to all of that. Whatever all of that is.*

I ask how this shows up in the school, and he answers, "It would affect the atmosphere of the school, I guess."

Jennifer Perrotto, a mother from Los Angeles who chose a private Catholic school for her children, explains why she thinks it is a good school: "There's other mothers there that have the same desires as I do, and they all have the same faith." I ask Jennifer to expand, and she explains why buying into a community is more important than education for her:

> *I want my children to marry someone Catholic, so I need to expose them to other Catholic children. They also, their family values are the same. And to me it's no longer education, it's the community that it brought. . . . So there is education there, but the number one thing is the community that I receive from there. And then education.*

Black families often spoke of similar considerations when discussing what kind of schools they want for their children. Yvette and Elesey Medina are African Americans living in a black middle-class suburb in St. Louis with 13-year-old Elesey Jr. and 11-year-old Dwan. Yvette talks about why she is thinking about moving to a white middle-class suburb so her sons can attend better schools:

> *If we were talking about the neighborhood that I really wanted to move in, it would probably be in Maryland Heights. Those are some really nice homes. And I think that's the Parkway school district, which probably is a better school district. I'm not sure if it's Parkway or one of the other school districts. But I'm sure it's a pretty good school district, because they have really, really nice homes.*

I ask if she assumes schools are better because homes are better.

*Probably so. . . . I mean, it's West County. Everybody out there is rich. My doctor's kids go there. And I know he's got money. He's a specialist. . . . So I know he's got plenty of money.*

Angela Slater, a black middle-class mother from Los Angeles who sends her children to private school, explains how important school environment is:

*It's not only the academics that I'm concerned about. You know, I have to be concerned about the environment, the community, you know? Because who is to say where her attention will lie, you know? I have hopes that it will lie on the books and academics, but they're kids, you know? They are influenced by their peers. So I have to be concerned about that as well.*

The kinds of schools black middle-class families want for their children are similar in most ways to what white middle-class families want. One big difference, however, is that black families consistently brought up diversity as an important and positive factor when they look at schools. Just like white families, they do not want their kids in all-minority schools. Unlike white families, blacks purposefully seek racial and cultural diversity. Susan Molloy, a middle-class black St. Louis mother, explains why she thinks her kids attend a good school: "Well, it's a very diverse school—economically, socially, and racially—and I like that a lot." Meta Joseph, a middle-class black mother from Boston, explains why she thinks her daughter attends a good school:

*Diversity. A lot of kids from lots of different places—which I like. . . . She's made a lot of friends from a lot of different places, and I like that. Black, white, Asian, Hispanic. I like that. I think that's important.*

Some academics and politicians find comfort in attitude and opinion surveys that most whites no longer reveal anti-integration sentiments; they use this as evidence that America is now a post-racial society where race no longer matters.[7] However, actual survey data disclose that what whites mean by integration and diversity is something quite different from what blacks do. For instance, hardly any whites object to schools with just a few black children, but almost half say they would object to a school that is more than 50 percent minority.[8] Although our interviews did not inquire about statistical levels of diversity, it is nonetheless abundantly clear how much it is on their minds, since most white parents become apprehensive with schools that have more than a few minorities. The difference is that white parents say they want their kids "exposed" to a few black classmates while black parents want their children to know how to perform in white-dominated settings. Effectively, what is the beginning point of diversity for African American parents is a tipping point for most white parents; that is, a handful is not enough for blacks, but more than a handful is too many for whites, and they look to exit the system. Thus, whites' concern about school composition and peers is a prime motivation for residential moves and school maneuvering that keep schools segregated.

Current school reform initiatives take place in a context of educational inequality and highly unequal conditions of education. The United States lacks the political commitment to mix poor urban and disadvantaged children into better schools, and we choose not to make the financial commitment necessary to equip urban schools with what we know works. In this context, choices are not taking place among equitable schools, and that is unlikely to change in the near future.[9]

We met the Conways, a white middle-class family living in Los Angeles, in Chapter 3. Since they were married, they have happily lived in a modest middle-class section of Los Angeles that is predominantly African American. As their daughter, Logan, approaches school age, however, they anguish over their school options. For them, the critical choice boils down to two. They can stay where they are and try to get Logan into a magnet school for gifted children, which has a waiting list of about 100. The local schools simply are not an option for them. The second option they are considering is to buy a home in South Pasadena, where the schools have an excellent reputation. South Pasadena encompasses three and a half square miles, with a population of approximately 25,000. It is known for its tree-lined streets, historic California Craftsman–style homes, unique small businesses, award-winning public library, and outstanding public schools. All of these things combine to maintain the small-town atmosphere that makes South Pasadena one of Southern California's most desirable locations for families raising children. It also is expensive. This is not a "choice" that most Americans have, because most of the single-family homes in South Pasadena cost over half a million dollars.

Throughout the interview, much of our conversation revolved around the educational issue and the Conways' sense of choices. Later, when I listened to the interview and read the transcript, something about their story just did not seem to fit. Their anguish about moving, clearly entailing moving from a modest middle-class community to an affluent and whiter community, was palpable. The language they used about moving to South Pasadena was anchored in terms of their daughter: The move, the schools, everything was being considered for Logan's sake. We had heard parents talk about community and school issues this way many times before. We often wondered about a family's motives: Was all this really being done for the sake of the kids, or was it a justification for seeking higher status? Frank and Suzanne Conway clearly stated their dilemma and choices, like others I interviewed, yet they seemed overly solicitous in their efforts to make me believe that their motivations were altruistic. Throughout the interview, the talk was about the horror of the local public schools and the difficulty of getting a child into a school for gifted children, as opposed to the exceptional public schools in South Pasadena. The way they posed their dilemma sounded as if they had made their minds up already. They also made it seem as if they had thoroughly researched and analyzed all the elementary schools within a reasonable commuting distance from their jobs, selected the best schools, and then looked for homes in those school jurisdictions. In fact, we did hear stories from real estate agents and others of families bringing newspaper lists of statewide school test scores into real estate offices and specifically asking to see property only in a certain school district. Let's see how Frank and Suzanne Conway made their decision.

They say their present neighborhood

*really is terrific. I think we have almost everything that we need, except for maybe a Starbucks and a Trader Joe's* [a popular gourmet food store] *in our neighborhood, to make us happy,* if we had a good elementary school and a good high school [emphasis added]. *And I think that all kids should have a good elementary school and high school to go to, but I'm not sure that I'm able to fight the system that much.*

The comment about not being "able to fight the system" illustrates an irony of educational reform. For at least the past decade, an educational reform agenda has focused on testing, quality, and how to make schools better and more accountable. At least in rhetoric, this discussion is about how best to deliver quality and effective educational practice to weak schools, particularly substandard urban schools with minority and disadvantaged students. This reform agenda, and the intense controversy that swirls in its wake, centers on how to make schools more effective. For most families I interviewed, however—even though they may be invested in this debate, because they want better schools for their children—solutions within their reach result from individual decisions and dealings, not educational reform or collective action. The point I heard over and over again from parents is that they feel disengaged from discussion about how to make schools better; instead they search for ways to get their kids into better schools. The educational reform agenda for the Conways—and, I suspect, most Americans—is not about how to make schools better but about how to get to better schools. Topics like educational reform, making schools better, or even joining the PTA to work for improved schools usually did not come up in our conversations; sometimes, however, bringing about educational reform seems too daunting, which is behind Suzanne Conway's comment that she is "not sure I am able to fight the system that much." From her perspective, it does not make sense to fight the system when you can acquire a better system.

It was one of those revealing moments. The interview was over, but I said I had one last question and asked if they had visited schools in South Pasadena. Suzanne said, "Mostly what we did was we decided that we were pretty much interested in the Pasadena area, and then we started asking around about the schools. No, not yet." Their presumption that South Pasadena schools are high quality is completely accurate in this case, but they decided on the community first without visiting or investigating schools. This is not unusual but typical. Educational researcher Jennifer Holme reports that only 1 of 20 parents she interviewed who moved out of neighborhoods because they were dissatisfied with their children's school actually visited the rejected school. Most, 34 of 42, had not obtained test-score data for schools they moved away from. She interviewed 36 parents who bought homes for the schools, but very few actually visited their child's new school before buying the home, and most had not obtained test-score data for their new school before they moved.[10]

Another mother with a different set of circumstances is working on another kind of game plan. Sandra McCord lives in the Crenshaw area of Los Angeles with her daughters, 11-year-old Kalila and 15-year-old Myisha. Her neighborhood is poverty stricken and African American. Sandra has worked at various low-level, poverty-wage jobs, but she went back to school full-time and is about to earn a degree. She has zero financial assets, owes money on some store charge cards, and patches together less than $7,000 in social assistance, food stamps, and school grants. Hers is not an easy life.

> I am living right now off a very, very tight budget. Sometimes, to be honest with you, since the new [welfare reform] laws were implemented, I am not receiving food stamps for myself, but I'm receiving it for both of my kids, because they are citizens and I am not. Due to that fact, I am not receiving food stamps. So that has really put a tremendous dent in my food budget. When it comes to the last week of the month and onto the first couple days into the month, I go through a rough time providing food for my kids. We really sometimes have to struggle. Sometimes I have to go to like these different church centers [food pantries].

In the midst of these daily struggles, Sandra is more troubled about her daughters' future.

> 'Cause like, right now, like two of the schools that my two kids were assigned to, I didn't send them to those schools, because I went and I checked the schools out and I wasn't satisfied with the program that they offered. Along with the program, I wasn't satisfied with the environment. So I just got them out, and my kids, they are going to school out of their district. I had to go get a release from the Board of Education and send them to school outside the district.
> The youngest one, she is going to Culver City Middle School. I'm very happy with her going there. I like their programs. It's a small community.

*They look out for each other in their community, and the teachers there are into giving the children a good education. My eldest daughter, she is going to Fairfax High School, and to me that's a pretty decent school, where I like the educational system there. To me, they offer the kids a lot. There is a lot for the kids to choose from. And if the kids want to do good and make something of themselves, they are given the opportunity to do so. They are really behind the kids, where they push them to do good.*

I ask why she chose two different, faraway school districts; neither is in their local jurisdiction nor even close to where they live.

*Okay, at the time, when I didn't want my kids to go to the school that they were assigned to, and when I got my youngest daughter into Culver City Middle School, at the time, there wasn't a space for the older girl. So I decided that I certainly didn't want her to go to L.A. High, and I didn't want her to go to any other high school, and I had the opportunity to get her into Fairfax, and that's what I chose.*

I ask how she heard about these schools. How did she know they were good places?

*A friend. . . . Plus I have an in-law, he does janitorial services up there. And then Culver City, my husband-to-be, my fiancé, he coaches at Culver City, and that's how I got my daughter in. I got her in through his work permit. Then my eldest daughter, he has a friend that works at Fairfax, and he told us about Fairfax, and we went and looked at the program, and we got her into Fairfax.*

I ask about their commute.

*If you don't send your kids to the school that your kids are being assigned to, you are not allowed to have the opportunity to have your kid bused. You have to find your own transportation. Well, I have to send both of my kids on the city bus. Well, the younger one, she . . . ends up taking like three buses to school—no, she does take three buses to school every day, because she has to take the sixty-eight, which is the Metro to the Fairfax transit station. Then she picks the number one up, and that doesn't take her exactly to her school.*

*That drops her off at [the] half point. And from there, Washington and Overland, she takes the number three that takes her to her school, and she walks like two blocks. Then the older girl, she takes two buses. She takes the sixty-eight to the Fairfax transit station, and from there she takes the two seventeen that takes her directly in front of her school.*

Sandra tells me that it takes over an hour for them to get to school each morning and that she is afraid of violence she has seen at some bus stops and transfer points along their route. Finally, I ask her if it is hard sometimes to come up with the fares.

*Sometimes, to be honest, sometimes, sometimes, when I have to wait for my check on the fourth, sometimes my kids will have to* miss a couple days of school [emphasis added], *or sometimes if I could get friends to drop them off, I'll have friends drop them off. Or like, the youngest one, what I do, my fiancé picks her up, so this way I don't have to pay for her to come back home. I just have to find the fare for her to go to school in the morning time. And then, what I did, I applied for half fare for kids. I went to the MTA* [Metropolitan Transit Authority] *and I got the forms from their school and I applied for a low bus rate for them where I just have to pay half fare for the month. But even with that, at times it's still very difficult.*

  *Or sometimes I would even have my kids and we would get up a little earlier and I would have them, instead of paying the fare on the Metro, we would walk from here to Fairfax and then just pick up the other bus where we don't have to pay the first fare. So that's how I do it sometimes.*

Because of their class and race legacies and the effects of inequality, the Conway and McCord families have different game plans, and Logan and Kalila and Myisha most certainly face divergent futures.

As the last chapter suggested, to understand the implications of our findings one does not need to believe that a majority of parents are racist. Rather, their actions take place in a context of high-quality education's increasing importance for economic success in the global economy. Middle-class parents, in particular, frequently talked about wanting not just to give their children opportunities but to cultivate competitive edges. In this context, a highly stratified educational system and middle-class social apprehension combine to produce an environment where parents feel compelled to acquire opportunities and competitive advantages for their children. It follows that parents make individual decisions that make rational sense to them. The current parental frenzy over their children's schooling has broad implications. In the process of seeking educational advantages, whites resegregate themselves and their children overwhelmingly in schools and communities that look like them and perpetuate inequality. This advantage is secured in homeownership and is the most blatant way that transformative assets perpetuate inequality. If we as a society continue to take these moves for granted—even rewarding the action—then we sanction and extend patterns that reproduce class and race inequality. We must ask ourselves to look both at the current choices we would make and at the choices we would like to have available.

# Conclusion

## Assets for Equality

T HE ENORMOUS RACIAL WEALTH GAP perpetuates racial inequality in the United States. Racial inequality appears intransigent because the way families use wealth transmits advantages from generation to generation. Furthermore, the twenty-first century marks the beginning of a new racial dilemma for the United States: Family wealth and inheritances cancel gains in classrooms, workplaces, and paychecks, worsening racial inequality. I see no means of seriously moving toward racial equality without positive asset policies to address the racial wealth gap.

Diagnosing causes and effects of racial inequality, while difficult and controversial enough, is easier than the seemingly overwhelming task of reversing our direction toward more inequality. Connecting the thorny dots of racial inequality means no less than confronting our historical legacy of vast material inequality, massive residential segregation, and wide gaps in educational conditions. The racial wealth gap is more than an obdurate historical legacy that lives in the present, because it also springs from contemporary public policy and institutional discrimination, not to mention individuals' behavior. I will suggest policy initiatives and principles aimed at restoring ideals of equality, the American Dream, and democracy—what I call *assets for equality*.

I am convinced that asset policy can be an indispensable part of the march toward social justice. Over the past several years, I have participated with policy groups, community groups, advocacy organizations, and foundations whose work on asset policy has provided impressive results. In 1995 asset policy was virtually nonexistent. Today, it is an important part of state and federal policy agendas. We can draw upon the experience of those involved in important national demonstration programs on asset development, pilot programs, studies on the effects of assets, and state and federal legislation. At conferences on these programs, I have heard people's firsthand testimony about the galvanizing experience of asset-building programs helping them to buy a house or start a business that changed their lives. As families talked to me about impediments to their dreams, I was struck by the utter importance of remedying the racial wealth gap. I offer a strategy aimed simultaneously at assisting families in generating assets and in minimizing the advantages of wealth.

## The Road to Assets

In order to address the asset deprivation of two of every five American families, I want to propose or endorse several key policy initiatives. My policy proposals do not contest the right to succeed and reap the rewards of hard work. These are start-up policies that provide families with a chance to work toward the American Dream.

### Children's Savings Accounts

Children growing up in families with assets go to school secure in the knowledge that their families will support their dreams and future well-being. However, many children in America grow up without such confidence. The majority of children come from families who cannot provide a positive asset legacy. About 4 in 10 of all children grow up in asset-poor families. More distressing, over half of African American children grow up asset poor. What difference would it make if every child in America grew up knowing that (s)he had a nest egg to use to go to college, buy a home, or start a business? As a result of acquiring start-up money, they would be more confident and competent; they would feel more invested in themselves, their communities, and the future. They would have dreams and a way to risk making them come true. Benefits would accrue to individuals, families, and society as a whole.

Twelve-year-old Derek Tessler is being raised by his grandmother in the poor and black South Central section of Los Angeles. His grandmother works hard just to make ends meet and hopes the future will be better. Derek will be one of the lucky ones if he comes out of his community unscarred. Some start-up assets might keep his hopes alive and give him real choices about his life.

The Children's Savings Accounts initiative is the kind of idea that might work for Derek Tessler. There are many models for Children's Savings Accounts, such as initial government or private contribution at birth, matches of family contributions for low-income families throughout the child's formative years, and limited use of account balances at age 18 and older. Imagine, for example, that every child born in the United States had an initial deposit of $1,000 in such an account. Additional yearly deposits would be encouraged and possibly tied to achievements such as school graduations, summer employment, and community service. Acquiring financial literacy throughout the school years would be a strong program component, providing a relevant and stimulating educational context. Government funds would match contributions from low-income parents. Contributions to the account also could come from private, employer, or charitable sources. After high school, account holders could use funds for higher education or training. At age 25 or older uses of the funds might also include small-business capitalization and first-time home purchase. If accounts are still active by retirement age, people could use them to cover retirement expenses or pass them on to the next generation. With a $1,000 contribution at birth and $500 contributed annually by the family with half of that annual amount matched for poor families, a young adult by age 18 could have about $40,000 to start a productive life.

It is myopic not to support the aspirations and talents of those who are born with material disadvantages. There are sound practical as well as moral reasons for a policy that provides all children with a fair start in life and hope for the future. Children's Savings Accounts may just be one of those ideas.

The Corporation for Enterprise Development is planning a national Children's Savings Accounts demonstration program to put this idea in practice in 2003–4. Just as a national demonstration project for Individual Development Accounts provided empirical support for federal and state asset-building policies, this program will test policy designs, participation levels, uses, and effective match rates. In Great Britain a similar idea, dubbed Baby Bonds, was a popular centerpiece of Prime Minister Tony Blair's 2001 second-term election manifesto.[1]

*Individual Development Accounts*

The vast majority of Americans have not accumulated many assets and are not about to inherit a large nest egg. This lack of assets impedes them from moving ahead, and they watch people jumping ahead who they know have not worked harder, have not tried harder, and do not deserve financial success any more than they do. Start-up assets for opportunities like education, businesses, and retirement could improve dramatically the lives of average Americans.

Latoya Milton, who would do anything for her daughter's education, dreams of moving to a community with better schools, even calculating sacrifices like going without telephone service and auto insurance. If Latoya's job of managing a dry-cleaning establishment paid a living wage and offered health and pension benefits, moving to Kirkwood, Missouri, might not be just a dream. She is an ideal candidate for a program that motivates savings for future mobility. Smart and hardworking, she might use it for higher education or even start a dry-cleaning business of her own.

Individual Development Accounts (IDA) are the first and largest policy initiative in asset-development policy, spearheaded by Michael Sherraden's book *Assets and the Poor*, promoted by policy makers and advocacy groups, and backed by several national foundations. Individual Development Accounts reward savings by asset-poor families who aim to buy their first home, acquire postsecondary education, or start a small business. For every dollar a family saves, matching funds that typically come from a variety of private and public sources provide strong incentive. IDAs are usually managed by community-based organizations with accounts held at local financial institutions. In 1997 a multimillion-dollar IDA demonstration project, the American Dream Policy Demonstration, was launched and financed by private foundations and organizations. Since 1997 IDAs have made their way into federal policy in a wide range of federal programs. In 1998 a large federal demonstration was started through the Assets for Independence Act. Confusing many economists and others who claimed that poor people could not save because of their circumstances or values, the demonstration program provides compelling empirical evidence of poor families sacrificing to put aside money to create better lives for themselves.

The promise confirmed by privately funded national demonstration programs is now spreading to hundreds of thousands of American families through public policy. The Savings for Working Families Act was reintroduced in 2002, after Congress nearly passed it in previous sessions. It is part of a broad charitable giving bill known as the CARE Act. The legislation calls for $450 million dollars in IDA Tax Credits. If the bill passes in 2003, it would create 300,000 IDA accounts, beginning in 2004. And if it does not pass, it will be reintroduced again.

The IDA Tax Credit would work by providing financial institutions with a dollar-for-dollar tax credit for every dollar they contribute as matching funds for IDAs, up to $500 per IDA per year. The credit would substantially expand the amount of matching funds available for IDAs and cement them as an asset-building tool for low-income Americans in the federal tax system.

The bipartisan IDA Tax Credit proposal is backed by a coalition of organizations representing the financial, nonprofit, academic, and corporate sectors. It proposes to include married families earning up to $40,000. Allowable uses include first-time home purchase, small-business capitalization or expansion, and higher education or vocational training. Banks match savings on a dollar-for-dollar basis up to $500 per year for five years. Participating banks, in turn, receive federal tax credits. Funding accounts in this manner through the tax system means that the program is not dependent on annual federal budgets. There is no penalty for withdrawal of individuals' own savings, but the account holder loses corresponding matching funds for things other than allowed uses. The proposed legislation funds 300,000 accounts. Although this is a virtual drop in the bucket, if the program is successful and popular, popular pressure could mount to broaden it and start new ones. Peter Tufano of the Harvard Business School estimates that 40 million families would be eligible for IDAs under the act. At times, the asset movement comes under criticism for building big hopes around small programs that cannot bring about large-scale change. A strategy that reaches less than 1 percent is not an end point, but it is an important step in moving IDAs from demonstration programs to national policy, providing a model for public funding, and, maybe most significant, building a political constituency and momentum.

The political strategy behind IDA accounts has been diligently bipartisan, an approach that has been instrumental in gaining widespread support across party lines and ideologies. Getting new policy initiatives off the ground in an era of budget cutbacks, especially policies benefiting low- and middle-income families, is testimony enough to the success of this bipartisan approach. As these policies gain popularity and momentum, I think, strategy could shift to designing programs politicians will rush to support. Such an approach builds politics around programs.

### Down Payment Accounts

Homeownership is a signature of the American Dream and, as I have emphasized throughout this book, frames class status, family identity, and schooling opportunities. We also know that homeownership provides the nexus for transformative assets of family wealth. For this reason, and others, I think a hallmark policy idea is Down Payment Accounts for first-time homebuyers.

We met Vivian Arroya, who is working herself away from Watts and welfare to stable work and better communities. Now she wants to buy a house to solidify her social mobility and provide a stable environment for her teenage son and twin girls, but debts, no down payment money, and lack of assets preclude this possibility. She is everything welfare reform advocates want, but for her, as for others, working herself off the welfare roll has not meant an escape from poverty. Asset policies and some sort of down payment program would fit the aspirations of this working-poor family head well. Then she might be able to attack her debt problem and begin to look like the kind of credit risk that mortgage lenders would take.

Home equity accounts for 60 percent of the total wealth of America's middle class. The gap between rising home prices and incomes that barely keep pace has widened considerably since 1995, making it more difficult for families to buy a first home; not only must they qualify for larger mortgages, but steeper purchase prices require higher down payments. As we know, substantial parental financial assistance fills this breach for many young first-time homebuyers.

The chief purpose of Down Payment Accounts is to allow families to acquire assets for down payment and closing costs. How would these accounts work? Similar to the home mortgage interest deduction, renters could deduct a portion of their rent on their tax form and have it put aside in a dedicated account to match their own savings for homeownership on a one-to-one basis. This money would be used for first-time homebuyers. Say, for example, people could deduct 25 percent of their annual rent as a tax credit triggered into matching savings for home-ownership. All first-time homebuyers would be eligible. The amount of eligible tax credit should have yearly caps and a total cap of, say, $2,500 a year and $7,500 maximum matches. Thus, in as short as three years, family savings of $7,500 would become $15,000 toward down payment, points, and closing costs. A family could withdraw its own money and use it for any purpose at any time, but the matching tax credit would be lost for any use other than buying a home. The average rent in 2000 was about $7,500, so a 25 percent renter-to-homeowner tax credit amounts to $1,836.

Funding could also come from banks, lending institutions, and insurance companies as settlement from discriminatory lending and redlining practices. Cities could encourage new housing construction and community renovation by linking development and zoning policies with developer and construction industry participation in pooled down payment accounts. To encourage community stability, allowable uses for matching funds could include home repair and renovation for first-time homeowners. Such a program would include strong financial, home-ownership, and mortgage literacy components. Inherited wealth, parental financial assistance, and savings that do not come from earnings would not qualify for matching funds. Finally, use of Down Payment Accounts would not exclude using other IDA accounts for homeownership.

## Why Assets?

Contrary to political rhetoric and popular belief, the American welfare policy, particularly its safety net, is the most limited among Western industrialized countries.[2] Our record of helping lift families out of poverty to better lives is shameful, as measured in absolute terms or compared to other advanced democracies. U.S. governmental policy is ineffective in reducing poverty. In the United States, current government policies reduce poverty by about 38 percent. In stark contrast, among other Western industrialized countries, government social policies reduce poverty by an average of 79 percent. [3]

A revealing contrast is that in U.S. history government policies have been very effective in giving other kinds of families start-ups to acquire property and assets. I am thinking specifically of the Homestead Act, begun in 1862, which provided up to 160 acres of land, self-reliance, and ultimately wealth to millions of American families. This remarkable government policy set in motion opportunities for upward mobility and a more secure future for oneself and one's children by giving nearly 1.5 million families title to 246 million acres of land, nearly the size of California and Texas combined. One study puts the number of homestead descendents living today at 46 million adults.[4] This means that up to a quarter of the adult population potentially traces its legacy of property ownership, upward mobility, economic stability, class status, and wealth directly to one national policy—a policy that in practice essentially excluded African Americans.

I am thinking too of the Federal Housing Administration, which changed the rules under which Americans buy homes, provided the structural stability for America's middle class, and created inheritable wealth. And the GI Bill, which allowed millions of World War II veterans to attend college and acquire human assets that became the backbone for their economic success. And Veterans Administration home loans, which made low-interest mortgages and low down payments possible and thereby made homeownership accessible to millions.

My point is not just that America has had successful asset policies helping middle-class families acquire land, homes, and wealth for well over 150 years. The poor and disadvantaged—especially African Americans—were excluded from participation in those programs that helped others acquire land, property, homes, and wealth, stuck instead with welfare policies never meant to launch mobility out of the depths of poverty.

Michael Sherraden points out that a new shift to asset-security policy clearly has been under way in the United States since the early 1970s.[5] Asset accounts like 401(k)s, 403(b)s, IRAs, Roth IRAs, and the Federal Thrift Savings Plan are the most rapidly growing form of asset policy.

Some are private and some are public, but public subsidies through the tax system typically define them. In all likelihood this shift to asset-security policy will continue.[6] These accounts and policies protect and maintain assets of those who have accumulated assets already.

In fact, in its present form, the shift to asset accounts is potentially more regressive and will lead to greater inequality in the future. These current asset-security policies have the potential to exacerbate inequality, and indeed are doing so, because most Americans do not have enough assets to buy into these programs and are shut out.

Asset-building policies will most directly benefit the more than one in three American families (36 percent) falling beneath our conservative asset poverty line, those with less than $4,175 in financial assets. Less conservative estimates (like 125 percent of the poverty line or defining the financial safety net at six months instead of three) mean that close to one-half of American families would benefit from asset policy. An asset perspective draws the hidden fault line of inequality in a way that includes between one-third and one-half of Americans. In contrast, the more traditional income line draws the fault line more narrowly, at one in eight. Because African American families possess fewer financial resources than whites, asset policies will have greater impact in minority communities, but they will positively include millions of white families and thus address the sedimentation of both race and class inequality.

The concept of a stakeholder society—the individual can have a stake or feel invested in all aspects of society, whether financial or not—holds much promise. Although we should be cautious about the small number of studies, it is clear that building assets does far more than simply add money to bank accounts. Studies clearly indicate that families building assets experience more marital stability and move less, and their children perform better in school (as measured by fewer behavioral problems, better grades and test scores, and higher college attendance), compared to families of similar socioeconomic status but without assets. Families building assets participate more in community organizations like PTAs, vote more, and are more engaged in community and civic issues. Rates of spousal and child abuse are lower in families building assets.[7] As a sociologist, I am optimistic that families who accumulate assets and use them for social mobility also will start other related equity-based reforms in motion. For example, I am confident as families become more invested in their communities, as homeowners, stakeholders, and citizens, they will begin pressuring for improved civic services such as better schools, libraries, playgrounds, open spaces, police and fire protection, and other public services. As families begin expecting more of their communities and participate in community organizations to bring about these changes, they become powerful actors for social change.

Another reason for starting with asset-building policy is that it directly addresses an emerging new understanding of poverty. If welfare policy only targets those currently below the official poverty line, it focuses on about 1 in 8 Americans, but it neglects the nearly 6 in 10 Americans who will experience at least one year of poverty while they are adults. The economic fragility of those who will experience poverty would be improved vastly by building an asset safety net.

The euphoria associated with America's longest period of economic prosperity burst with the recession that began a few years ago. Prosperity created greater inequality, but recession has exposed rising unemployment, homelessness, and poverty and left welfare reform tattered. It does not take much hindsight to understand that virtually any welfare reform measure would have "worked" during a time when unemployment was diving to historical lows. In times like these, good timing masks bad policy, and we should not confuse the two. American welfare policies have not been effective in lifting families out of poverty. Even if welfare reform works on its own terms, the time has come for a serious consideration of asset policies to lift families out of poverty and address inequality.

## *Matching Social Assistance to Asset Policy*

Traditional welfare policies have failed to launch families out of poverty, just as they have failed to promote independence and self-reliance. Asset policies will not work by themselves, either. In tandem, asset and income policies promise supporting pillars for mobility. To make sure that asset-building policies do not become a shell game simply transferring costs from federal to state or from public to private—or creaming monies from social assistance—policy needs to be crafted so that asset and traditional social assistance policies synergize one another rather than cancel each other out. For example, Children's Savings Accounts should not replace a public commitment to higher education. Tuition at public institutions of higher education should not rise just because 18-year-olds have accumulated a small nest egg to make college afford-able. A worst-case-scenario involves a family raiding their fledgling IDA account, losing matching payments in the process, to buy food at the end of the month because their food stamp allocation was too small. Families should not miss medical appointments, delay renewing prescriptions, stretch out the time between dental visits, or skip meals to scrape together money for monthly IDA contributions. These sacrifices to contribute to asset accounts are damaging bargains families should not be forced to consider because of public policy failures. One lesson from the national IDA demonstration project indicates that these temp-tations are real and should be avoided.

Likewise, a commitment to child care support might allow Vivian Arroya to put money into an IDA or Down Payment Account for the home she wants to buy and not scrimp on her family's food or health care. Sandra McCord's choice at month's end of bus fare to send her daughters to school versus food on the table shamefully reveals back-ward public priorities. Social programs need to support families at levels that do not pose Faustian bargains between subsistence and health today versus a brighter tomorrow.

The asset-building policies I have discussed address low-asset fami-lies and can affect a majority of families. Unfortunately, in the early 2000s asset policies mainly benefit the wealthy 1 or 2 percent. More-over, asset policies will not work by themselves but will be most effective alongside equity-based reforms in other key areas.

## Inheritance and Wealth-Concentrating Policies

America draws from two philosophical and political traditions, dating back to the 1700s, when it comes to inheritance. One starts from John Locke and Edmund Burke and runs through conservatives including President George W. Bush. This tradition emphasizes the right to pass down property and generally advocates privileging the tax status of property and wealth, like abolishing the estate tax, or the "death tax," as it is currently being marketed. Another tradition stems from Jean-Jacques Rousseau and Thomas Paine and runs through liberal political thought, the New Deal, and the Great Society. FDR said, "The transmission from generation to generation of vast fortunes by will, inheritance, or gift is not consistent with the ideals of the American people." The matter, philosophically and politically, has never been settled; indeed, compromise seems to govern this issue. On three separate occasions, estate or wealth taxes were passed to fund military buildups and wars. In 1916 estate taxes became a permanent part of federal revenues, exempting the first $50,000. Subsequently Congress has revised estate taxes on several occasions, raising the exemption to $120,000 in 1976, $225,000 in 1981, and $600,000 in 1986 and phasing it to $3.5 million in 2009.

Inheritance is a vexing dilemma in building a case for asset policy. There is a strongly held belief in America that when financially successful individuals die they can pass wealth to their children to secure a better future for them. It would be one thing if this money bought fancier clothes, longer and plusher vacations, bigger houses, boats, expensive meals, or even freedom from work altogether. It is something quite different, however, if this unearned wealth buys advantages in schools, communities, jobs, businesses, and social networks. Standing up for American ideals, I firmly believe, means passing an Opportunity Act that taxes the inheritance of unearned property at, say, a flat 10 percent rate, after a reasonable exemption, with revenues earmarked for asset-building policies.

Washington is running in the opposite direction, with the push to repeal the estate tax at the top of the agenda that will worsen wealth inequality. The centerpiece of President Bush's political agenda, it provides an unfortunate context for current discussions about inheritance and the American Dream. The estate tax has come under severe political pressure precisely at a moment when the largest transfer of intergenerational wealth in American history is taking place. This is neither a surprise nor a time for political timidity. The Bush message advocates eliminating the estate tax, saying that it punishes those who succeed, especially small-business owners and farmers. Proponents of repeal tell us that children often are forced to sell family farms or businesses just to pay taxes. Is this true? One survey indicates that 37 percent of Americans think they or someone in their immediate family will have to pay an estate tax.[8] Whether this is hopeful dreams or benign ignorance, the reality is that only 2 percent of Americans leave large enough estates—over $1 million under current provisions—to fall within this tax. The same survey asked people if they favored or opposed repeal of the estate tax. This question was asked two times, once at the beginning of the survey and then again after other questions relayed accurate information about wealth and estates. With no information as context, 59 percent favored repeal and 33 opposed it. This 26 percent favorable margin changed within minutes to a 47–46 percent split, showing that once an informational context replaces a rhetorical, buzzword context, support for repeal quickly loses steam. Americans also were asked about reforming or eliminating the estate tax. The reform message highlights protecting family businesses and farms while taxing the estates of multi-millionaires. In this formulation, 60 percent favor reform and only 35 percent wish to abolish the estate tax.

The estate tax is more effective as a weathervane symbol in the struggle between inheritance and achievement than as a way of curtailing the practice of passing great fortunes to children and grandchildren. Only if your estate is worth $17 million or more do you fit the profile of an estate-tax payer. As part of its tax cut package in 2001, the Bush Administration phased in larger exemptions and lower rates, with exemptions rising to $1 million in 2003, $2 million in 2006, and $3.5 million by 2009. The law rescinds the estate tax temporarily in 2010, but it returns the following year, unless Congress permanently repeals it, as the Bush administration advocates. Estimates show that these changes cost the federal government $25 billion the first five years and $103 billion during the second five years when larger exemption and lower rates kick in. In the year of no estate tax, 2011, cost estimates balloon up to $54 billion. If repeal becomes permanent, the Joint Committee on Taxation estimates that it will cost $662 billion over 10 years. This is a lot of lost tax revenue, which, if not made up from other taxes, most likely will result in further budget and service cuts and even larger deficits.

Looking at who benefits from regressive changes in the estate tax highlights the fact that it is a reverse Robin Hood tax that further redistributes wealth to the richest. By 2009, less than one-half of 1 percent of Americans will be subject to the estate tax, due to changes Congress approved in 2001.[9] There is no evidence of family farmers in Iowa having to pay the estate tax. Only 4 percent of small businesses have a net worth of more than what the scheduled exemption will be in 2009, $3.5 million.

Instead of repealing the estate tax, I advocate reforming it to exclude family farms and small businesses and to progressively lower the exemptions while closing loopholes that allow the wealthiest families to evade this law. What is really at stake, it seems to me, is the power of very wealthy individuals to assure succeeding generations economic success and material comfort through unearned advantages, regardless of any achievements or contributions they may make. Kevin Phillips warns in his book *Wealth and Democracy* about this encroaching plutocracy. In thinking about racial inequality in particular and inequality in general, it makes a great deal of sense to draw political and philosophical lines around questions of inheritance and meritocracy. I am not disputing or discouraging the ability or right of innovative, hardworking, successful people to reap great wealth rewards from their own endeavors. Rather, to refocus us back to ideals and realities of equality, it is clear that passing unearned wealth and advantages results in greater inequality and is not consistent with the ideals of the American people. Seeing this issue as a struggle between inheritance and meritocracy not only returns the estate tax to its original purpose but also makes reform progressive and winnable.

Others, like New York University economist Edward Wolff, have proposed a wealth tax as a means of alleviating inequality and raising revenue.[10] As a way of rectifying the awesome concentration of wealth in American since the 1970s, no doubt such a tax would send a powerful democratic message. A wealth tax idea, unfortunately, does not distinguish between earned and inherited wealth. I think an Opportunity Act keeps this distinction clear. The estate tax is supposed to curtail passing dynasties down so that America does not become a plutocracy. Yet we have learned that massive amounts of wealth are transferred at times other than death; therefore, in keeping with the principle, the Opportunity Act would include large financial gifts. This symmetry links revenues from inheriting unearned wealth to matching asset-development funds.

The single most important housing policy is the home mortgage interest deduction. Because it lowers taxes in proportion to a family's tax rate, the majority of this $55 billion subsidy goes to the highest-income families; one-third of it goes to families in the top 10 percent. The home mortgage interest deduction promotes new home construction at the higher end of the housing market, which affects the availability of affordable housing. Others have pointed out the connection between stimulating the high end of the housing market and constricting the supply of low- and moderate-income housing, where most low-income renters pay more than half of their income in rent.[11]

The nation's housing priorities must change. First, the dynamic of housing markets—that is, laws of supply and demand, incentives for new housing construction, and the location of new housing—must change. Incentives should be redirected away from subsidizing homes for the affluent to making homeownership affordable. In present housing markets, the home-mortgage interest deduction is crucial to the nation's high homeownership rate, families' financial plans, and the homeownership aspirations of millions. An asset equity approach does not suggest throwing it out altogether, but it does suggest significant reforms to make it work equitably. I like an idea that, instead of rewarding taxpayers who pay higher marginal tax rates, converts the interest one can deduct into a flat percentage rate. All families, say, could take 25 percent of home mortgage interest off their taxes, regardless of earnings or whether they choose the standard deduction or the itemized tax schedule. More moderate-income families would be eligible, the subsidies of high-income families would be scaled back, and low- and moderate-income families would share in this housing policy. If the home mortgage interest deduction was converted into a tax credit, some families might even receive a refund.[12]

In the spirit of curtailing wealth-concentrating policies and creating a more level playing field, other policies that privilege wealth should be reexamined. The 2003 Bush tax cut package moves even further in the opposite direction because the capital gains and dividend provisions further privilege property and wealth. The capital gains portion of the new tax cut lowers tax bills considerably for those who sell property, stock, or mutual funds: It cuts the capital gains tax liability by one-half for those in lower tax brackets and one-quarter for those in higher tax brackets. The 2003 tax revision also lowers tax bills for the wealthy because qualifying dividends are taxed at much lower rates: The tax liability is cut by 61 percent at the highest bracket.

## Homeownership Discrimination

We met the middle-class Andrews family of St. Louis who send their children to private school because they feel that urban public schools serving their black community are substandard. They are urban pioneers, literally building a home from the ruin of past, failed public policies that created St. Louis's ghetto, and so many other ghettos just like it, yet their model risk-taking effort is capped by a home value ceiling that is typically found in African American communities and is rooted in the deep labyrinth of residential segregation.

Mortgage discrimination against African Americans is a major reason residential segregation remains persistently high. Fair housing laws do not allow judges immediate remedies or means to punish perpetrators. The onus is on individuals and community organizations to do the expensive and time-consuming work of law enforcement because people in office have little interest in or intention of enforcing fair-lending and fair-housing laws. A large part of the solution is an enforcement agenda.

A loan-approval decision rule that is affected by an applicant's membership in a minority group is discriminatory. Discrimination also occurs when a lender's decision is affected by the location of a property in a minority neighborhood. Fair-lending enforcement must become more aggressive and effective. We do not need new laws because the present system can be improved considerably. The Fair Housing Act of 1968 and the Equal Credit Opportunity Act of 1974 prohibit discrimination in mortgage lending. Ross and Yinger in *The Color of Credit* propose steps to make fair-lending laws more effective. The responsible enforcement agencies, the Department of Justice and the Department of Housing and Urban Development, must be given adequate staffing and resources to completely review and analyze mortgage applications; weak or ineffective enforcement negates law. While the political differences between former HUD Secretary Henry Cisneros (1993–97) and Attorney General John Ashcroft (2001– ) in their passion and commitment for enforcing fair lending are important, neither Democrats nor Republicans are very keen to take on banking and construction interests for the sake of fair lending or fair housing.

Given the increasing prevalence of automated underwriting systems in scoring mortgage applications, fair-lending enforcement agencies should develop tools to test for discrimination so that factors weighted against minorities do not become codified into uniform industry standards. Especially as loan pricing according to risk becomes common practice, lenders should be discouraged from generating greater profits by designing systems that make minorities appear to be riskier borrowers and then charge higher interest to justify supposedly riskier mortgages.

Mortgage lenders and insurance redliners should be held accountable for the racially specific damages they have imposed on communities of color. Why can't we sue predatory lenders and their suppliers of capital, mortgage and insurance redliners for what they have done to cities and communities?

Without these changes, the extra capital made available to families through various asset policies and other government policies would likely fail because the two-tiered housing market would still generate more wealth for the affluent.

## Educational Equity

The aspirations Clarisse and Dennis Lupi have for their children are like a poster for the American Dream. However, they feel a need to lie about where they live for the sake of their children's education. Public education has been a great democratic achievement and, in turn, nourishes democracy. For the Lupi children and 90 percent of American kids, the public education system is the place where hard work, merit, and talent lead to individual success and democratic participation. But in the real-world context of educational inequality, driven by race and class anxieties, a market for quality schooling is created where financial resources buy opportunities. The failure of public policy forces the Lupis to lie just to seek educational opportunities for their children.

The Andrews family story illustrates a special burden faced by middle-class African Americans who plant roots in their communities but feel betrayed by weak public education. Unlike similarly successful white families, they must use private wealth accumulated in home equity to offset failed public schools in their community. The Andrewses do not need "help" from anybody, but they would be better off if they did not feel forced to pay for schooling. This is a kind of segregation tariff many middle-class black families pay.

Movement toward equality requires shrinking advantages of wealth and turning around our national drift toward plutocracy. Although we understand that awesome wealth inequality is not likely to end anytime soon, even as we work to reverse this trend, it is important to work vigorously to narrow the advantages of wealth and birth in communities and schools. Living in whatever community one wants is not in question, even using wealth to move into a higher-status community. However, public policy should work toward equity of condition in schools and communities. This means that moving to wealthier communities should not be the publicly supported ticket to higher-quality schools. Family moves from Watts to Santa Monica, Dorchester to Harvard, or St. Louis to Sappington are not in question; the gap in school quality and resources should be in question so that these family moves do not automatically confer huge educational advantages with lifelong consequences. Clearly, this means a renewed commitment to equity-based educational reform. The way to leave no child behind in this approach is to ensure high-level equity in educational conditions, to take the school advantage out of moving to wealthier communities. Present conditions of educational inequality create reasons for families to seek richer educational environments and establish artificial markets to carry out this inequality mechanism. Public sectors like education should not legitimize, reward, and exacerbate private inequalities.

School reform is a most vexing issue because we have uncovered how educational inequality perpetuates inequality and promotes a restless nation of movers. Where a family lives largely determines school quality, and family wealth largely determines where people live. Local property taxes fund the leading portion of school finances, 45–50 percent; therefore, it is easy to understand how the wealth of a community, its resource base, governs educational resources and the opportunities that go with them. (The federal share is actually only about 5–10 percent, with the state contributing the remaining 45–50 percent.) The disadvantage of low-resource communities and the advantage of higher-resource communities can be addressed by shifting local school financing to state and federal levels.

It would be a mistake to read this as a case for vouchers. The ostensible appeal of educational vouchers is that they compensate for educational inequities by subsidizing student movement to better schools. Even if this were the real intent behind the voucher effort, the colossal mismatch between the number of students currently languishing in substandard schools and the number of open spots in high-quality schools demonstrates the folly of vouchers. In Los Angeles, one estimate is that 230,000 children occupy seats in substandard schools while there are only 100 openings in high-quality schools.[13]

From my asset perspective, and from the lessons learned through the research and understanding of findings in this book, the fundamental issue is condition of education and how best to foster high-quality schools. Reforms that lead to better schools also can come from within schools and outside of schools. From smaller classes to better-trained and better-paid teachers to smaller administrative units, much room exists for improving what goes on inside schools. From increased parental participation to connecting learning with working to longer and more school days, much room also exists for improving the value of education in society. Unfortunately, current choice programs like magnet schools, charter schools, and similar creative reforms, when they work, produce small islands of quality but come with a large equity price tag. Research has shown that choice programs lead to greater inequality both in who participates and in results.[14] We need to question seriously policies that result in greater inequality. However, I believe that within a context of equal conditions, all sorts of choice programs could flourish with different results. Arts-oriented schools, technology-oriented schools, math and science schools, language-immersion schools, and many other kinds could offer meaningful choices sculpted to the needs of children and parents in the context of equal educational conditions.

The goal is to achieve educational equity at a high quality level. Greatly increased educational resources more fairly distributed is the means to this goal. Since school resource levels reflect community wealth, new and significantly enhanced resources must come from federal and state governments. It is difficult to improve upon the words of educator Deborah Meier: "The primary national responsibility is to narrow the resource gap between the most and least advantaged, both between 9 A.M. and 3 P.M. and during the other five sixths of their waking lives when rich and poor students are also learning—but very different things."[15] Educational equity takes rewards out of moving for the schools, cancels advantages of community wealth, and undermines benefits of residential segregation.

## The Challenge for Middle-Class America

The discussion in the Hadley household provided a revealing moment. As Jan was justifying their white neighborhood and school, "it just happens to work out that way," Steve interrupted and began to openly question how and why they ended up in a white environment, realizing that it is neither what he intended nor the way he wants his children to grow up.

Part of the big picture I have been describing is how communities, families, and individuals try to trap resources and hoard them for their own benefit. Because individuals believe they can personally benefit from it, and because they do not trust government to act in the civic interest, they attempt to buy their way out of social problems on a one-at-a-time basis. This encourages a privatized notion of citizenship at the expense of solutions that work for all. It creates artificial demand and artificial sources of profit, such as when people pay larger amounts for suburban homes, private schools, gated communities, car alarms, home security systems, and private police services because they feel threatened by city life. A far more cost-effective system—and a far more democratic approach—is to build an infrastructure that would help everyone. None of this can happen without an activist agenda that puts these issues on the table in a way that makes sense to people.

This agenda poses two challenges for the middle class. The first recognizes that government built the pillars of middle-class life in America by policies such as FHA and the home mortgage interest deduction that put homeownership within the reach of most families, policies from which those families personally benefit. Without family legacies of head-start assets, middle class status would not be a realizable dream for millions of Americans, especially young families. But the government-sponsored mobility ladder does not help families with few financial assets. The challenge for the middle class is to support policies that extend similar mobility opportunities to less fortunate families and do not saw off the mobility ladder behind themselves. If government policies and head-start assets are key reasons behind the success of middle-class Americans, then we need to recognize that most middle-class families, particularly white families, do not achieve that status on their own. It is time to extend those opportunities to all.

The second tough challenge for middle-class America is to participate in rebuilding a civic infrastructure for the common good. Through a steady erosion under Republican and Democratic administrations alike, our commitment to and resources targeted for building high-quality, democratic public education, supporting community development, stability, and prosperity, and enforcing civil rights, fair-housing, and fair-lending laws has deteriorated considerably. As a result, success is tougher and exacts a larger toll, quality of life declines for many, and the American Dream becomes more elusive. Largely due to deteriorating civic infrastructure, a privatized notion of citizenship—where communities, families, and individuals seek private solutions for public problems—is gaining prominence among a large portion of the middle class. Given the current choices, perhaps this is understandable, and I do not mean to assess individual responsibility or assign personal guilt. Whether it is buying out of weak schools or moving for the schools, hiring tutors and coaches, building gated communities, investing in security for cars, homes, and communities, or shunning diverse communities and schools, middle-class citizens are buying into private solutions for their own benefit that further deteriorate the civic infrastructure and make social problems worse. The answer lies in rebuilding our civic infrastructure so that what makes sense to one family does not disadvantage others. A robust, durable, opportunity-laden civic infrastructure is the best asset for equality.

It is a measure of our times and how far we have strayed from American ideals that awarding achievement and merit, not birth, sounds radical. Policies should simultaneously begin to build asset ladders out of poverty, reward achievement while narrowing inequality, and uphold rights to fair opportunity over the privilege of wealthy dead people to permanently advantage their children by giving them property. My cousin Jimmy has asked me what is wrong with improving your family. Nothing, except when improving your children's opportunities means disadvantaging others, and when inherited wealth disenfranchises the American Dream. I believe that we want to be defined as a society whose values, structures, incentives, customs, policies, and laws encourage equality of opportunity, achievement, and reward.

We can no longer ignore tremendous wealth inequities as we struggle with the thorny issue of racial inequality. Without attending to how equal opportunity or even equal achievement does not lead to equal results—especially concerning wealth—we will continue to repeat the deep and disturbing patterns of racial inequality and conflict that plague our republic. A just society would not wish racial legacies and inheritance to block opportunities and make a mockery of merit, and just individuals will rejoice to give merit and democracy a fairer chance to triumph.

# Appendix I

Table A.1: What Accounts for Wealth Changes, 1989–1999?

|  | Net Worth | Net Financial Assets |
|---|---|---|
| White | 41707 | 45565 |
| Live in/Moved to South | 15096 | 13259 |
| Gained/Retained Degree | 43295 | 34375 |
| Become/Remained Middle Class | 30721 | 37842 |
| Change in Number of Children | −6453 | −9273 |
| Became/Remained Widowed | 34384 | 12153 |
| Became/Remained Married | 24879 | −821 |
| Became/Remained Female Headed | 24767 | 17601 |
| Became/Retained Unemployed | −35161 | −32785 |
| Became/Remained Retired | 18870 | 33393 |
| Gained/Retained Homeownership | 59908 | 34531 |
| Change in Income Since 1989 | 3.22 *** | 2.97 *** |
| Inheritance Received Since 1989 | 0.60 * | 0.62 * |
| CONSTANT | −72166 | −41474 |
| N | 2838 | 2909 |
| R Squared | 0.151 | 0.134 |
| Adjusted R Squared | 0.147 | 0.130 |
| Total Model Significance | *** | *** |

+ < = .10;  * < = .05;  ** < = .01;  *** < = .001
Source: PSID, 1989–1999

### Table A.2 What Accounts for Changes in Family Wealth for White and Black Families, 1989–1999?

|  | Net Worth | | Net Financial Assets | |
|---|---|---|---|---|
|  | WHITE | BLACK | WHITE | BLACK |
| Live in/Moved to South | 17576 | 9218 | 15610 | 1030 |
| Gained/Retained Degree | 44870 | 10897 | 35193 | 10624 |
| Become/Remained Middle Class | 37563 | 8116 | 48553 | 2932 |
| Change in Number of Children | −4583 | −8029 | −8686 | −7565 |
| Became/Remained Widowed | 46336 | 10080 | 10451 | 11216 |
| Became/Remained Married | 36064 | −4804 | −1445 | −5341 |
| Become/Remained Female Headed | 2679 | 15244 | −7970 | 12507 |
| Became/Retained Unemployed | −59891 | 35267 | −59635 | 37426 |
| Became/Remained Retired | 16283 | 210 | 34151 | 4898 |
| Gained/Retained Homeownership | 90556 | 7606 | 57838 | −3500 |
| Change in Income Since 1989 | 3.224 *** | 2*** | 2.981 *** | 1.891 *** |
| Inheritance Received Since 1989 | 0.593 * | −0.273 | 0.612 * | −0.092 |
| CONSTANT | −67,453 | −2,797 | −18,537 | 1,169 |
| N | 2135 | 703 | 2169 | 740 |
| R Squared | 0.155 | 0.023 | 0.138 | 0.017 |
| Adjusted R Squared | 0.150 | 0.006 | 0.133 | 0.001 |
| Total Model Significance | *** | NS | *** | NS |

+ < = .10;  * < = .05;  ** < = .01;  *** < = .001
Source: PSID, 1989–1999

**Table A.3  Where Do Families of Children Move?***
**1984–1994, By Income of Neighborhood**

| 1984 Residence | Poverty Level+ | 1994 Residence | | High+ | Total |
| | | Lower Middle+ | Upper Middle+ | | |
| | (n) | (n) | (n) | | (n) |
| **WHITE** | | | | | |
| **Poverty Level** | 63.6% | 18.2% | 18.2% | – | 100.0% (11) |
| **Lower Middle** | 5.8% | 68.1% | 21.0% | 5.1% | 100.0% (138) |
| **Upper Middle** | 0.4% | 15.4% | 69.6% | 14.3% | 100.0% (259) |
| **High** | – | 3.4% | 21.4% | 75.2% | 100.0% (145) |
| **TOTAL*** | 2.9% (16) | 25.5% (141) | 43.9% (243) | 27.7% (153) | 100.0% (553) |
| **BLACK** | | | | | |
| **Poverty Level** | 59.5% | 33.9% | 6.6% | – | 100.0% (121) |
| **Lower Middle** | 25.4% | 52.6% | 20.2% | 1.7% | 100.0% (173) |
| **Upper Middle** | 3.4% | 31.5% | 57.3% | 7.9% | 100.0% (89) |
| **High** | 5.6% | 16.7% | 27.8% | 50.0% | 100.0% (18) |
| **TOTAL*** | 29.9% (120) | 40.6% (163) | 24.7% (99) | 4.7% (19) | 100.0% (401) |

Source: PSID, 1984–1994
*Census data, 1984–1994
+Poverty level < = $24,311; Lower Middle = $24,312–$36,394; Upper Middle = $36,395–$54,911; High = > $54,912

# Appendix II

## Methodological Appendix

THIS BOOK ATTEMPTS TO PROVIDE CLEAR EXAMPLES of the connections between family wealth, opportunities, and racial inequality. Other scholars arrived at a similar understanding of what the emerging field of wealth studies needed before we could grapple adequately with such significant questions. The sociologist Dalton Conley noted in his book *Being Black, Living in the Red* that a definitive study really is not feasible using information surveys, the traditional method of gathering data on these topics. The information needed for this examination could only come from thorough, in-depth interviews that sought to understand if and how families make decisions to use their assets to promote mobility. Sociologist Lisa Keister concluded her book *Wealth in America* by noting that we need data that track family wealth over time to answer basic questions about how families use wealth and that even then underlying processes "may not be evident without complementary in-depth investigation into the lives of both those who are upwardly mobile and those who are downwardly mobile." The research that undergirds this book is complex, lengthy, labor intensive, and quite costly. I have been fortunate that the Ford Foundation made this venture possible and a superb research team assisted me at every turn.

Who are the families that provided so much insight and guidance for us into these themes? The families were chosen using what is called a snowball sampling method in which we asked families to suggest other families who also might want to participate in the study. We used census tract data to identify residential neighborhoods in the metropolitan areas of Boston, St. Louis, and Los Angeles according to race and class criteria. Using 1990 census data, the most recent available, we mapped these metropolitan areas for white and black middle-income and lower-income communities. I spent several days investigating and observing areas that matched our criteria so I could select a few communities within each city in which to interview families. I wanted to talk to a number of white middle-class families in Boston, for instance, who had experiences in similar neighborhoods, real estate markets, and schools. In Los Angeles, I drove around several areas with an urban studies professor from UCLA. We stopped and talked to real estate agents, shopkeepers, and people on the street about the community, housing prices, what the schools were like, and who lived there, checking census data against my sociological eye.

Since the study called for interviewing families with young, school-age children, I decided to recruit families initially through day care facilities. I drew up a list of day care facilities in target areas, visited them, introducing the study and myself, and then asked permission to use their centers to let families know about the study. Only 1 of the 10 centers I visited refused to cooperate. At the end of each interview, we asked families if they knew others in their immediate neighborhood who were facing similar community and school issues. In this way, the sample snowballed to include chains of families not initially recruited through day care centers. Because I wanted families to speak as freely as possible about their children's school experience, we decided not to contact families through the schools. In addition, I did not want to deal with school bureaucracies to meet families.

The group included approximately one-half black and one-half white families from a broad socioeconomic spectrum ranging from poor to working class to middle and upper-middle class. In Boston and Los Angeles we also interviewed a subset of Hispanic families. From January 1998 through June 1999 we interviewed couples and single heads-of-households in these three cities. Interview participants were all parents of school-age children. Approximately one-fifth of the families were sending their children to private schools (secular and parochial), and the rest were sending their children to public schools (both urban and suburban). Interviews took place in the participants' homes or in another place of their choosing and lasted one to three hours each.

The interviews were recorded and transcribed, then coded using NUD*IST qualitative data analysis software. The interview transcripts produced over 7,000 pages of reading and are the foundation of the first-ever qualitative research database on this subject.

A lack of longitudinal data with adequate coverage has stymied empirical analysis and understanding. Therefore, we examined two large national databases: the Survey of Income and Program Participation (SIPP) and the Panel Survey of Income Dynamics (PSID). PSID is a household survey that interviews families every four months over two and one-half years; the first information about family wealth came from the 1984 survey. We organized a database of family information from 1984 to 1999. Using the survey data, we have the unique ability to examine the changing wealth status of white and black American families over a fifteen-year window from 1984 to 1999.

The Panel Study of Income Dynamics is especially well suited to explore residential mobility. We also contracted with PSID to obtain Geocode Match Files. These files allowed us to link PSID families with their census tracts. We used these geocodes to append 1990 Census Extract Files obtained from ICPSR to the PSID families in our sample.

# Notes

## Introduction

1. Joint Center for Housing Studies of Harvard University (2002); Ross and Yinger (2002); Boshara (2001). Data for 2002 from the third-quarter report from the Census Bureau, Department of Commerce.
2. Data from Mishel, Bernstein, and Boushey (2003). The increase in work hours primarily comes from wives working more hours and more weeks per year. The actual figure is 660 more hours worked.
3. See Otto (1999).
4. See Wedner (2002) and Andrews (2003).
5. See Avery and Rendall (1993).
6. Avery and Rendall (1993).
7. Most particularly, Steele (1990) and Thernstrom and Thernstrom (1997).
8. The narrowing of the earnings gap during the 1990s appears to have centered on black men with relatively low educations. Altonji and Blank (1999) review the economics literature on the racial earning gap.
9. Data from Mishel, Bernstein, and Boushey (2003). The specific data refer to the ratio of black-to-white median family income.
10. Data from Shkury (2001).
11. Western (2001); Western and Pettit (2002).
12. Figure from Mishel, Bernstein, and Boushey (2003).
13. Patillo-McCoy (1999) contains a good discussion of the growth and condition of the black middle class. For a statistical profile, see Smith and Horton (1997).
14. Patillo-McCoy (1999) makes this case strongly.
15. In addition to the income literature already cited, see Jargowsky (1997) for increased African American labor force participation; Grodsky and Pager (2001) for African Americans' demonstrable gains in occupational attainment; and Hout (1984) on occupational mobility. Jencks and Phillips (1998) argue that the black-white education gap has narrowed since 1970, even though large differences remain. The black-white score gap at the end of high school, for example, has narrowed substantially since 1965.
16. On employment, see Kirschenman and Neckerman (1993); Moss and Tilly (2001); Hill (1993); Feagin and Sykes (1994). On education, see

Orfield, Eaton, and Jones (1997). On environment, see Bullard (1997). For residential segregation, see Massey and Denton (1993).

17. See Harrison and Weinberg (1992).

18. See Oliver and Shapiro (1995).

19. Simmel (1978).

20. Harvey (1985).

21. Lipsitz (1998).

22. After the publication of *Black Wealth/Wealth* in 1995, I set out on this journey of understanding because these interviews are the most appropriate way to find out the inner workings, dynamics, strategies, and decisions involving how families use their wealth. I use these interview data to learn the structured and intimate details around private wealth and then to give human face and voice to otherwise abstract social processes. More powerfully, this sort of data can be used to search for recurring themes and trends, to discover patterns, and to test explanatory ideas and theories. For this book, I do not use more than a sprinkling of the Hispanic interviews mainly because I need to keep the racial inequality focus on black-white issues. See the Methodological Appendix for a fuller description of methodological procedures.

23. See the Methodological Appendix for descriptions of the Survey of Income and Program Participation (SIPP) and the Panel Survey of Income Dynamics (PSID) databases.

## Chapter 1: The Color of the Safety Net

1. Miller and McNamee (1998).

2. Johnson and Eller (1998).

3. An emerging body of work and policy initiatives takes up this challenge. I have in mind here the work of Dalton Conley, Lisa Keister, Edward N. Wolff, and others.

4. See the work of Oliver and Shapiro, Conley, Keister, and Wolff.

5. Strong evidence for a narrowing black-white hourly wage gap is found in Card and Lemieux (1994) and discussed in Altonji and Blank (1999). In contrast, the annual earnings gap results from number of hours worked, job status, working at a second job, and self-employment. See Bluestone and Stevenson (2000).

6. Keister (2000), 10. Indeed, when asset income is not included, the correlation between income and net worth is only .26.

7. The official government poverty line is pegged to the price of food at a minimal diet, based on the assumption that the average family spends one-third of its income on food. Most poverty analysts think this produces an official poverty line that excludes a large portion of needy families. These experts suggest that the "real" poverty line should be 125 percent to 150 percent of the official poverty budget.

8. Rank (2004).

9. This line of theorizing owes much to the work of Amartya Sen, particularly *Development as Freedom*.

10. *Black Wealth/White Wealth* developed an early version of this idea. Haveman and Wolff developed the notion further in their 2001 paper "Who Are the Asset Poor? Levels, Trends, and Composition, 1983–1998." Our notions of Asset Poverty Line or Index are quite similar in concept. The calculations differ somewhat in that Haveman and Wolff use three months at the poverty line as a standard, and they measure net worth. Because the largest component of net worth for most American families is their home equity, I do not think this is the appropriate measure. Instead, I use the net financial asset measure of wealth resources. The issue, I suppose, is whether a family should sell their home or take out a home equity loan before falling into the asset poverty category. If selling of homes were required, of course, the family would have to replace their housing. My assumption for using the net financial asset measure is to preclude forced home sales or home loans. Our notion takes it out to three months but leaves the official poverty level unchanged. In any case, our figures differ because I use a different assumption, net financial assets, and a three-month threshold and because the databases are not the same. We can have a healthy academic discussion about which measure to use, threshold levels, and datasets, but the most important outcome would be adoption and reporting of any standard measure, because that would give us a yardstick to measure the direction asset poverty is heading.

## Chapter 2: The Cost of Being Black and the Advantage of Being White

1. See James P. Smith (2001) for a clear statement of this position.
2. Data from the Panel Study of Income Dynamics.
3. See Keister (2000) and Wolff (2002) for data.
4. Ibid.
5. *Federal Reserve Bulletin*, January 2003. Figures from a Federal Reserve survey released in January 2003 as reported in Andrews (2003).
6. African Americans had roughly 10 cents for every dollar of median net worth that white Americans possessed in 1993, $4,418 compared to $45,740. See Eller and Fraser (1995); Flippen and Tienda (1997); O'Toole (1998); Grant (2000).

   In *Black Wealth/White Wealth*, comparable figures for family income show that African American families earned 62 cents for every dollar that white families earned. The much greater wealth gap revealed new dimensions of racial inequality. In 1988, even among the black middle class, levels of net worth and net financial assets lagged drastically behind those of the white middle class. College-educated African Americans had 24 cents on the dollar, and for dual-earning black couples the figure reached 37 cents. Clearly there are factors other than what we normally understand as educational and job achievements that led to low levels of asset accumulation for African Americans. If blacks and whites went to similar schools, had similar jobs, and earned similar incomes, then the racial wealth gap should effectively disappear or at least narrow significantly. We gave black and white families the same income and educational levels, family characteristics, region of the country, and other important characteristics. A $43,143 net worth gap between whites and blacks remained even when factors were identical. Matching important features could not explain nearly three-quarters (71 percent) of the net worth racial gap. Similarly, it only explained about one-quarter of the racial net financial asset difference. Taking the average black household and endowing it with the same income, age, occupation, education, and other attributes as the average white household still left a $25,794 gap in net financial assets.

Similar findings show gross differences between Hispanics and whites. Hispanics have slightly higher net worth figures than African Americans. However, these findings are not sufficiently nuanced to really capture the diversity of the Hispanic population in the United States. A 2000 study showed substantial differences in assets between recent immigrants, who are primarily from Mexico and Central America, and Hispanics born in the United States. Recent immigrants are poorer and have fewer assets than Hispanic families who have lived in the United States for one or more generations.

Flippen and Tienda (1997) argued that discrimination in housing markets is more costly to black families than Hispanics. While "white Hispanics" may not face such discrimination, it may not be the case for black Puerto Ricans, who share social space with blacks and therefore may be the target of institutionalized racism in housing markets and financial institutions. O'Toole's data from the Greater Boston Social Survey (O'Toole 1998) suggest that Latinos in that region, the majority of whom are Puerto Rican, have even lower levels of net worth and financial assets than African Americans.

The case of Asian Americans is quite similar to that of Hispanics in that we need to be mindful of their diversity, in terms of both national origin and immigrant status. See Flippen and Tienda (1997) and O'Toole (1998). For example, changes in immigration rules have favored those who bring assets into the country over those without assets. Consequently, recent Asian immigration, from Korea, for example, is composed of individuals and families with assets who once they arrive convert these assets into other asset-producing activities, e.g., small businesses. Bates (1998) points out that Koreans who started businesses had significant assets and were able to use those assets to secure loans for business start-ups. Grant's 2000 report from Los Angeles again underscores the importance of immigrant status and nativity. Native-born Asians have assets approaching those of white Los Angelenos, while foreign-born Asians report lower wealth than native-born Asians but higher than all other ethnic and racial groups.

7. See James P. Smith (2001).

8. I switch the data in this table to SIPP because in my estimation this dataset is more appropriate for detailed breakdowns, especially if one wants to include useful information on Hispanics. The lowest income quintile includes the elderly; thus the wealth figures for this quintile appear larger than one might otherwise expect.

9. Yet another way to test this, almost to the point of absurdity, compares wealth controlling for white and black income distributions. Calibrating the white-to-black income distributions means, for example, comparing the 25th percentile of the white wealth data to the 45th in the black distribution, the 50th white to the black 70th, and the white 75th to the black 88th.

These results show, for example, that at the 25th percentile (white), median white NW is $7,671, but the black NW now adjusts upward to $3,548. At the 50th white percentile, white NW is $52,944, compared to $30,000 for equivalent earning blacks. At the 75th percentile, white wealth stands at $141,491 versus $72,761 for blacks.

At the 50th percentile, then, the original uncontrolled gap weighs in at $46,817 with a ratio of .12. Controlling for income reduces this gap to $22,944. The black-white wealth ratio closes as well to .57.

10. Shapiro (2001).

11. Authors analyzing this issue include Blau and Graham (1990); Oliver and Shapiro (1995); Conley (1999); and Keister (2000).

12. These tables are unweighted PSID data. Social scientists disagree about whether regressions like these should be weighted and/or logged. We examined every combination possible. We present the unweighted data because it allows us to preserve as many cases as possible. In addition, results from the weighted data are not much different from the unweighted, although more factors become significant. Using the logged data does not allow us to discuss the dollar contribution of each factor to wealth accumulation.

13. PSID has collected information on family assets since 1984, asking questions that are more comprehensive about family assets and liability issues every five years, and thus we can examine changes in family wealth over a 15-year period, 1984–99. For technical reasons, we use the most recent 10-year period, 1989–99. The 1984 survey reported too many families who did not answer some critical wealth questions for us to use the 1984 survey with confidence.

14. Of course, this longitudinal window is another way to examine racial differences and see if the most significant factors—income, middle-class occupations, and inheritance—remain the same. We can examine whether the wealth gap between equally achieving families narrows, stays the same, or increases over time. Do the disadvantages and advantages wealth confers accumulate, magnify, and sediment into racial stratification? We compute changes in wealth accumulation by subtracting a family's 1989 wealth from their reported wealth in 1999. We regressed the same set of independent variables identified in our previous regression on the 10-year change in family wealth. Now we convert these factors to changes because we want to know, for example, how change in family income between 1989 and 1999 affects a family's wealth.

15. In a different regression model, not shown here, receiving an inheritance between 1989 and 1999 added $131,000 net worth for white families.

## Chapter 3: Inheritance—"That Parent Thing"

1. See Modigliani (1988a).
2. See Kotlikoff and Summers (1988).
3. Gale and Scholz (1994).
4. PSID families were asked questions concerning parental wealth only if they had at least one living parent. Unfortunately, the collection method for this information is less than optimal. If respondents said their parents had positive assets, they were asked how much. Those who knew approximate dollar amounts specified the figures, while those who did not know or were hesitant about answering were then given wide bracket choices and dollar figures that did not require specific amounts. The available data, then, reflect this two-tiered approach: Some families specified amounts, some gave brackets, and still others combined both methods. In our reporting for the brackets, we used figures for each bracket. For example, if a family reported that their parents' wealth fell in the $1,000 to $25,000 range, we used $12,500 as the mean. The total effect of this procedure raises the floor and lowers the ceiling; that is, amounts tend to compress to the middle.
5. See Gale and Scholz (1994).
6. Economists disagree on whether payments of college expenses are intergenerational transfers. Most exclude parental payments of college expenses because the children are regarded as dependents. Asking if private school payments should be considered shows this validity of this position, as if the child actually receives this wealth and then can decide what to do with it. They also disagree about whether college expenses are fungible; that is, is this given money that can be freely spent?
7. See Engelhardt and Mayer (1994).
8. In the inheritance tabulations from our interviews we did not count college expenses as a direct inheritance partially because I decided not to spend the time required in each interview for people to remember and calculate the exact dollars.
9. Lareau (2000).
10. Bourdieu (1973); Miller and McNamee (1998); Keister (2000).
11. See Wilhelm (2001).
12. Avery and Rendall (2002).
13. These data are taken from Wilhelm (2001).
14. In some ways, these 1987 data are as disturbing as the bequest data because the $2,000 racial difference represents a single year's financial assistance. Suppose this $2,000 racial difference recurred every year?
15. See Jayakody (1998). Methodological differences, particularly in how Wilhem and Jayakody define families, most likely account for the variation in dollar amounts.
16. Gale and Scholz (1994). One reason the figures differ from these in previous studies is that the dataset they used asked about gifts amounting to $3,000 or more.
17. These questions also were asked during the annual interview, which gave

us a chance to double-check the annual data against the five-year block and verify the information.

18. This procedure pertains to inheritances received between 1984 and 1999. Inheritances received before 1984, which are recorded in the PSID data file, were adjusted as if they were received in 1984. We tallied the inheritance information for all these years and adjusted inheritance figures to reflect 1999 buying power. This, of course, has the rough effect of appreciating wealth received to reflect the increasing value of those assets. Thus a family inheritance of $5,000 in 1990 appreciated to $6,373 in 1999.

19. PSID first asked this question in 1984, asking if the respondent or anybody in his or her family had ever inherited any money. No floor was put on this question, so no matter how small the inheritance, it was recorded. The same set of inheritance questions was repeated every five years (1989, 1994, and 1999) but asked if the respondent or anybody in his or her family had inherited a substantial sum of money during the past five years. A substantial inheritance was pegged at $10,000; however, if a family volunteered that they had inherited a sum of money that was less than $10,000 and gave an exact figure, this information was recorded.

20. An examination of inheritances among those 65 and older reveals both the highest incidence levels and lowest amounts. The low level of bequests most likely results because parents of those 65 or older spent a good portion of their work lives in the Depression of the 1930s and during World War II, before they could take advantage of the long postwar prosperity and accumulate much wealth. For the parents of black Americans, of course, incidence and levels of inheritance reflect the direct legacy of discriminatory economic life in the past, especially among those parents whose work careers started before major civil rights legislation in the mid-1960s.

21. Again, see Wilhelm (2001).

22. See Weitzman (1985) for instance.

23. See Johnson (2001). Her insights were critical in shaping my interest in this material.

24. Mitchell (1998) discusses this notion.

## Chapter 4: Middle Class in Black and White

1. Remembering the connection that wealth grows with income, an income-bound middle-class definition with an upper limit of $79,000 may impose a ceiling effect on wealth that pertains only to income definitions of class. The education and occupation criteria do not impose similar ceiling effects.

2. Building wealth into the middle-class definition, for instance, has the effect of equating professional black American families with lower-blue-collar white families.

3. See the work of Charles Murray, especially *Losing Ground.*

4. See Blau and Graham (1990).

5. Gittleman and Wolff (2000).

6. To give an idea of our coding procedures, Barry Pullman's answer that he

helped people by working on fixing a roof was recorded as giving assistance. An overwhelming majority of the positive answers, though, involved money.

7. See Stack (1978). Jayakody's 1998 article on racial differences in financial assistance contains a good test and discussion of the cultural argument.
8. Edsall and Edsall (1992).
9. See Edsall and Edsall (1992) and Schuman, Steeh, Bobo, and Krysan (1997).
10. See (Bobo 2001) and Bobo, Kluegel, and Smith (1996).
11. I have in mind the works of David Wellman, Edwardo Bonnilla-Silva, Joe Feagin, Lillian Rubin, and others who have produced a rich interpretation concerning racial inequality and black disadvantage.
12. Indeed, the work of Feagin, for instance, provides abundant evidence concerning continual, everyday discrimination faced by even middle-class black Americans.
13. See Edsall and Edsall (1992) and Lipsitz (1998).
14. Lipsitz (1988).

## Chapter 5: The Homeownership Crossroad

1. See Eller and Fraser (1995).
2. The 1998 Survey of Consumer Finances is the source for these data. Middle class here is the middle three quintiles.
3. Jackson (1985) documents this story well in *Crabgrass Frontier*, and Massey and Denton (1993) expand on important themes in their book *American Apartheid*. Guy Stuart's book on the mortgage lending industry and discrimination, *Discriminating Risk: The U.S. Mortgage Lending Industry in the Twentieth Century* (2003), is an excellent analysis.
4. See Oliver and Shapiro (1995); Yinger (1995); and Massey and Denton (1993).
5. See Stuart (2003).
6. Ibid.
7. John Yinger's work has been critical in this documentation; especially 1986, 1995.
8. See Munnell et al. (1996) for the basic documentation, Oliver and Shapiro (1995) and Ladd (1998) for a discussion.
9. In results entirely consistent with Federal Reserve Board studies, Charles and Hurst (2002) produce very similar numbers. They find that black households are 87 percent more likely to be rejected by banks than similarly qualified white households. Since their analysis uses PSID data, and not official mortgage application information, the closeness of these rejection rate numbers to ours gives reason for confidence.
10. The best discussion of these issues is in Ross and Yinger (2002).
11. See discussion in Ross and Yinger (2002).
12. Looking at similar data in 1995, *Black Wealth/White Wealth* showed that the mortgage rate difference is not due to where the home is located, purchase price, or year bought.

13. Joint Center for Housing Studies at Harvard University (2002).
14. Ibid., 10.
15. See Linneman and Wachter (1989).
16. See Gyourko, Linneman, and Wachter (1999).
17. Munnell et al. (1996).
18. However, homes in poor neighborhoods, particularly poor black neighborhoods, do not typically increase in value. On this issue, see Denton (2001).
19. See Oliver and Shapiro (1995).
20. Rusk (2001).
21. See Yinger (1995) and Massey and Denton (1993) for neighborhood preferences.
22. On neighborhood preferences, see Krysan and Farley (2002) and Charles (2003).

## Chapter 6: Where People "Choose" to Live

1. Jasper (2000), 243.
2. The best accounts are: Jackson (1985) and Massey and Denton (1993).
3. Basic facts taken from Zepezauer and Naiman (1996).
4. See Gyourko and Sinai (2001).
5. Ibid.
6. See Boshara (2001).
7. See Gyourko and Sinai (2001).
8. See Howard (1997).
9. See Zepezauer and Naiman (1996).
10. See Schuman, Steeh, Bobo, and Krysan (1997).
11. See South and Crowder (1998).
12. Gramlich, Laren, and Sealand (1992). This study looks at movement in and out of poverty areas. No analysis that we are aware of has examined the longitudinal residential mobility of young families or looked at the income levels of communities.
13. The Panel Study of Income Dynamics is especially well suited to explore residential mobility.

    The sample from PSID is constrained in several ways. First, we want to use census data from 1990, the most recent extract file available to date, to analyze PSID families. We also want to look at as long a time span as possible to capture residential mobility. Thus we selected 1984 and 1994. This 10-year span is the longest possible to ensure a valid analysis of census tracts. Our sample includes only those families who have census data for both periods. Second, we are interested in tracking family mobility, not simply that of individuals. This approach ensured we would capture those families who went through some household change, like marital dissolution, during this time span and would retain as many families as possible by looking at family heads from either 1984 or 1994. Third, we wanted to look at families with children to ensure an analysis of families who might be making school decisions for their children.

14. This understates actual moves because we looked only at moves between census tracts, thus not counting moves within the same census tract. A typical census tract is about 1,500 individuals.

15. In 1994 poverty level is family incomes of less than $24,311. Lower middle ranges between $24,311 and $36,394. The upper-middle income range starts at $36,395 and goes up to $54,911. Upper income is above $54,911. We arrived at these numbers by dividing income levels into four percentile categories—the top and bottom 15 percent of incomes and the top and bottom of the remaining middle 70 percent, yielding rough "poverty level," "lower-middle," "upper-middle," and "high" income groupings.

    The economic profile of the census tract could change between 1984 and 1994, so a small fraction of the upward and downward movement could reflect area changes, not residential moves.

16. See Iceland et al. (2000). Social scientists use what is known as a "segregation index" to assess residential segregation, ranging from 0 for full integration to 100 for complete segregation. Anything above 60 is considered a high level of residential segregation. The 2000 figure for the United States was 74.

17. On this point, see Waters (1999).

18. See Patillo-McCoy (1999).

19. See Harrison and Weinberg (1992) and Rusk (2001).

20. On discrimination in real estate markets and mortgage approvals, see Turner et al. (2002); Ross and Yinger (2002). On racial neighborhood preferences, see Krysan and Farley (2002); Charles (2003); and Yinger (1995). Massey and Denton (1993) analyze the policy issues.

21. See Harris (1999) for a review of this issue.

22. Waters (1999), 244.

23. Orfield (2001).

24. Ibid.

25. Orfield (2001), Oakes (1985), Oakes et al. (1992), and Mickelson (2003).

26. Rates are 61 percent compared to 8.5 percent. See Mortenson (2000) for figures on college graduates. Wealthier families are those in the top 25 percent; poorer families are those in the bottom 25 percent. On troubles with the law, see Coalition for Juvenile Justice (2001).

27. Lee and Burkam (2002), 84.

28. See Young and Smith (1997).

29. Using data from Chubb and Moe's highly regarded 1990 book (Table 4-3, p. 107), I recalculated family incomes to 2002 dollars. I simply want to point out the connection between family income, community wealth, and educational quality, not defend their specific methods.

30. Information and data on desirable class size from Mayer and Mullins et al. (2001). Kindergarten data from Lee and Burkham (2002).

31. March 29, 2000.

32. See Schofield (1989, 1991) and Wells and Crain (1994). For the controlled study on black students, see Rubinowitz and Rosenbaum (2000).

33. For the impact of learning in integrated schools, see Braddock (1980); Crain and Mahard (1983); Wells and Crain (1997); and Hallinan (1998).

## Chapter 7: "Getting a Decent Middle-Class American Education"

 1. Especially, see Julia Wrigley's foreword to the second edition.
 2. This point is explored in Lareau (2002).
 3. Ibid.
 4. See National Center for Educational Statistics (1995).
 5. Data on who goes to private school from our analysis of the PSID dataset. The table is not shown because all data is in the text.
 6. Mayer and Mullins et al. (2001).
 7. See Thernstrom and Thernstrom (1997).
 8. See Schuman, Steeh, Bobo, and Krysan (1997).
 9. For a discussion of this argument, see Hochschild and Scovronick (2003).
10. Holme (2002).

## Conclusion

 1. More information about this type of account can be found at www.cfed.org.
 2. Rank (2004) reviews the most recent data describing the minimalist American welfare state and showing the ineffectiveness of social policy in lifting families out of poverty.
 3. This is measured by looking at pretransfer poverty rates versus posttransfer poverty rates. Countries include Canada, Finland, France, Germany, the Netherlands, Norway, Sweden, and the United Kingdom. See Rank (2004) discussion of results from the Luxembourg Income Study.
 4. Williams (2000).
 5. Sherraden (2001).
 6. At this writing, the Bush administration is suggesting a reform that would not shield the tax status of income deposited into these accounts. In return, when money in the account is withdrawn, it would not be taxable.
 7. For a superb summary of existing studies, see Scanlon and Page-Adams (2001).
 8. Greenberg Quinlan Rosner Research conducted the survey for OMB Watch. See http://www.ombwatch.org.
 9. See http://www.ombwatch.org site for data.
10. See Wolff (2002).
11. See Jargowsky (1997) on the connection between the lack of affordable housing and stimulating the high end of the real estate market. On who benefits most from the home mortgage interest deduction, see Howard (1997).
12. This proposal is very similar to one outlined by Paul Jargowsky (1997). One can make a strong argument to end the home mortgage interest deduction entirely. While I am sympathetic to its merits, repeal would need to be phased in over a 25-year period until those owing mortgages have paid them off.

13. Huffington (2002). There may be some severe methodological problems with this estimate, but the point about the inability of any voucher plan to match needs to solutions illustrates the very limited scope of such plans. These estimates come from looking at the number of students in low-performing schools and the number of open spots in high-performing schools.
14. This research includes Lee and Burkam (2002); Lee, Croninger, and Smith (1994); Wells and Crain (1997); and Lee (1993).
15. Meier (2000).

# Bibliography

Aizcorbe, Ana M., Arthur B. Kennickell, and Kevin B. Moore. 2003. "Recent Changes in U.S. Family Finances: Evidence from the 1998 and 2001 Survey of Consumer Finances." *Federal Reserve Bulletin*. January.

Altonji, Joseph, and Rebecca Blank. 1999. "Race and Gender in the Labor Market." In *Handbook of Labor Economics*, vol. 3, ed. Orley Ashenfelter and David Card. Amsterdam: Elsevier.

Andrews, Edmund. 2003. "Economic Inequality Grew in 90s Boom, Fed Reports." *New York Times*. January 23.

Avery, Robert, and Robert Rendall. 1993. "Estimating the Size and Distribution of the Baby Boomers' Prospective Inheritances." In *Proceedings of the Social Science Section of the American Statistical Association*. Alexandria, Va.: American Statistical Association.

———. 2002. "Lifetime Inheritances of Three Generations of Whites and Blacks." *American Journal of Sociology* 107, no. 5: 1300–1346.

Bates, Tim. 1998. *Race, Self-Employment, and Upward Mobility: An Illusive American Dream*. Baltimore: Johns Hopkins University Press.

Bier, Thomas. 2001. "Moving Up, Filtering Down: Metropolitan Housing Dynamics and Public Policy." Washington, D.C.: Brookings Institution Center on Urban and Metropolitan Policy Discussion Paper.

Blau, Francine D., and John W. Graham. 1990. "Black-White Differences in Wealth and Asset Composition." *Quarterly Journal of Economics* 105, no. 2: 321–39.

Bluestone, Barry, and Mary Huff Stevenson. 2000. *The Boston Renaissance: Race, Space, and Economic Change in an American Metropolis*. New York: Russell Sage Foundation.

Bobo, Lawrence D. 2001. "Racial Attitudes and Relations at the Close of the Twentieth Century." In *America Becoming: Racial Trends and Their Consequences*, vol. 1, ed. Neil Smelser, William Julius Wilson, and Faith Mitchell. Washington, D.C.: National Academy Press.

Bobo, Lawrence, James R. Kluegel, and Ryan A. Smith. 1996. "Laissez-Faire Racism: The Crystallization of a 'Kinder, Gentler' Anti-Black Ideology." New York: Russell Sage Foundation. June.

Bonilla-Silva, Eduardo. 2001. *White Supremacy and Racism in the Post–Civil Rights Era*. New York: Lynne Rienner.

Boshara, Ray. 2001. *Building Assets: A Report on the Asset-Development and IDA Field.* Washington, D.C.: Corporation for Economic Development.

Bourdieu, Pierre. 1973. "Cultural Reproduction and Social Reproduction." In *Knowledge, Education, and Cultural Change,* ed. R. Brown. London: Tavistock.

Braddock, J. H. 1980. "The Perpetuation of Segregation Across Levels of Education: A Behavioral Assessment of the Contact-Hypothesis." *Sociology of Education* 53, no. 3: 178–86.

Brenner, Robert. 2002. *The Boom and the Bubble: The U.S. in the World Economy.* London and New York: Verso.

Bullard, Robert, ed. 1997. *Unequal Protection: Environmental Justice and Communities of Color.* San Francisco: Sierra Club.

Card, David, and Thomas Lemieux. 1994. "Changing Wage Structure and Black-White Wage Differentials." *American Economic Review* 84, no. 2: 29–33.

Charles, Camille Z. 2003. "The Dynamics of Racial Residential Segregation." *Annual Review of Sociology* 29.

Charles, Kerwin Kofi, and Erik Hurst. 2002. "The Transition to Home Ownership and the Black-White Wealth Gap." *Review of Economics and Statistics* 84, no. 2: 281–97.

Chubb, John, and Terry Moe. 1990. *Politics, Markets, and America's Schools.* Washington, D.C.: Brookings Institution Press.

Coalition for Juvenile Justice. 2001. *Abandoned in the Back Row: New Lessons in Education and Delinquency Prevention.* Washington, D.C.: CJJ.

Conley, Dalton. 1999. *Being Black, Living in the Red.* Berkeley: University of California Press.

Crain, Robert L., and R. Mahard. 1983. "The Effect of Research Methodology on Desegregation-Achievement Studies: A Meta-analysis." *American Journal of Sociology* 88, no. 5: 839–54.

Denton, Nancy. 2001. "Housing as a Means of Asset Accumulation: A Good Strategy for the Poor?" In *Assets for the Poor,* ed. Thomas Shapiro and Edward Wolff. New York: Russell Sage Foundation.

Edsall, Thomas, and Mary Edsall. 1992. *Chain Reaction.* Rev. ed. New York: Norton.

Ehrenreich, Barbara. 2001. *Nickel and Dimed.* New York: Metropolitan Books.

Eller, T. J., and Wallace Fraser. 1995. "Asset Ownership of Households: 1993." Washington, D.C.: U.S. Bureau of the Census, *Current Population Reports,* Household Economic Studies, Series P70–47.

Engelhardt, Gary, and Christopher Mayer. 1994. "Gifts for Home Purchase and Housing Market Behavior." *New England Economic Review* (May/June): 47–58.

Feagin, Joe. 2000. *Racist America.* New York: Routledge.

Feagin, Joe, and Melvin Sykes. 1994. *Living with Racism: The Black Middle-Class Experience.* Boston: Beacon.

Flippen, Chenoa, and Marta Tienda. 1997. "Racial and Ethnic Differences in

Wealth Among the Elderly." Paper presented at the 1997 annual meeting of the Population Association of America, Washington, D.C.

Gale, William, and John Scholz. 1994. "Intergenerational Transfers and the Accumulation of Wealth." *Journal of Economic Perspective* 8, no. 4: 145–60.

Gittleman, Maury, and Edward Wolff. 2000. "Racial Wealth Disparities: Is the Gap Closing?" Levy Institute Working Paper no. 311. Available online at http://econpapers.hhs.se/paper/levwrkpap/311.htm.

Goldman, Victoria. 1998. *Los Angeles Guide to Private Schools.* New York: Soho Press.

Gramlich, Edward, Deborah Laren, and Naomi Sealand. 1992. "Moving into and out of Poor Urban Areas." *Journal of Policy Analysis and Management* 11, no. 2: 273–87.

Grant, David. 2000. "A Demographic Portrait of Los Angeles, 1970–1990." In *Prismatic Metropolis: Analyzing Inequality in Los Angeles,* ed. Larry Bobo, Melvin Oliver, James Johnson Jr., and Abel Valenzuela. New York: Russell Sage Foundation.

Grodsky, Eric, and Devah Pager. 2001. "The Structure of Disadvantage: Individual and Occupational Determinants of the Black-White Wage Gap." *American Sociological Review* 66: 542–67.

Gyourko, Joseph, Peter Linneman, and Susan Wachter. 1999. "Analyzing the Relationships Among Race, Wealth, and Home Ownership in America." *Journal of Housing Economics* 8, no. 2: 63–89.

Gyourko, Joseph, and Todd Sinai. 2001. "The Spatial Distribution of Housing-Related Tax Benefits in the United States." Washington, D.C.: Brookings Institution Center on Urban and Metropolitan Policy Discussion Paper.

Hallinan, Maureen. 1998. "Diversity Effects on Student Outcomes: Social Science Evidence." *Ohio State Law Journal* 59, no. 3: 733–54.

Harris, Cheryl. 1993. "Whiteness as Property." *Harvard Law Review* 106 (June): 1709–91.

Harris, David. 1999. " 'Property Values Drop When Blacks Move in, Because . . .': Racial and Socioeconomic Determinants of Neighborhood Desirability." *American Sociological Review* 64: 461–79.

Harrison, Roderick, and Daniel Weinberg. 1992. "Racial and Ethnic Segregation in 1990." Washington, D.C.: U.S. Bureau of the Census Working Paper.

Harvey, David. 1985. *Consciousness and the Urban Experience.* Baltimore: Johns Hopkins University Press.

Haveman, Robert, and Edward Wolff. 2001. "Who Are the Asset Poor? Levels, Trends and Composition, 1983–1998." Institute for Research on Poverty Discussion Paper.

Hill, Herbert. 1993. "Black Workers, Organized Labor, and Title VII of the 1964 Civil Rights Act." In *Race in America: The Struggle for Equality,* ed. Herbert Hill and James E. Hones Jr. Madison: University of Wisconsin Press.

Hochschild, Jennifer, and Nathan Scovronick. 2003. *The American Dream and the Public Schools*. New York: Oxford University Press.

Holme, Jennifer Jellison. 2002. "Buying Homes, Buying Schools: School Choice and the Social Construction of School Quality." *Harvard Educational Review* 72, no. 2: 177–205.

Hout, Michael. 1984. "Occupational Mobility of Black Men, 1962 to 1973." *American Sociological Review* 49: 308–22.

Howard, Christopher. 1997. *The Hidden Welfare State*. Princeton: Princeton University Press.

Huffington, Arianna. 2002. "When 'Back to School' Means 'Tough Luck, Kid.'" http://www.ariannaonline.com/columns/files/090202.html. September 2.

Iceland, John, et al. 2000. "Racial and Ethnic Residential Segregation in the United States: 1980–2000." *Census 2000: Special Report 3*. Washington, D.C.: U.S. Bureau of the Census.

Jackson, Kenneth T. 1985. *Crabgrass Frontier: The Suburbanization of the United States*. New York: Oxford University Press.

Jargowsky, Paul. 1997. *Poverty and Place*. New York: Russell Sage Foundation.

Jasper, James M. 2000. *Restless Nation: Starting Over in America*. Chicago: University of Chicago Press.

Jayakody, Rukmalie. 1998. "Race Differences in Intergenerational Financial Assistance." *Journal of Family Issues* 19, no. 5: 508–33.

Jencks, Christopher, and Meredith Phillips, eds. 1998. *The Black-White Test Score Gap*. Washington, D.C.: Brookings Institution Press.

Johnson, Barry, and Martha Eller. 1998. "Federal Taxation of Inheritance and Wealth Transfers." In *Inheritance and Wealth in America*, ed. Robert K. Miller Jr. and Stephen J. McNamee. New York and London: Plenum Press.

Johnson, Heather. 2001. "The Ideology of Meritocracy and the Power of Wealth." Ph.D. dissertation, Northeastern University.

Joint Center for Housing Studies of Harvard University. 2002. *The State of the Nation's Housing 2002*. Cambridge: JCHD.

Keister, Lisa. 2000. *Wealth in America*. New York: Cambridge University Press.

Kirschenman, Joleen, and Kathryn M. Neckerman. 1991. "We'd Love to Hire Them, But ...": The Meaning of Race for Employers." In *The Urban Underclass*, ed. Christopher Jencks and Paul E. Peterson. Washington, D.C.: Brookings Institution Press.

Kotlikoff, Laurence J., and Lawrence H. Summers. 1988. "The Contribution of Intergenerational Transfers to Total Wealth: A Reply." In *Modelling the Accumulation and Distribution of Wealth*, ed. Denis Kessler and Andre Masson. Oxford: Clarendon Press.

Krysan, Maria, and Reynolds Farley. 2002. "The Residential Preferences of Blacks: Do They Explain Persistent Segregation?" *Social Forces* 80: 937–80.

Ladd, Helen. 1998. "Evidence of Discrimination in Mortgage Lending." *Journal of Economic Perspectives* 12, no. 2: 41–62.

Lareau, Annette. 2000. *Home Advantage: Social Class and Parental Intervention in Elementary Education.* 2d ed. Lanham, Md.: Rowman & Littlefield.

———. 2002. "Invisible Inequality: Social Class and Childrearing in Black Families and White Families." *American Sociological Review* 67: 747–76.

Lee, Valerie. 1993. "Educational Choice: The Stratifying Effects of Selecting Schools and Courses." *Educational Policy* 7, no. 2: 125–48.

Lee, Valerie, and David Burkam. 2002. *Inequality at the Starting Gate.* Washington, D.C.: Economic Policy Institute.

Lee, Valerie, R. Croninger, and J. Smith. 1994. "Parental Choice of Schools and Social Stratification in Education: The Paradox of Detroit." *Educational Evaluation and Policy Analysis* 16, no. 4: 434–57.

Linneman, Peter, and Susan Wachter. 1989. "The Impact of Borrowing Constraints on Homeownership." *AREUEA Journal* 17, no. 4, 389–402.

Lipsitz, George. 1998. *The Possessive Investment in Whiteness.* Philadelphia: Temple University Press.

———. 2001. *American Studies in a Moment of Danger.* Minneapolis and London: University of Minnesota Press.

Massey, Douglas, and Nancy Denton. 1993. *American Apartheid.* Cambridge: Harvard University Press.

Mayer, D. P., J. E. Mullens, et al. 2001. *Monitoring School Quality: An Indicators Report 2000.* Washington, D.C.: U.S. Department of Education, National Center for Education Statistics.

Meier, Deborah. 2000. *Will Standards Save Public Education?* Boston: Beacon Press.

Meyers, Laura. 1998. "The High Five." *Los Angeles Magazine.* January.

Mickelson, Roslyn. 2003. "The Subversion of Swann: How First- and Second-Generation Segregation Undermined Educational Equity in Charlotte." In *Bring Equity Back In,* ed. Amy Stuart Wells and Janice Petrovich.

Miller, Robert K., Jr., and Stephen J. McNamee. 1998. "The Inheritance of Wealth in America." In *Inheritance and Wealth in America,* ed. Robert K. Miller Jr. and Stephen J. McNamee. New York and London: Plenum Press.

Miller-Adams, Michelle. 2002. *Owning Up: Poverty, Assets, and the American Dream.* Washington, D.C.: Brookings Institution Press.

Mishel, Lawrence, Jared Bernstein, and Heather Boushey. 2003. *The State of Working America, 2002–2003.* Ithaca: Cornell University Press.

Mitchell, Lawrence. 1998. *Stacked Deck: A Story of Selfishness in America.* Philadelphia: Temple University Press.

Modigliani, Franco. 1988a. "Measuring the Contribution of Intergenerational Transfers to Total Wealth: Conceptual Issues and Empirical Findings." In *Modelling the Accumulation and Distribution of Wealth,* ed. Denis Kessler and Andre Masson. Oxford: Clarendon Press.

———. 1988b. "The Role of Intergenerational Transfers and Life-Cycle

Saving in the Accumulation of Wealth." *Journal of Economic Perspectives* 2, no. 2: 15–40.

Mortenson, Tom. 2000. Bachelor's Degree Attainment by Age 24 by Family Income Quartiles, 1970 to 1999. Washington, D.C: Postsecondary Education Opportunity. http://www.postsecondary.org.

Moss, Phillip, and Chris Tilly. 2001. *Stories Employers Tell: Race, Skill, and Hiring in America.* New York: Russell Sage Foundation.

Munnell, Alicia H., Geoffrey M. B. Tootell, Lynne E. Browne, and James McEneaney. 1996. "Mortgage Lending in Boston: Interpreting HMDA Data." *American Economic Review* 86, no. 1: 25–53.

Murray, Charles. 1984. *Losing Ground: American Social Policy, 1950–1980.* New York: Basic Books.

National Center for Educational Statistics. 1995. *The Condition of Education, 1995.* Washington, D.C.: NCES.

———. 2000. *The Condition of Education, 2000.* Washington, D.C.: NCES.

Oakes, Jeannie. 1985. *Keeping Track: How Schools Structure Inequality.* New Haven: Yale University Press.

Oakes, Jeannie, Molly Selvin, Lynn Karoly, and Gretchen Guiton. 2000. *Educational Matchmaking.* Santa Monica: RAND.

Office of Trust Responsibilities. 1995. *Annual Report of Indian Lands.* Washington, D.C.: U.S. Department of the Interior.

Oliver, Melvin, and Thomas Shapiro. 1995. *Black Wealth/White Wealth: A New Perspective on Racial Inequality.* New York: Routledge.

Orfield, Gary. 2001. *Schools More Separate: Consequences of a Decade of Resegregation.* Cambridge, Mass.: Harvard University Civil Rights Project.

Orfield, Gary, Susan Eaton, and Elaine Jones. 1997. *Dismantling Desegregation: The Quiet Reversal of Brown v. Board of Education.* New York: New Press.

O'Toole, B. 1998. "Family Net Asset Levels in the Greater Boston Region." Paper presented at the Greater Boston Social Survey Community Conference, John F. Kennedy Library, Boston. November.

Otto, Mary. 1999. "The Working Homeless Is a Growing Reality." *Miami Herald.* December 26.

Patillo-McCoy, Mary. 1999. *Black Picket Fences.* Chicago: University of Chicago Press.

Phillips, Kevin. 2002. *Wealth and Democracy.* New York: Broadway Books.

Portes, Alejandro, and Reuben Rumbaut. 1990. *Immigrant America.* Berkeley: University of California Press.

Rank, Mark. 2004. *One Nation, Underprivileged: How American Poverty Affects Us All.* New York: Oxford University Press. Forthcoming.

Ross, Stephen, and John Yinger. 2002. *The Color of Credit: Mortgage Discrimination, Research Methodology, and Fair-Lending Enforcement.* Cambridge, Mass., and London: MIT Press.

Rubin, Lillian. 1994. *Families on the Faultline: America's Working Class Speaks About the Family, the Economy, Race, and Ethnicity.* New York: HarperCollins.

Rubinowitz, Leonard, and James Rosenbaum. 2000. *Crossing the Class and Color Lines*. Chicago: University of Chicago Press.

Rusk, David. 2001. "The 'Segregation Tax': The Cost of Racial Segregation to Black Homeowners." Washington, D.C.: Brookings Institution Center on Urban and Metropolitan Policy.

Scanlon, Edward, and Deborah Page-Adams. 2001. "Effects of Asset Holding on Neighborhoods, Families, and Children: A Review of Research." In *Building Assets: A Report on the Asset-Development and IDA Field*, ed. Ray Boshara. Washington, D.C.: Corporation for Economic Development.

Schachter, Jason. 2000. "Geographical Mobility." *Current Population Reports*, P20–538. Washington, D.C.: U.S. Bureau of the Census. May.

Schofield, J. W. 1989. *Black and White in School*. New York: Teachers College Press.

———. 1991. "School Desegregation and Intergroup Relations: A Review of the Literature." In G. Grant, ed., *Review of Research in Education* 17: 335–409. Washington, D.C.: American Educational Research Association.

Schuman, Howard, Charlotte Steeh, Lawrence Bobo, and Maria Krysan. 1997. *Racial Attitudes in America: Trends and Interpretations*. Rev. ed. Cambridge: Harvard University Press.

Sen, Amartya. 2000. *Development as Freedom*. New York: Knopf.

Shapiro, Thomas M. 2001. "The Importance of Assets." In *Assets for the Poor*, ed. Thomas Shapiro and Edward Wolff. New York: Russell Sage Foundation.

Shapiro, Thomas M., and Edward Wolff. 2001. *Assets for the Poor*. New York: Russell Sage Foundation.

Sherraden, Michael. 2001. "Asset-Building Policy and Programs for the Poor." In *Assets for the Poor*, ed. Thomas Shapiro and Edward Wolff. New York: Russell Sage Foundation.

———. 1991. *Assets and the Poor*. New York: Sharpe.

Shkury, Shimon. 2001. "Wage Differences Between White Men and Black Men in the United States of America." Master's thesis, Department of Sociology, University of Pennsylvania.

Simmel, Georg. 1978. *The Philosophy of Money*. Trans. T. Bottomore and D. Frisby. Boston: Routledge & Kegan Paul.

Smith, James P. 2001. "Race and Ethnicity in the Labor Market: Trends over the Short and Long Term." In *America Becoming*, vol. 2, ed. Neil Smelser, William J. Wilson, and Faith Mitchell. Washington, D.C.: National Academy Press.

Smith, Jessie, and Carrell Horton. 1997. *Statistical Record of Black America*. 4th ed. Detroit: Gale Research Press.

South, Scott J., and Kyle D. Crowder. 1998. "Leaving the 'Hood: Residential Mobility Between Black, White, and Integrated Neighborhoods." *American Sociological Review* 63: 17–26.

Stack, Carol. 1978. *All Our Kin*. New York: Basic Books.

Steele, Shelby. 1990. *The Content of Our Character: A New Vision of Race in America*. New York: St. Martin's.

Stoesz, David. 2000. *A Poverty of Imagination: Bootstrap Capitalism, Sequel to Welfare Reform*. Madison: University of Wisconsin Press.

Stuart, Guy. 2003. *Discriminating Risk: The U.S. Mortgage Lending Industry in the Twentieth Century*. Ithaca: Cornell University Press.

Thernstrom, Stephan, and Abigail Thernstrom. 1997. *America in Black and White: One Nation, Indivisible*. New York: Simon & Schuster.

Turner, Margery Austin, et al. 2002. "Discrimination in Metropolitan Housing Markets." At www.huduser.org/publications (visited February 28, 2003).

Waters, Mary. 1999. *Black Identities*. Cambridge: Harvard University Press and New York: Russell Sage Foundation.

Wedner, Diane. 2002. "Mortgage Delinquency Rates Reach 30-Year High." *Los Angeles Times*. September 10.

Weitzman, Lenore. 1985. *The Divorce Revolution*. New York: Free Press/ Macmillan.

Wells, Amy Stuart, and Robert L. Crain. 1994. "Perpetuation Theory and the Long-Term Effects of School Desegregation." *Review of Educational Research* 64, no. 4: 531–55.

———. 1997. *Stepping over the Color Line: African-American Students in White Suburban Schools*. New Haven and London: Yale University Press.

Western, Bruce. 2002. "The Impact of Incarceration on Wage Mobility and Inequality." *American Sociological Review* 67: 526–46.

Western, Bruce, and Becky Pettit. 2002. "Black-White Wage Inequality, Employment Rates, and Incarceration." Department of Sociology, Princeton University. At www.princeton.edu/~western/.

Wilhelm, Mark. 2001. "The Role of Intergenerational Transfers in Spreading Asset Ownership." In *Assets for the Poor*, ed. Thomas Shapiro and Edward Wolff. New York: Russell Sage Foundation.

Williams, Trina. 2000. "The Homestead Act: A Major Asset-building Policy in American History." Paper commissioned for "Inclusion in Asset Building: Research and Policy Symposium," Center for Social Development Washington University, St. Louis. September 21–23.

Wolff, Edward N. 2002. *Top Heavy*. New York: New Press.

Yinger, John. 1986. "Measuring Racial Discrimination with Fair Housing Audits: Caught in the Act." *American Economic Review* 76, no. 5: 881–93.

———. 1995. *Closed Doors, Lost Opportunities*. New York: Russell Sage Foundation. 1995.

Young, B. A., and T. M. Smith. 1997. *Issues in Focus: The Social Context of Education*. Washington, D.C.: National Center for Education Statistics.

Zepezauer, Mark, and Arthur Naiman. 1996. *Take the Rich off Welfare*. Tucson: Odonian Press.

# Index